# DEMOCRATISING

# PARTICIPATORY RESEARCH

# Democratising Participatory Research

## Pathways to Social Justice from the Global South

*Carmen Martinez-Vargas*

OpenBook
Publishers

ISBN Paperback: 9781800643086
ISBN Hardback: 9781800643093
ISBN Digital (PDF): 9781800643109
ISBN Digital ebook (epub): 9781800643116
ISBN Digital ebook (mobi): 9781800643123
ISBN Digital ebook (xml): 9781800643130
DOI: 10.11647/OBP.0273

Cover image: Sander van Leusden (Studio SanArt), *Transmorphosis* (2016), all rights reserved. Cover design by Anna Gatti.

# Table of Contents

Acronyms                                                                      vii

Acknowledgements                                                               ix

1.  Introduction                                                                1
2.  Coloniality and Decoloniality in the Global South Higher-                  29
    Education Context
3.  Traditions and Limitations of Participatory Research                       41
4.  Democratising Participatory Research: A Capabilitarian                     75
    Conceptualisation
5.  Co-Researchers' Valued Capabilities                                       105
6.  The South African DCR Project: Undergraduates as Researchers              135
7.  Broadening Our Participatory Evaluations: A Southern                       171
    Capabilitarian Perspective
8.  DCR for Socially Just Higher Education: Perspectives from the             203
    South
9.  Redrawing Our Epistemic Horizon                                           229

List of Figures                                                               237
List of Tables                                                                239
Index                                                                         241

# Acronyms

AR – Action Research

ARNA – Action Research Network of the Americas

CA – Capabilities Approach

CARN – Collaborative Action Research Network

CPAR – Critical Participatory Action Research

DCR – Democratic Capabilities Research

EAR – Educational Action Research

HDCA – Human Development and Capabilities Association

PA – Participatory Approaches

PALAR – Participatory Action Learning Action Research

PAR – Participatory Action Research

PR – Participatory Research

PRIA – Participatory Research in Asia

UFS – University of the Free State

# Acknowledgements

A multiplicity of people and entities has enhanced my capabilities, allowing me to embark on this exciting and exhausting book. Firstly, for funding, I am grateful to NRF Grant No. 86540 which funded my research under the SARChI Chair in Higher Education and Human Development, without which this study would not have been possible. Equally, I am enormously grateful to Alessandra Tosi, the commissioning editor of Open Book Publishers, for making open access publications possible for early-career scholars like me. Similarly, I should also thank Melissa Purkiss, Luca Baffa and Anna Gatti for all your support and hard work during the production process of this book. It has been a pleasure working with all of you. Further, my most sincere appreciation to the two anonymous reviewers for their deep and generous engagement with my work. Thank you for believing in this book and making it even better.

I am equally indebted to Melanie Walker not only for helping me tirelessly with this study and my professional development, but for being more than a mentor in my life. I am grateful for all you have done for me before, during and beyond this book. I would also like to thank Talita Calitz and Nelson Masanche Nkhoma for guiding and supporting me during this study and subsequent book—your support throughout this work and your friendship are much appreciated. Thank you for all your help and inspirational conversations over many years. Thank you to Alejandra Boni for introducing me to the Capabilities Approach as well as providing the link to become part of this amazing research programme in South Africa. Without your guidance and leadership in the years prior to this book, my work would not have been possible. To all my colleagues from the HEHD research group, but especially Mikateko Mathebula and Faith Mkwananzi, thank you for your support and help, in addition to our friendship. Your kindness, selflessness and hard work have been a constant source of inspiration to me. Thank you for this and our long conversations about Africa, South Africa and social injustices, which helped me to develop many of the ideas in this book. To my beloved husband, Sander van Leusden, thank you for remaining supportive and caring despite my ups and downs throughout this book. The journey has not been easy, but I could not imagine undertaking it without you. You have been a central pillar of strength for my work. Finally, but not least, to all the DCR co-researchers that took part in the collaborative inquiry, thank you for your enthusiasm, dedication and hard-work despite your academic commitments. Without you this book would not have been possible. I feel grateful for our friendships and to have shared with you all this time during and since the project.

*For Sphe*

# 1. Introduction

## 1.1 This South African Story Matters to All of Us

As a young, working-class girl who grew up in a mono-parental family in the South of Spain, knowledge meant something simple but also something unattainable. First, it was clear to me that we all have the capacity to know many things to a certain extent. Back then, I thought my mother knew a lot, many adults did as well. They knew how to do things and how things worked in the local context. However, there was another kind of knowing that was relegated to others, especially not for a family like mine, the knowing from universities and what is usually understood as scientific or academic knowledge.

University knowledge, the knowledge nourished within universities' walls, was a mystery to me and many of the members of my family and friends, however, somehow whoever was able to access it or embodied it through university degrees or any diploma would become something 'more'. This 'more', was not a distinction between which kinds of academic knowledge we were talking about. It was an intrinsic value that raised the person possessing scientific knowledge to a level of dignity that was strange to imagine for someone who had never been seen in that light. Equally, becoming 'more' meant of course, we were 'less'; less respectable, less educated, less intelligent, and less dignified than those who were part and parcel of these elitist institutions.

And all this became overwhelmingly clear when I first entered university at the age of eighteen and, as expected, I failed, and I dropped out during my second year. I was constantly wondering: how do I not belong in this university when everyone said (directly or indirectly) to me that this is what I have to do to become a dignified human being in my society? To have opportunities, to have a voice, to have freedoms,

 https://doi.org/10.11647/OBP.0273.01

to become the person I wanted to be. At that time, it was not yet the moment to understand but to experience that other worldview so different from the one I grew up with and I lived in. It was not yet the time to deconstruct all these underlying assumptions, until I overcame certain structural barriers.

I was not meant to become an academic, not meant to complete my university degree, masters or PhD, but the fact that I did positioned me in this world with a slightly different perspective, understanding the intersecting disadvantages I experienced, as well as my privileges as a white and European member of our global and unequal society. Of course, it was not only my educational path that foregrounded this understanding, but many other encounters, experiences and reflections about who am I and what dignity, humanity, knowledge, justice and universities are, and ought to do.

Having faced many structural constraints in my educational and academic path, I was sure that universities ought to do better, but this became even clearer when I landed in South Africa more than six years ago and started my research career in the field of Higher Education and Human Development. In a country where aberrant inequalities are lived and experienced on a daily-basis, I became aware that universities were not only excluding working-class students in Europe, but that this exclusion becomes more nuanced and profound in post-colonial contexts such as South Africa. Many students and their communities are not just marginalised because of socio-economic class, nationality or gender, but also because of race, culture, language or religion, among many others. This can make them become the 'other' to an extreme, such that they are detached from their most fundamental humanity, their recognition as humans, and as humans who belong (Mpofu & Steyn, 2021). Being estranged from one's humanity also equates to being estranged from knowledge, thereby jeapordising one's recognition as a dignified human who knows and who deserves to be listened to (Ndlovu-Gatsheni, 2018). And this is precisely my concern in this book. Recognising the importance of higher education and knowledge processes in defending the humanity, dignity and knowledge agency of those situated on the margins, whoever they are. Those who were thought not to know at all by modernist thinking, especially in post-colonial contexts such as South Africa. As maintained throughout this book, we cannot talk about knowledge in the singular, but rather we must talk about knowledges because they are relational, cultural, intuitive, scientific, Indigenous and more. Despite scepticism in academia, the ultimate 'knowledge' is not only possessed by one group behind university walls, nor is there a finite and perfect underline of universal truth. 'Knowledges' are incomplete pieces of partially knowing that need to be connected in networks with others, as De Sousa Santos (2014) claims. Thus, in order to connect them we need to look beyond our constraints and limited logics, allowing us to expand our conceptions of what reality is (what I refer in this book as ontology), and what knowledge is (epistemology). But especially important in this book is the means by which we obtain knowledge (methodology) having an underlying critical and historical perspective that acknowledges power and oppression.

Connecting knowledge is not building networks of abstract objectivities where knowledge is aseptically carried. Connecting knowledges is what De Sousa Santos (2014) calls 'Ecology of Knowledges'. It is the recognition that we carry rooted knowledges. As such, different collectives, communities and peoples need to be involved in the knowledge creation process that universities lead. However, involvement does not mean the instrumentalisation of people. What participatory research promotes is the centrality of participation and democratisation of the knowledge production processes (Kemmis, McTaggart & Nixon, 2013). Democratising research is not only about providing open access to scientific knowledge or access to universities, which is also important, but beyond that the equal and as just as possible involvement of other collectives, individuals and the knowledges which they carry as central to a multi-epistemic knowledge production.

While this is an issue of concern for all of us, it certainly needs special attention in Global South contexts and what I also refer to here as post-colonial spaces. In referring to the Global South, I do not designate a geographical area but rather a cultural, cosmological, metaphysical and ontological space, which is dominated by Western standards of living that minimise and jeopardise other valued ways of being, living and doing in the world. The Global South, and South Africa in particular, as explored in this book, have been subjected to complex historical processes of deprivation not only at the individual level but at the community cosmological level, which have repressed and invalidated local languages, knowledges and cultures. These oppressions have tremendous consequences for social justice aims, including the freedoms of communities in the Global South and processes of democratisation of knowledge, which are needed to overcome global epistemic barriers.

Therefore, in this book my aim is to build a theoretical and practical foundation based on these ideas and discussions, named Democratic Capabilities Research. It defends the use of participatory research in scientific projects, but also expands and enhances what is currently carried out as participatory research beyond Western applications, situating this in a Global South context. In a way, this book is a methodological discussion between different academic fields of study, transgressing assumptions about what knowledge is, what reality is, and how we obtain knowledge. The point is to use a moral and evaluative framework such as the Capabilities Approach to advance towards more, rather than less, democratic knowledge production. It acknowledges our imperfection as human beings and researchers, but also acknowledges the plurality of voices from the Global South that should be heard. This is ultimately a pathway to enhancing human capabilities and human well-being, and therefore, to assisting higher-education institutions and participatory research practitioners to reflect on social justice aims, which they claim to do, but perhaps are not doing so well.

Hence, while this book is a deep and normative critique of scientific scholarship and the limitations it has placed on knowledge production through the modernist tradition, it also engages with the language, theories and discourses of different academic fields. The objective is to speak directly to an academic audience who are starting to use participatory research, or who have used it, without considering their Western limitations. I hope this book, therefore, clarifies what might be called an imperfect but meaningful democratisation of knowledge, and elaborates how this would look in practice within and beyond what we understand as 'research'.

On the other hand, structures of oppression and the unfreedoms of post-colonial contexts are central to this book. In this book I use the term 'conversion factors' to represent structures of privilege and exploitation, however these are not divided between individual, social and environmental conversion factors as they tend to be within capabilitarian literature (Robeyns 2005). For many communities in the Global South individual and social factors are intrinsically bound, and individual 'normalcy' is socially created and therefore indivisible (Ndlovu 2021).

Equally, central to my idea of conversion factors is its colonial element in the Global South. This is why I use 'colonial conversion factors' as a merged category. With colonial conversion factors, I refer to post-colonial effects on individuals' freedoms. Colonial conversion factors have disproportionately deprived targeted groups, impacting their freedoms negatively while giving huge privileges to other groups. These colonial conversion factors create an abyss between dominant and subordinate groups with various shades of grey between them. The central point of this conceptualisation is that we really do have good reasons to acknowledge post-colonial oppression. Examples of colonial conversion factors and their degenerative consequences on students' freedoms might be the use of foreign languages by universities to teach local students or when university knowledge is foreign to local students.

In these institutions students are seen as receivers and passive agents of their university experiences, however this study confirms that students know which capabilities matter for them and that they are active agents against aberrant oppression through insurgent capabilities. Hence, this book stresses that full (not partial) access to the Western epistemic system is fundamental and necessary in order for students to exercise other valued capabilities. Nevertheless, this alone is not sufficient. The process of accessing the epistemic system does not only relate to accessing direct academic knowledge, but to understanding and taking part in the processes of knowledge generation, through multi-epistemic knowledge platforms. Therefore, epistemic freedoms depend not only on access to a Western epistemic system, but also the power to overcome colonial conversion factors jeopardising students' valued capabilities.

Hence, the case investigated shows that involving university students in a knowledge production process, such as Democratic Capabilities Research, permits us to expand significant freedoms through functionings such as voice or participation, beyond the invaluable importance of becoming dignified members of their university community. We know that participatory research, as well as universities, cannot resolve all of the colonial oppressions that these students experience before, during and after their higher-education paths. To advance towards social justice in a broad and open-ended way, the point is to identify practices that help us create local and contextual spaces of epistemic resistance and transformation, even if they are imperfect, through plural and contextualised participatory processes. Further, in this book the Capabilities Approach supports and defines the evaluative and moral understanding of what our path towards more socially just universities might mean in democratising knowledge production.

Therefore, the three main aims of this book are:

- To engage with decolonial and participatory approaches literature to unpack the different natures of knowledge and knowledge production in academia. This analysis presents a Global South basis on which to position a more democratic epistemic platform, which acknowledges the plurality of knowledges.

- To explore the conceptualisation and implementation of a participatory capabilities-based research (Democratic Capabilities Research), which links the Capabilities Approach, participatory approaches and decolonial debates.

- To explore the opportunities, challenges and lessons with regard to the democratisation of knowledge and promotion of socially just higher education from a Global South perspective that emerges from a DCR case study with undergraduate students in South Africa.

To conclude this section, and before exploring the context of this book, I would like to remark that this book is inevitably a reproduction of epistemic inequalities. It is immersed in knowledge asymmetries, with some still more capable than others to be heard and to be believed as worthy testifiers (Fricker 2015). I am aware that in my positionality as a white European woman, I continue to reproduce epistemic inequalities when talking in the name of Global South populations and in the name of black students. I am certainly using my privilege of voice in the academic space as a white woman. However, it is true that beyond that reproduction of white privilege, I intend to partially overcome these challenges. And I say partially because if things were the way they were supposed to be, I would not be the one writing this book, or this book would not need to be written at all. That is why I see myself as an imperfect ally and as a comrade in my own privilege and discomfort with that privilege. However, I see the need to raise concerns about participatory research in powerful circles so as to advance critiques already identified by Indigenous scholars and critical participatory practitioners (Coombes, Johnson & Howitt 2014; Chilisa 2013; Kovach 2009; Ritchie et al. 2013; Santos 2012; Smith 1999). This is in my view a combination of forces, strengthening these scholars' arguments and criticism from an alternative framework, such as a capabilitarian perspective. It confirms that we might succeed in transforming the 'decolonial' research practices of which we dream.

Thus, I hope this introduction has encouraged most of you to continue reading this book, and to understand the importance of listening and overcoming whiteness and Western thinking about university experiences and participatory research in the Global South 'to the extent that we are able to do so'. I hope my work can transcend and challenge Western academic understandings as much as possible. Hence, I ask you to read this work as my own personal struggle to unlearn my privileges and biases. This is a work in progress embedded in my personal and professional struggle of becoming aware of and challenging my inherited whiteness and Eurocentrism in my interpretations of the world.

## 1.2 The Context of this South African Story: Getting to Know the Post-Colonial Complexities in Higher Education

The South African higher-education context presents an invaluable object of study for this book. Its colonial past and current debates about decolonisation from grassroots movements and scholars (Pithouse 2006; Botha 2007; Luckett 2016; Butler-Adam 2016) sustain and justify the need for this type of research. The South African context, although different and specific, shares similar challenges with other higher-education institutions in the Global South. Thus, the Global South perspective is therefore important for visualising and claiming to Global North scholars and international scholars as a whole that these issues cannot be resolved without their critical engagement and alliances in seeking out alternatives. Therefore, I will start with a short contextualisation of the higher-education system in South Africa.

Traditionally, higher education in Africa has been emblematised by its modern and colonial higher-education institutions. However, it is nowadays well known that pre-colonial Africa developed its own Indigenous educational systems equivalent to modern higher-education institutions, with methods based mostly on oral transmission of knowledge (Diop 2010). For instance, Oyewumi (2016) explored the role of motherhood in a particular knowledge system, that of the Yoruba, investigating how knowledge was transmitted orally through a system of divination, and that, although matriarchal, it did not exclude males from the educational endeavour. Ndlovu-Gatsheni (2018) furthers these ideas, introducing the role of extended family and traditional intellectuals into the Indigenous educational systems as part of the collectives in charge of transferring knowledge to the younger generations. Further, scholars situate the first universities in Africa around the time when African Indigenous systems intersected with Islam/Arabic systems of education, resulting in the University of Qarawiyyin in Fes, Morroco (AD 859), the University of Al-Azhar in Cairo, Egypt (AD 972) and the University of Timbuktu in Mali (twelfth century). What is controversial is that none of them have survived or resisted the imposition of the modern Western university, due to the intervening slave trade and savage exploitation of the continent.

In this historical phase, Africa and its African peoples were considered inferior, meaning that all their traditions, beliefs, languages and knowledges were replaced by those of the colonisers. However, as stated above this did not apply to all countries in the Global South context, and there were great differences between their experiences. In Latin America the isolation of certain tribes and communities allowed for the preservation of some of these cultures; and the earlier decolonial process promoted the flourishing of alternative and insurgent educational projects around the continent. In comparison with African nations, the Latin American context is composed of alternatives to mainstream educational programmes, although not without challenges (Mato 2014). However, in Africa there has been a more significant move towards Western educational systems, sustained by international aid and development interventions, which are still central to current social and political transformations, even if in the last years there has been vigorous debate about these inherited aspirations. This proves that the diversity of the Global South is clear, and that the responses against the hegemonic system differ from context to context. When I talk about the Global South I do not talk about a unified space. In Africa, and particularly South Africa, the fight was and still mainly is leading towards assimilation with mainstream Western educational systems, due to the division imposed by the apartheid regime and the global neoliberal pressure to situate South Africa in an international economic market. Hence, although there are differences, what is common in these post-colonial spaces is the imposition of a Western educational system, that ignores citizens' local and rooted knowledge systems and their need to defend their fundamental non-Western or alternative educational aspirations and freedoms.

Switching now in particular to the South African context and its 'modern' educational system, the 'modern' higher-education system in South Africa was established under colonial rule in 1829 with the South African College in Cape Town. In 1910, three establishments existed in the country (the University of Cape Town, Stellenbosch University and the University of South Africa), which expanded with affiliated colleges in every region of the country, creating the current higher-education network (Pithouse 2006; Cloete et al. 2006). In 1953, the Bantu Education Act (1953) enacted legislation to racially segregate all educational facilities in the country (Tabata 1960). The apartheid regime used higher-education institutions as an instrument to achieve their political aspirations. They developed into strong institutions internationally up until the 1960s, when the international community began to question the legitimacy of the segregated system, provoking an academic boycott (Badat 2008; Bunting 2006). Additionally, resistance against apartheid flourished in South African universities during this period, with grassroots movements[1] that positioned themselves as

---

1   Student movements played a crucial role in the historical transformation of universities in the country. Educational activism took place in South Africa during the 1970s and 1990s. Student associations such as the South African Students Organisation (SASO) or Black Consciousness Movement (BCM) nurtured intensive debates about policy, transformation and practice (Naidoo 2015; Karodia et al. 2016) which continue today. During 2015 and 2016 diverse protests took place in different universities all around the country, and fourteen institutions were shut down in

opponents of the National Party prior to the release, and subsequent ascent to the presidency, of Nelson Mandela (Naidoo 2015; Karodia et al. 2016).

After 1994, a new South Africa was born with the first democratic elections, which reflected an aspiration to transform the nation and its higher-education system, as prescribed by the White Paper of 1997.[2] Nevertheless, as Badat (2008, 19) corroborated, 'social, political and economic discrimination and inequalities of race, gender, institutional and spatial nature profoundly shaped and continue to shape South African higher education'. Certainly, many posterior studies have corroborated this, mapping a higher-education context in which a significant part of the student body lives under severely deprived conditions and clear post-colonial marginalisation. A significant number of students survive on government bursaries or face daily issues related to food security on campuses around the country (Breier 2010; Firfirey & Carolissen 2010). As Walker (2020, 66) corroborates, 'It is very clear that students do not leave socio-economic inequalities behind when they come to university, that student hardship is a reality'.

The recent emergence of student demands for the decolonisation of universities in South Africa is one indicator of the fact that this issue remains unresolved in the country, as well as internationally.[3] The different protests since 2015 have brought about a public debate in South Africa, with calls to challenge the ways in which we think about colonisation, and its influence on how knowledge is produced in higher-education institutions (Karodia, Soni & Soni 2016; Bosch 2017; Luescher, Loader & Mugume 2016; Naicker 2016). Moreover, the academic debate on decoloniality has been active internationally for decades, with many demanding that academia ought to be liberated from hegemonic structures (De Sousa Santos 2010; Hall & Tandon 2017; Leibowitz 2017).

Thus, all these historical and present challenges have fuelled public scrutiny of the functions and aims of public higher-education institutions in the country, as reinforced by scholars and the student

---

the largest and most effective student campaign post-1994, #FeesMustFall. This campaign opened up latent debates about the role of universities and the heritage of the colonial institution.

2    See the link for more information http://www.che.ac.za/sites/default/files/publications/White_Paper3.pdf.

3    See https://www.bbc.com/news/world-africa-34615004 for more information.

body (Badat 2008; Luescher et al. 2016; Msila & Gumbo 2016; Postma 2016; Van der Merwe & Van Reenen 2016). These features make the higher-education context especially relevant for this study, advancing the current debate on alternatives that could challenge persistent injustices in the area of knowledge production. Furthermore, the South African case can be used to critically examine post-colonial challenges in higher-education systems around the world. It is necessary to open up this debate to an international audience and especially international scholars in powerful institutions, where many decisions severely impact on Global South universities. Hence, South African higher-education institutions are crucial because their decolonial project is not a parallel system, but an integrated solution 'within', which is not found in other post-colonial contexts. This is an essential platform through which we can form alliances and start conversations with the Global North about real plurality and the real introduction of Southern perspectives into their higher-education institutions.

## 1.3 The Baseline of this Book

To conclude this introductory chapter and for the sake of clarity, it is necessary to provide some explanations of the terminology used and ideas driving the argument before outlining its structure.

The word 'research' in this book is understood broadly, as 'knowledge'. Research is one of the most contested words in academia, as many Indigenous scholars have pointed out. Research seems to be as much an ideological as a political term, which is signified by what lies behind it; its historical and philosophical tradition (Smith 1999). For this reason, in this book, research should be understood as having an open-ended definition, which considers research beyond a disciplinary contribution to academic knowledge, although its academic component is still present. In this way, research is—in many parts of this book—a general capacity for investigating things that we need to know (Appadurai 2006). As Appadurai claims, '[i]t is the capacity to systematically increase the horizons of one's current knowledge, in relation to some task, goal or aspiration' (2006, 176) beyond any disciplinary or academic contribution to the body of knowledge. Hence, although the case study explored in the second part of this book can be regarded as a conventional piece of research, especially through the qualitative exploration of valuable capabilities (Chapters Five, Six and Seven), the proposed Democratic Capabilities Research (DCR) case study and its practice needs to be understood in this broader way. DCR is a pedagogical space in which the investigation itself goes beyond scientific standards of research because knowledges other than the scientific one are used and assessed in the process.

Accordingly, the word 'knowledge' is used in a similar way. Just as the outcome of scientific research is scientific knowledge, in expanding the meaning of research I do the same with the knowledge resulting from the enquiry process. Epistemic injustices are based on the dominance of one epistemic system over others that are thought unworthy and unreliable (De Sousa Santos 2014). Therefore, when referring to knowledge, I designate a multiplicity of systems that are rooted in different cultural traditions as well as diverse processes of knowledge creation, rationality and relationalities (Mignolo & Walsh 2018). This is to understand rationality in a broad sense that goes beyond the modern understanding, embracing other means of understanding and producing knowledge. To do so means acknowledging what lies beneath the broadest meaning of knowledge as including—but not limited to—scientific, conceptual, experiential, intuitive, local, spiritual, Indigenous and cultural knowledge. It is in this space, where knowledge creation seems to merge with a learning process, that there is no clear difference between a process of knowledge production and a process of active learning, so both go hand in hand.

Secondly, the decolonial claim throughout this study does not represent a radical perspective, even if it might be considered that way. Conversely, this critical positionality understands the importance of scientific knowledge and is under no circumstance trying to invalidate it. The case presented in this book clarifies the invisibility of other knowledge systems and other means of research that have historically been invalidated. These knowledge systems need to be acknowledged if we want to advance towards epistemic and global social justice (De Sousa Santos 2014). Therefore, the argument sustains the creation of spaces within, as well as outside academia to promote other knowledge systems and other research processes. As Mignolo (2007) corroborates, it is not a question of a new hegemony that is different from the old one, but of how we are able to create bridges between all the different traditions of knowledge and apply them on a more egalitarian terrain. Furthermore, to acknowledge this positionality, the book makes use of the terminology 'decolonial debate' in order to clarify the particular vision of decoloniality sustained in this study. This refers to the preservation of diversity and the multiplicity of practices for knowledge creation, not as a single theory but as an open-ended debate with different and compatible positionalities. Methodologically, that is why we undertake an open-ended participatory process with undergraduate students as well as using qualitative techniques. The inquiry process explores students' valued capabilities and how researchers and practitioners can overcome Western participatory processes using the Capabilities Approach, as part of the DCR role of the facilitator.

Regarding the terminology used, namely 'coloniality', 'decolonisation', 'decolonial', 'decoloniality' and 'post-colonial', I would like to clarify several aspects, especially regarding the distinction between 'decolonisation' and 'decoloniality'. As many societies and groups have been exposed to and oppressed by colonial powers, their resistance to these can take on different names and features. This is important to highlight because these collectives, populations and experiences are different and their responses to it are equally distinct. This variety of experiences has resulted in numerous terminologies for naming resistance to hegemony. In a bright attempt to classify them, Ndlovu-Gatsheni (2018, 49–53) identifies at least twenty decolonial intellectual currents, movements or philosophies in this diversity of resistances. For instance, these include Rastafarism, Garveyism, Black Consciousness, Black Feminism, Dependency Theory, Afrikology, and many others. What differentiates one from another is the central focus of their resistance, which is defined by the persistent inequalities affecting the particular collectives, although somehow all share a common resistance to the dominant Western system. In this classification, decoloniality and decolonisation are situated in a single category, which is the way I use both terminologies in this book. However, it is worth mentioning that some scholars do differentiate between them. Mignolo and Walsh (2018) refer to decolonisation as overcoming the territorial dominance of the old colonies. For many scholars in the Latin American and African traditions, decolonisation was the territorial process, and thus coloniality comes after that as a structure of power that was preserved after independence from the colonies (Tamale 2020). This is the reason why the use of 'decoloniality' instead of 'decolonisation' refers to the will to overcome colonial thinking and to act in decolonial terms. Furthermore, as Mignolo and Walsh (2018) insist, decolonisation means a final point at which we will ultimately get rid of colonial domination which, for them, is not achievable. They sustain that we need to act in favour of decoloniality, not as overcoming coloniality—this will never happen in their view—but as thinking and acting in ways that help us to achieve certain steps without reaching the end of the road. Although I agree with much of this argument, I still use the word 'decolonisation' because the prevalence of this concept (rather than 'decoloniality') in the South African higher-education context is significant. In using it, I believe I am conserving the meaning that is attached to the term locally, whilst defending the term not only as meaning territorial independence but also as meaning a process (that is always incomplete) towards an ecology of knowledges, democratisation of knowledge and the social justice aim thereof.

Thirdly, this book refers to participatory approaches as participatory practices that can be applied on three levels, namely participatory methods, participatory methodologies, and participatory research processes. This division is acknowledged intentionally to help the reader to understand the different categories and their various implementations. When we refer to participatory methods—which are residual in this book—we highlight a specific use of a participatory element within a larger study, which aims to collect data sets for the researchers to analyse. For instance, a quantitative research team working on food security wants to have a participatory workshop with a particular community to better understand food habits and food availability. In this case, the research team prepares a series of participatory activities and implements them in order to acquire some data about how to improve the following methodological step or just to collect data using different methodological strategies. In these cases, there is a clear participatory component, although this is only as a punctual strategy for the researchers to collect data. This is a common practice, especially in development studies, but it does not deal with the many dilemmas in how knowledge is produced. Due to this, the outcome of the workshop is only a preparatory step or a process of innovatively gathering data, and does not involve any further philosophical questions about knowledge production. Therefore, when referring to participatory methods, we refer to this type of practice or similar examples, such as not necessarily involving communities in designing the research project, not analysing together and so on.

On the other hand, this book is more strongly focused on participatory methodologies and research processes. Surprisingly, the differences between them are not really clear in the literature and they tend to be mixed unintentionally, due to the significant differences between academic fields and their conceptualisation of 'research' and use of methodologies. For instance, the majority of social sciences research or educational research will see the process of enquiry as linear, from conceptualising the issue, to finding the academic gap, to designing an adequate research design, to applying it, to analysing and concluding it. This is not the same process for other disciplines such as anthropology, in which, for instance, the case of grounded research challenges a linear structure. Therefore, due to the transdisciplinary nature of participatory approaches and the different influences in their practices, the division seems not to be sufficiently clear. Therefore, as a clarification for this book, when the text refers to 'methodology' it does not necessarily imply that the community or group of individuals participating have been deciding the issue under research, although this may be possible in some cases. On the contrary, it mainly refers to when the scholar frames the issue under research and implements a participatory methodology that can be composed of diverse participatory techniques that are enacted by the community, resulting in a collaborative knowledge production process. And finally, when referring to the participatory research process, the text acknowledges a collaborative process from beginning to end, in which the individuals (meaning community members and researchers) are those who define and propose the issue under research and implement the research process in a collaborative study. Therefore, the conceptualisation of the capabilities-based participatory practice (see Chapter Four) shall be framed and referred to throughout this book as a 'research process', rather than a methodology.

It is due to this ambiguity that some scholars may consider this book a methodological discussion, instead of seeing it as a new conceptualisation of an alternative research process and of the principal role of the facilitator. I will argue that this book proposes a research process which is informed by the Capabilities Approach and a particular decolonial debate to explore Southern processes of knowledge generation. In this way, what I am claiming is not only the methodological space—the strategies to create knowledge—but the collaborative formulation of the issue under research. This is a major statement, as it assumes that the conceptualisation of the issue is a political, metaphysical, ontological and cosmological statement that may highly affect and/or misdirect the research process as a whole. Furthermore, the role of the facilitator as a qualitative researcher is still present, not only in order to value scientific knowledge but as a way to enhance contextual knowledge creation in the field of capabilities. This is equally a way to promote an ecology of knowledges, as a whole, combining grassroots research processes and qualitative research processes.

Equally, terms such as 'North', 'South', 'voiceless', 'democracy', and 'social justice' need to be clarified in this section, in order for the reader to anticipate their meaning throughout this book. First, the distinction between 'North' and 'South' in this book refers more to a geopolitical space, as clarified in the first section of this chapter. North and South are understood more as a mindset than as a geographical space. These terms do not represent a static or well-defined territory; they represent different logics, which give sense to the way we live and act in the world. This vision, in a way, implies a controversial territorial division that contradicts many of the arguments supported and defended in this work. I do not consider any of these categories as internally homogeneous. As highlighted above, the South, as a geopolitical space, has been subject to diverse and varied forms of oppression, and thus the experiences and responses to these are different from context to context. What this case helps us to do is to re-think. It does not universalise experiences in the Global South, but pays attention to contextual specificities and how we can challenge these tensions from a Global South positionality, with an open-ended epistemological basis.

On the other hand, the term 'voiceless' is here used with a particular meaning, which it is also necessary to comment on. When students are referred to as a 'voiceless' group, it does not assume they do not have a voice. Actually, the argument supported here is that they do have a voice in diverse ways and express it by different means—such as for instance through student protests, or their capacity to choose those capabilities that they deem valuable. Conversely, the term 'voiceless' refers to the difficulties they have accessing and contributing to powerful or dominant structures of knowledge production. In this case, I acknowledge that they produce knowledge in their own ways and have a voice in certain marginal spaces due to many Western epistemic oppressions. Thus, this project seeks to link and build bridges between diverse areas of knowledge production. It creates a more—although not perfectly—equal terrain, especially for those that have historically been excluded from powerful spaces. Thus, this project enhances their capacities to participate in those epistemic systems to which they did not have access due to their colonial epistemic marginalisation.

The terms 'democracy' and 'social justice' also need further clarification. Both terms are used in this book from a capabilities and Southern perspective. First, 'democracy' is understood in a broad sense, as Sen claims (2009). He asserts that democracy needs to be assessed by 'the capacity to enrich reasoned engagement through enhancing informational availability and the feasibility of interactive discussion. Democracy has to be judged not just by the institutions that formally exist but by the extent to which different voices from diverse sections of the people can actually be heard' (Sen 2009, xiixiii). In this way, democracy in this study is understood in terms of the extent that individuals from diverse sectors are scrutinising for a better decision- and knowledge-making process. This includes the extent to which different Southern populations and groups can be heard and the relevance of participatory research to enhance these marginal voices.

On the other hand, the term 'social justice' is equally framed from the Capabilities Approach and a Southern perspective. In this sense, I am not trying to identify the perfect society or pursue a theory of justice. Conversely, I am looking for 'deplorable situations that leave individuals with few choices to exercise their reasoned agency', such as epistemic injustices (Sen, 1999; Fricker, 2015). Therefore, injustices refer to situations where individuals are not able to enjoy their valued capabilities, or their valued freedoms, and cannot become the individuals they want to be. In this sense, I am not talking about a unique way of achieving justice but rather an incomplete sense of justice that needs to be guided by the lives that different individuals and communities have reason to pursue. Hence, it should be guided by lives as valued by Southern perspectives and by the question of how well their institutions and systems are protecting these valued lives. Furthermore, as Drydyk (2012, 32) corroborates, 'Acting justly, according to the Capabilities Approach, aims not merely for people to rise above capability deprivation, but to do it through processes that are empowering for them, so that they have become better able to shape their own lives'. Thus, these ideas are where the Democratic Capabilities Research practice and its orientation towards Southern social justice align. It is not only about enhancing capabilities, but rather about doing so by means of a process that empowers and prepares individuals and groups to better shape their own lives in their own valuable ways, thereby overcoming Western ways of being and doing, as imposed by the Global North.

As a final point, in capabilitarian literature, the Capabilities Approach is also referred to as the Capability Approach, and both (singular and plural) terminologies are used indistinctly (Nussbaum 2011). However, this book uses the plural formulation of the term, 'Capabilities Approach', throughout the text to highlight and emphasise the plurality of capabilities that are valuable for diverse and heterogeneous individuals and collectives as well as the different interpretations of the Capabilities Approach.

Therefore, after some initial clarifications, the final part of this introductory chapter will summarise the book and briefly explore the different chapters of which it is comprised.

This book is divided into nine chapters, with each drawing on different aspects of the exploration. Short excerpts from the collaborative book written by the co-researchers of the DCR project are also introduced at the beginning of each chapter. The DCR collaborative book *Narratives on Social Injustices: Undergraduate Voices* was one of the outcomes of this participatory research process. The twelve undergraduate students decided to write pieces (in different languages) narrating their diverse experiences of social injustices and of what it is to be a young South African undergraduate student. Their stories not only recount current events, but also events and experiences that informed their understandings of their context and life as young university students in South Africa. They explore intersectional issues such as gender inequalities, racism experienced by them and others they knew, and their struggles to be recognised as dignified human beings in their universities. In this book, I present their stories at the beginning of each chapter as 'rooted moments' for the reader. They are flashbacks into students' minds, which allow us to understand the complexities of the contexts in which these students have grown up and continue to live. The narrative pieces are presented anonymously, as this was the students' preference when co-authoring their collaborative book in 2018. Equally, the students' names have been anonymised through pseudonyms, as agreed with them for this research project. The collaborative book, titled *Narratives on Social Injustices: Undergraduate Voices*, was distributed, as decided by the team, as an open-access resource among attendees of the book launch and other individuals on campus in 2018. Therefore, some stories have been selected and included in this book, in line with our open-access ethos, as a way of enhancing the reach of students' voices. For more information about the collaborative book and other research outcomes, please refer to Chapter Six.

This book commences with a broad exposition of basic elements and theoretical points of this study. It situates this study in the South African higher-education context, presenting an historical review of this country's institutions and their current challenges. The text explores the students' claims for decolonisation and the subsequent revitalisation of the academic literature. The second chapter ('Coloniality and Decoloniality in the Global South Higher Education Context') continues examining and presenting the particular decolonial debate defended in this book. Different aspects are examined, clarifying concepts, ideas and the central vision of decoloniality in higher education.

The third chapter ('Traditions and Limitations of Participatory Research') explores the scholarly work on participatory approaches. This analysis helps us to better understand the academic gap between capabilities and human development literatures, identifying a space for the conceptualisation of this innovative research process, 'Democratic Capabilities Research'. It lays the foundation on which the capabilities-based research proposal is situated, challenging some Western participatory tendencies in the field.

The fourth chapter ('Democratising Participatory Research: A Capabilitarian Conceptualisation') poses the question that if the colonial challenge is central to participatory practices—as the literature in the field claims—how can we resolve the limitations and controversies in the field? For this reason, this chapter introduces the Capabilities Approach, linking its foundational elements with those of decolonial debates. This chapter aims to illustrate the current commonalities between both positions, and the potential of the Capabilities Approach to fill some of the gaps in the field of participatory practices. To this end, the chapter uses an open-ended version of the Capabilities Approach defended by Amartya Sen (1999; 2009) as a way to understand the multiple kinds of life (beyond the Western lifestyle) that different individuals have reason to value. In short, the Capabilities Approach is used as a framework to understand human development, leading us to ask the question: 'What are the real freedoms an individual has to lead the life she/he has reason to value?' This provides us with a theoretical foundation that can accommodate different lifestyles around the world which do not necessarily fit into the hegemonic capitalist/neoliberal/patriarchal/ Christian and heteronormative perspectives, thus highlighting this aspect's centrality to the achievement of social justice from a Southern perspective.

Hence, the chapter introduces the participatory, capabilities-based research proposal as Democratic Capabilities Research (DCR) through five open-ended principles that can accommodate the variety of practices and implementations needed to democratise participatory research from a decolonial capabilities perspective. This perspective is flexible and context-dependent—thus, open-ended—as is the view of the Capabilities Approach used throughout this book. The five DCR principles discussed in this chapter are: (1) injustice as an initial issue that unites a group of individuals to research things that matter to them; (2) uncertain horizons, such as the promotion of democratic spaces for knowledge production, beyond simple participation, situating agency at the core of the research process; (3) internal/external diversity, in the sense of allowing the space for an ecology of knowledges or epistemic diversity within knowledge production; (4) resituating the voiceless as knowledge creators, including collectives and individuals excluded from official spaces of knowledge creation and considering them as worthy contributors of knowledge; and (5) the process of knowledge production as a space for the expansion of an individual's valued capabilities.

The second part of the book is composed of five chapters, three of them dedicated to evidence based on the DCR experience in South Africa, such as exploring capabilities and the role of the facilitator (Chapters Five, Six and Seven); and two of them dedicated to discussion of and conclusions on the DCR case study (Chapters Eight and Nine).

Chapter Five ('Co-researchers' Valued Capabilities') is centred around the debate on the universalisation of capabilities—the creation of universal capabilities for all (Nussbaum 2011)—in relation to the evidence that arose from the case study in South Africa. Firstly, using a prospective application of the Capabilities Approach, the chapter argues for the need to identify the valued capabilities of a group of co-researchers before undertaking participatory practices. The analysis is made by exploring the valued capabilities for the twelve students participating in the case study explored in this book. It incorporates the fluid aspect of capabilities and presents the four central capabilities for this group: Epistemic, Ubuntu, Human Recognition and Self-Development capabilities.

Furthermore, contextual capability choices, instead of a universal list (Nussbaum 2011), are used to compare and understand their differences. Thus, the chapter argues that despite the contribution this universal list makes to the capabilitarian field, we still have good reason to scrutinise it, as many cultural and contextual specificities of the Global South can be lost in these types of aggregation. For instance, the Ubuntu capability identified in this group exposes current understandings of care and support from the Global North that in its Western form limits a contextual vision of this freedom. Further, the chapter presents conceptualisations such as 'Insurgent capabilities' and 'Colonial conversion factors', discussing their relevance in a Global South context such as South Africa. Hence, it provides Southern perspectives as an alternative to normative, Western, liberal ways of seeing and understanding the Capabilities Approach. The final section of the chapter focuses on the actual prospective frame designed prior to the participatory project in this DCR case study, as part of the facilitator's role. The frame highlights the strategies drafted according to the most valuable capabilities among the group of participants. These strategies are presented in order to show how the author—as facilitator—applied the different recommendations from the prospective plan during the DCR project following Principle 5 from the DCR practice.

Chapter Six ('The South African DCR Project: Undergraduates as Researchers') clarifies how the DCR process took place and what the DCR team did in each of the workshops, with emphasis on the valued capabilities highlighted in the previous chapter. Thus, this chapter presents the participatory project, focusing on the data from interviews and students' perspectives on the participatory project, as collected by the facilitator during and after the project. Nevertheless, data from journals and participant observation are also displayed in order to problematise the power imbalances within the group and within wider debates on participatory literature. Furthermore, the chapter discusses tensions in the application of Principle 3 with regard to the ecology of knowledges and practical imbalances due to contextual variables.

Chapter Seven ('Broadening our Participatory Evaluations: A Southern Capabilitarian Perspective') explores the cases of two students from the wider group of twelve using the qualitative data collected in the case study. These two cases were chosen due to the students' uneven levels of enjoyment in their capabilities sets when they first became part of the project. The two students had really different lives, coming from different cultural and economic backgrounds, and being of different genders. The lives they had reason to value had commonalities and divergences that are worthy of exploration when using capabilities to guide our participatory practices. Their actual freedoms were distinct and thus they had dissimilar valued capabilities. Hence, individual choices about valued capabilities and the initial enjoyment of those capabilities are important sources of information when it comes to assessing participatory practices such as DCR.

Therefore, this chapter highlights what a capabilities analysis of DCR adds to current evaluative spaces. It provides a more people-centred analysis, but at the same time avoids paternalistic assessments. That is, instead of using generic capabilities to understand what impact the participatory project had on students, the chapter presents students' valuable capabilities as an evaluative space.

Subsequently, Chapter Eight ('DCR for Socially Just Higher Education: Perspectives from the South') focuses on the idea of justice and the challenges and lessons learned from the South African case study (Sen 1999). Firstly, the chapter combines conceptual and empirical elements, prompting a conversation between the five principles presented in Chapter Four and elements from the data in this project to conceptualise this DCR practice. Thus, the five DCR principles are taken from its initial conceptualisation and reviewed after the case study implementation, exploring their actual application in the South African case as well as their contribution to social justice and decoloniality.

The chapter therefore begins with an exploration of social justice as a contested term that has been influenced historically by various dominant visions and perspectives (Capeheart & Milevanovic 2007). However, these positionalities have tended to universalise just criteria in order to assess and impose a 'perfect society' from above—usually originating from an elitist and paternalist social class that took it upon themselves to speak in the name of everyone. Hence, justice is in this chapter conceptualised as an incomplete vision that must be contextualised in order to understand its meaning at different points in time and in different contexts, and that must scrutinise perspectives that do not necessarily need to be unified (Sen 2009). In this way, to achieve social justice in knowledge production within higher education we do not need to create a universal way of applying DCR or participatory research. Conversely, we need to contextualise the research, focusing on the moment, place and individuals with whom we are working.

The final chapter (Chapter Nine, 'Redrawing our Epistemic Horizon') focuses on the main contributions, general reflections and conclusions of this book. It also elaborates on the specific contributions this book makes to bodies of scholarly knowledge. Firstly, it starts by looking at the conceptual/empirical contributions linking the empirical and theoretical debates developed in the book. The chapter concludes by focusing on pedagogical contributions and applications in the classroom, as well as possible applications in educational policies. Here, diverse uses and applications are highlighted, broadening the use of DCR beyond its central aim. In summary, this section contemplates the implications of using DCR for institutional practices and policies. Furthermore, the chapter outlines the future directions of DCR and how these practices may be expanded and further theorised in the area of participatory research. It highlights the centrality of networks for the progression and application of this tool in the future as a way to democratise participatory research from a Southern perspective.

# References

Appadurai, A. (2006). The right to research. *Globalisation, Societies and Education*, *4*(2), 167–177. https://doi.org/10.1080/14767720600750696.

Badat, S. (2008). Redressing the colonial/apartheid legacy: Social equity, redress and higher education admissions in democratic South Africa. In Hasan & Nussbaum (eds). *Conference on Affirmative Action in Higher Education in India, the United States and South Africa.* New Delhi: Oxford University Press (pp. 19–21). https://www.ru.ac.za/media/rhodesuniversity/content/vc/documents/Redressing_the_Colonial_or_Apartheid_Legacy.pdf.

Bosch, T. (2017). Twitter activism and youth in South Africa: The case of #RhodesMustFall. *Information, Communication & Society*, *20*(2), 221–232. https://doi.org/10.1080/1369118x.2016.1162829.

Botha, M. M. (2007). Africanising the curriculum: An exploratory study. *South African Journal of Higher Education*, *21*(2), 202–216. https://doi.org/10.4314/sajhe.v21i2.25630.

Bunting, I. (2006). The higher education landscape under apartheid. In Colete, Maassen, Fehnel, Moja, Gibson & Perold (eds). *Transformation in Higher Education, Global Pressures and Local Realities* (pp. 35–52). Dordrecht: Springer Netherlands. https://doi.org/10.1007/1-4020-4006-7_3.

Butler-Adam, J. (2016). What really matters for students in South African higher education? *South African Journal of Science*, *112*(3–4), 12. https://doi.org/10.17159/sajs.2016/a0151.

Breier, M. (2010). From 'financial considerations' to 'poverty': Towards a reconceptualisation of the role of finances in higher education student drop out. *Higher Education*, *60*(6), 657–670. https://www.jstor.org/stable/40930317.

Capeheart, L., & Milovanovic, D. (2007). *Social Justice: Theories, Issues, and Movements.* London: Rutgers University Press. https://doi.org/10.36019/9780813541686.

Coombes, B., Johnson, J. T., & Howitt, R. (2014). Indigenous geographies III: Methodological innovation and the unsettling of participatory research. *Progress in Human Geography*, *38*(6), 845–854. https://doi.org/10.1177/0309132513514723.

Chilisa, B. (2013). *Indigenous Research Methodologies.* Thousand Oaks: Sage Publications.

Cloete, N., Maassen, P., Fehnel, R., Moja, T., Gobbon, T. & Perold, H. (2006). *Transformation in Higher Education: Global Pressures and Local Realities.* Amsterdam: Taylor & Francis. https://doi.org/10.1007/1-4020-4006-7.

De Sousa Santos, B. (2010). *Descolonizar el saber, reinventar el poder*. Montevideo: Ediciones Trilce. http://www.boaventuradesousasantos.pt/media/Descolonizar%20el%20saber_final%20-%20C%C3%B3pia.pdf.

De Sousa Santos, B. (2014). *Epistemologies of the South: Justice against Epistemicide*. New York: Routledge. https://unescochair-cbrsr.org/pdf/resource/Epistemologies_of_the_South.pdf.

Diop, C. A. (2010). The meaning of our work. In R. Grinker, S. Lubkemann & C. Steiner (eds). *Perspectives on Africa: A Reader in Culture, History and Representation* (pp. 44–47). Oxford: Wiley-Blackwell.

Drydyk, J. (2012). A capability approach to justice as a virtue. *Ethical Theory and Moral Practice, 15*(1), 23–38. https://doi.org/10.1007/s10677-011-9327-2.

Firfirey, N., & Carolissen, R. (2010). 'I keep myself clean... at least when you see me, you don't know I am poor': Student experiences of poverty in South African higher education. *South African Journal of Higher Education, 24*(6), 987–1002. https://journals.co.za/doi/10.10520/EJC37654.

Fricker, M. (2015). Epistemic contribution as a central human capability. In George Hull (ed.). *The Equal Society: Essays on Equality in Theory and Practice* (pp. 73–90). Lanham: Lexington Books. https://rowman.com/ISBN/9781498515719/.

Hall, B. L., & Tandon, R. (2017). Decolonization of knowledge, epistemicide, participatory research and higher education. *Research for All, 1*(1), 6–19. https://doi.org/10.18546/rfa.01.1.02.

Karodia, A. M., Soni, D., & Soni, P. (2016). Wither higher education in the context of the Feesmustfall campaign in South Africa. *Research Journal of Education, 2*(5), 76–89. https://ideas.repec.org/a/arp/rjearp/2016p76-89.html.

Kemmis, S., McTaggart, R., & Nixon, R. (2013). *The Action Research Planner: Doing Critical Participatory Action Research*. New South Wales: Springer Science & Business Media. https://doi.org/10.1007/978-981-4560-67-2.

Kovach, M. (2009). *Indigenous Methodologies: Charasteristics, Conversations and Contexts*. Toronto: University of Toronto Press. https://doi.org/10.1111/j.1541-0064.2012.00420.x.

Leibowitz, B. (2017). Power, knowledge and learning: Dehegemonising colonial knowledge. *Alternation, 24*(2), 99–119. https://journals.ukzn.ac.za/index.php/soa/article/view/1322.

Lincoln, Y. S., Lynham, S. A., & Guba, E. G. (2011). Paradigmatic controversies, contradictions, and emerging confluences, revisited. In Denzin & Lincoln (eds). *The SAGE Handbook of Qualitative Research*, 4 (pp. 97–128). Thousand Oaks: Sage Publications.

Luckett, K. (2016). Curriculum contestation in a post-colonial context: A view from the South. *Teaching in Higher Education, 21*(4), 415–428. https://doi.org/10.1080/13562517.2016.1155547.

Luescher, T., Loader, L., & Mugume, T. (2016). #FeesMustFall: An internet-age student movement in South Africa and the case of the University of the Free State. *Politikon, 44*(2), 231–245. https://doi.org/10.1080/02589346.2016.1238644.

Mato, D. A. (2014). Universidades indígenas en América Latina: Experiencias, logros, problemas, conflictos y desafíos. *ISEES: Inclusion social y equidad en la education superior, 14,* 17–45. https://ri.conicet.gov.ar/handle/11336/50938.

Mignolo, W. D. (2007). DELINKING: The rhetoric of modernity, the logic of coloniality and the grammar of de-coloniality. *Cultural Studies, 21*(2-3), 449–514. https://doi.org/10.1080/09502380601162647.

Mignolo, W. D., & Walsh, C. E. (2018). *On Decoloniality: Concepts, Analytics, Praxis.* Durham: Duke University Press.

Naidoo, L. A. (2015). The role of radical pedagogy in the South African Students Organisation and the Black Consciousness Movement in South Africa, 1968–1973. *Education as Change, 19*(2), 112–132. https://doi.org/10.1080/16823206.2015.1085614.

Naicker, C. (2016). From Marikana to #feesmustfall: The praxis of popular politics in South Africa. *Urbanisation, 1*(1), 53–61. https://doi.org/10.1177/2455747116640434.

Ndlovu, S. (2021). Humanness and ableism: Construction and deconstruction of disability. In Steyn & Mpofu (eds). *Decolonising the Human: Reflections from Africa on Difference and Oppression* (pp. 65–85). Johannesburg: Wits University Press.

Ndlovu-Gatsheni, S. J. (2018). *Epistemic Freedom in Africa: Deprovincialization and Decolonization.* New York: Routledge.

Mpofu, W. & Steyn M. (2021). *The Trouble with the Human.* In Steyn & Mpofu (eds). *Decolonising the Human: Reflections from Africa on Difference and Oppression* (pp. 1–24). Johannesburg: Wits University Press.

Msila, V., & Gumbo, M. T. (eds) (2016). *Africanising the Curriculum: Indigenous Perspectives and Theories.* Johannesburg: African Sun Media.

Nussbaum, M. C. (2011). *Creating Capabilities: The Human Development Approach.* Cambridge: Harvard University Press.

Oyewumi, O. (ed.) (2016). *African Gender Studies: A Reader.* New York: Springer.

Pithouse, R. (ed.) (2006). *Asinamali: University Struggles in Post-Apartheid South Africa.* Johannesburg: Africa World Press.

Postma, D. (2016). An educational response to student protests: Learning from Hannah Arendt. *Education as Change, 20*(1), 19. http://dx.doi.org/10.17159/1947-9417/2016/1042.

Ritchie, S. D., Wabano, M. J., Beardy, J., Curran, J., Orkin, A., VanderBurgh, D. & Young, N. L. (2013). Community-based participatory research with

Indigenous communities: The proximity paradox. *Health & Place, 24,* 183–189. https:// 10.1016/j.healthplace.2013.09.008.

Robeyns, I. (2005). The capability approach: A theoretical survey. *Journal of Human Development, 6*(1), 93–117. https://doi.org/10.1080/14649880520003 4266.

Santos, D. (2012). The politics of storytelling: unfolding the multiple layers of politics in (P) AR publications. *Educational Action Research, 20*(1), 113–128. https://doi.org/10.1080/09650792.2012.647695.

Sen, A. (1999). *Development as Freedom.* New York: Random House.

Sen, A. (2009). *The Idea of Justice.* Cambridge, MA: Belknap.

Smith, L. (1999). *Decolonizing Methodologies: Research and Indigenous Peoples.* London: Zed Books.

Tabata, I. B. (1960). *Education for Barbarism.* London: Unity Movement of South Africa.

Tamale, S. (2020). *Decolonization and Afro-Feminism.* Ottawa: Daraja Press.

Van der Merwe, J. C., & Van Reenen, D. (2016). *Transformation and Legitimation in Post-Apartheid Universities: Reading Discourses from 'Reitz'.* Bloemfontein: Sun Media.

Walker, M. (2020). The well-being of South African university students from low-income households. *Oxford Development Studies, 48*(1), 56–69. https:// doi.org/10.1080/13600818.2019.1672143.

# 2. Coloniality and Decoloniality in the Global South Higher-Education Context

Universities have embraced or preached transformation and integration policies. These are unseen or even unheard of for many students within universities. They feel prejudiced because of certain actions portrayed by universities and other students different from them.

In January 2012, Thabang Makhoang from North-West University in Potchefstroom drowned in the campus swimming pool in what was alleged to be initiation activities. Instructions were in Afrikaans and it is said that he did not understand them well. The university claims that he had the option of saying yes or no to the activity, he might have agreed or not but the fear of isolation after not agreeing to the group activities was much higher than the fear of being unable to swim.

Keith Arlow of St John's College was alleged to have made racist remarks to pupils over an extended period of time. Despite being found guilty of serious misconduct, he was said to have remained, as the school stated that it is a result of mitigating factors.

This problem has also occurred at the University of the Free State where students and workers were harassed, violated and arrested for seeking the implementation of a presidential commission on in-sourcing.

The alleged victim of racism at the University of Pretoria is a Kenyan national. In 2012, a black parent was killed in a stampede at the gates of the University of Johannesburg, where crowds of students had gathered in the quest to gain admission into this university.

These are just a few of many incidents that have occurred and they have had huge impacts on people's lives. It all goes back to the issue of racism, which occurs within South African universities. It simply shows how much has not changed as much as people say things have changed.

*Excerpt from Narratives on Social Injustices: Undergraduate Voices, the collaborative book by DCR members, 2018*

 https://doi.org/10.11647/OBP.0273.02

## 2.1 Coloniality in the Global South

There is a significant body of knowledge highlighting the social, political and epistemological transition that old colonies need to overcome in order to liberate their communities and cultures (Mbembe 2001). Nowadays this process seems to be central for many scholars and grassroots movements, as many countries in the Global South, while having overcome territorial or political domination, have, however, not succeeded in some other important aspects, such as the social, economic or epistemological areas. This includes processes of knowledge generation as well as higher-education institutions in general (De Sousa Santos 2014; Dussel 2007; Mignolo 2007).

In brief, since the fifteenth century, colonialism and imperialism have played a major role in the Western conquest of other nations and the expansion of Western power across the world (Parra-Romero 2016). Mignolo (2010; 2007) conceptualises this Western idea as the North Atlantic block, arguing that the Western space has been historically repositioned to the geographical point of the North Atlantic, which represents the domination of a European-American system. Furthermore, for post-colonial scholars, this phenomenon, as stated above, goes beyond the initial colonial aim of conquering territory; it is a political and intellectual invasion and exploitation of other cultures (Chilisa 2012; Wa Thiong'o 1986). Chilisa (2012, 29) states that colonialism was 'a brutal process through which two-thirds of the world experienced invasion and loss of territory accompanied by the distribution of political, social, and economic systems, leading to external political control and economic dependence on the West'. For Chilisa, this power over territories accelerated not only the loss of territory but the loss of local knowledge systems, cosmovisions,[1] and beliefs. Further, Wa Thiong'o (1986) supports a similar perspective, stating that it was a psychic and mental conquest, appropriating the wealth of other societies, their territories, and goods, thus establishing a colonised universe in which culture, institutions, languages and social and political systems are imposed as a unique and hegemonic world paradigm.

---

1    A cosmovision is the way in which an individual and/or a society perceives and interprets the world.

For post-colonial scholars, the colonial question remains a present and urgent issue. Wa Thiong'o (1986) uses the term 'neocolonies' to refer to the current situation of domination and injustices maintained through cultural and political constraints, such as colonial language and identity formation in the Global South. On the other hand, Mbembe (2001; 2015) names this state of affairs 'postcolony', referring to present colonial spaces which continue to sustain identity assimilation under a 'regime of violence' (1992, 3). Appiah (1993) and Wa Thiong'o (1986) use the term 'neocolonial territory', where identities are constructed through the codes of the coloniser, using their languages and admiring their historical figures as tools to construct a single, exceptional, valid history.

In brief, for many of these scholars, what is currently problematic is the maintenance of this system of domination, which is not colonial per se, but preserves dominant colonial elements across the world, especially in the academic field and the ways in which scholars produce knowledge and understand reality (Smith 1999). This Eurocentric domination is related to the onto-epistemological challenges highlighting the need to understand and critically analyse epistemic inequalities, which dominate in present-day higher-education institutions.

## 2.2 Deciphering the Global North Codes

The onto-epistemological challenges can be summed up by two demands: the universal ontological claim of Western sciences by Castro-Gomez (cited in Soldatenko 2015) and epistemic killing—epistemicide—by De Sousa Santos (De Sousa Santos 2014). Both critiques are substantial in order to understand the decolonial debate and the proposals for social justice and democratisation of knowledge in higher-education institutions. Firstly, these two colonial challenges perpetuate colonisation as a way to sustain hegemony (Escobar 2007). Hegemony is here conceptualised as a dominant system that establishes and balances two dimensions—'the good life' and 'the valid life'—inadvertently imposing them on everyone (Dussel 2007; Joseph 2002). These two dimensions represent a normative position, which is culturally related and attached to a clear Western colonial, and subsequently capitalist, tradition that conceptualises reality (the ontological position), whilst understanding knowledge creation and its use in a particular way (the epistemic system).

Firstly, the ontological narrowness is based on a Western conceptualisation of reality as universal, which is incapable of understanding its own positionality. This idea is called 'zero-point' by Castro-Gomez and explained by Soldatenko (2015) as an 'imaginary position of objective neutrality that enlightenment science took for itself by displacing other epistemic frameworks in the colonial world as primitive, irrational and religious' (Soldatenko 2015, 140). To a certain extent, this Western tradition conceptualises nature as detached from individuals and assumes a universal, disembodied reality (Mignolo 2007). This stands in contrast with other perspectives such as, for instance, those of Indigenous communities who regard nature and human beings as deeply interconnected (Smith 1999). Hence, the problem itself is not this particular positionality, which is as valid as any other, but its imposition on others due to its self-proclaimed status as the only objective perception and investigations of our reality as human beings, despite our cultural and cosmological differences. Therefore, this critique is based on the influence of the unquestioned universality and superiority of Western ontological positions. Further, as Mignolo and Walsh (2018) recently argued, this ontology is, in itself, a Western and Eurocentric term, as it assumes that objects and subjects create reality instead of knowledge. Mignolo and Walsh (2018) clarify that in order to find a more accurate terminology, we will need to think about cosmologies instead of ontologies, as the former are able to overcome the limitation of meaning to objects, despite having other cultures that attach meaning to relationalities.

On the other hand, ontological or cosmological domination is linked to the epistemological challenge because, as Mignolo and Walsh confirm, 'ontology is an epistemological concept' (2018, 135). Hence, the imposition of Western ontology as superior also sustains a particular way of understanding the nature of knowledge and the processes in which it is produced, thus maintaining a hegemonic epistemological system. This issue has been named 'epistemological blindness' by Hlela (2018) or 'epistemicide' by De Sousa Santos (2014). Both terms refer to the destruction or invisibility of other knowledge systems due to the 'universal' perception of the Western epistemological canon as superior (De Sousa Santos 2014) or the inability to recognise other knowledge systems as valid (Hlela 2018). For instance, one example broadly referred to in the literature is the fact that Indigenous people need to validate their knowledge as rigorous, and therefore universal, by means of scientific procedures (Cooper & Morrell 2014). As Berenstain (2016, 571) clearly states:

> This creates a burden on the marginalised to educate and enlighten. Though the privileged demand the epistemic labour of the marginalised, they often perpetuate epistemic oppression by dismissing the knowledge produced. The marginalised are excluded from the realm of recognised knowledge creators despite contributing novel conceptual resources and epistemic frameworks.

Hence, epistemic oppressions highlight how hegemonic epistemic perspectives have narrowed the richness of human knowledge and wisdom beyond the Western epistemic system (Zibechi 2015).

Furthermore, these scholars do not deny the importance of Western thought or its philosophical tradition, conversely; they believe that this tradition is rich and has generated valuable knowledge, from other cultures and civilisations too (Dussel 2007; Mignolo 2007). Their issue lies in the fact that this system does not understand its own superior positionality and does not allow for a space in which knowledge could be considered or produced differently (De Sousa Santos 2014). Therefore, these cosmological and epistemological gaps provide the foundation for alternative pathways towards decoloniality, from a Global South perspective, that these scholars articulate.[2] Moreover, as higher education is the central interest of this book, the following section will explore universities with a particular decolonial project for social justice through the use of participatory research practices and its role in these debates.

---

2     It is important to mention that there are many other decolonial perspectives supported by other scholars but that this book, due to its aim, supports and explores this particular one. I will only refer to the pluriversal project as a higher-education, decolonial perspective from the South in this book.

# 2.3 Transforming Our 'Uni-Versity' into a 'Pluri-Versity'

In light of the complexity outlined above, what the universal project, the hegemonic project, ignores is the diversity of perspectives (cosmologies) and knowledges (epistemic systems) beyond itself. Therefore, a group of scholars (Boidin, Cohen & Grosfoguel 2012; Dussel 2007; Mignolo 2007; Escobar 2018) have developed a perspective that provides the heterogeneous foundation needed to reverse these colonial challenges; this is called the 'pluriverse' project. This project aims to transform a universe into a pluri-verse better capable of accommodating the diversity that has historically been excluded due to structures of domination. Although the pluriversal project is extensive and fertile, I will focus here on its educational derivative, the 'pluriversity', in order to understand the foundational ideas.

In this pluriversity model, the idea is to transform a monolithic university institution into a less provincial one (Boidin et al. 2012). In addition, in this project, the fight against epistemic coloniality is substantial for the transition to an academic model which is capable of challenging academic knowledge production and practice (Tamdgidi 2012).

In this matter, the concept of an 'ecology of knowledges'—epistemic multiplicity—coined by De Sousa Santos (2014) is helpful for understanding the equal relevance of different knowledge systems and the possibility of bringing them together as a way of cooperation. De Sousa Santos (2010; 2014) asserts that every knowledge system is incomplete, due to its own internal and external limitations. Therefore, the incompleteness of all knowledge systems—including the Western epistemic system—necessitates an epistemological dialogue between them, which is called an ecology of knowledges. When scholars are able to interrogate their knowledge system and bring it into conversation with others, an ecology of knowledges is stimulated, and this is a necessary condition in promoting a pluriversity. Thus, this is a way to include Southern perspectives long ignored by the Global North.

The pertinent questions are: what are universities currently doing to challenge these colonial issues, and how can these strategies be improved or reformulated, if necessary? Do we decide to propose a solution 'within' or 'outside' our higher-education institutions? Is it even possible to achieve a decolonial project in the Western higher-education system?

This book seeks to conduct an internal analysis of what higher-education institutions are doing so far, and how these practices, specifically participatory practices, can be improved and stimulated by new theoretical insights, bringing methodological plurality into our research processes from a Southern perspective. However, before analysing and assessing different participatory practices, it is necessary to investigate how, if at all, participatory approaches are aligned with decolonial debates.

## 2.4 Participatory Approaches in the Twenty-First Century: A Decolonial Intention

Certainly, participatory approaches are related to certain values of togetherness, democracy, inclusion, heterogeneity and social justice, which are strongly represented in many categories such as Participatory Action Research, Participatory Research, Educational Action Research or Community Based Action Research, among others. These discourses are especially visible within the Action Research family, which, despite being part of the industrial strand, and the more conventional line of practices, nowadays embraces all participatory typologies. Hence, scholars tend to refer to many participatory practices as Action Research. For example, we may consider the many handbooks exploring different participatory practices that use Action Research in their titles, such as *The Palgrave International Handbook of Action Research* (2017). Further, these handbooks tend to claim decolonial aims in different ways and among different families of participatory approaches. One of the latest compilations about the diverse practices of AR claims in its preface:

> We believe Action Research has a crucial role to play in the work of creating, an 'alternative globalisation' that counters the standard view being propagated by those whose interest lies in maintaining the status quo of colonial domination largely by the global North at the expense of the peoples, cultures, resources, and epistemologies of the global South. (Rowell et al. 2017, xii)

Equally, they state that '[they] represent efforts to push against various forms of colonisation of hearts and minds' (Rowell et al. 2017, xii). *The SAGE Handbook of Action Research* (2008), another reference for AR practitioners, states:

> Most of us educated within the Western paradigm have inherited a
> broadly 'Cartesian' worldview, which channels our thinking in significant
> ways. It tells us the world is made of separate things [...] and it tells
> us that mind and physical reality are separate [...] This split between
> humanity and nature, and the abrogation of all mind to humans, is what
> Weber meant by the disenchantment of the world. As Fals Borda has
> put it, participation is one way through which we may 're-enchant' our
> plural world. (Reason & Bradbury 2008, 8)

These works incisively expose the Western worldview, calling for a shift
towards a more plural world. This is especially relevant for many of
the decolonial arguments, which acknowledge the colonial imposition
of reason over tradition in modern Cartesian thinking as a Western
creation, and emphasise its perpetuation through imperialism. This is
why they confirm that:

> Action Research without its liberating and emancipatory dimension is a
> shadow of its full possibility and will be in danger of being co-opted by
> the status quo. (Reason & Bradbury 2008, 5)

Thus, despite the diversity of practice within participatory approaches,
current discourses of AR sustain and support the use of these practices
as a way to move towards decoloniality. Further, the role of epistemic
justice is central to this debate. These AR-focused handbooks expose
the invisibility of other knowledge systems that are dominated by the
technocratic and objectivist perspectives sustained by a hegemonic
academic system. Additionally, the same book, in its most recent edition
published in 2015 (Bradbury 2015), maintains similar ideas:

> While our theoretical groundings are informed by the post-modernist
> deconstructing of classical theorising, which privileged the objective
> observer with his ostensibly value-free language and logical deduction/
> generalisation, we also know that criticism is not enough. (Bradbury
> 2015, 3)

Hence:

> When action researchers think of epistemology, we understand the
> impoverishment of having only the objective voice of conventional
> social science. We are called to consider how multiple epistemological
> voices can be better integrated to serve our inquiry and our co-inquirers.
> (Bradbury 2015, 4)

And finally, the Educational Action Research Family pursues these critiques eloquently, expressing that AR aims to:

> Promote decolonisation of lifeworld that has become saturated with bureaucratic discourses, routinised practices and institutionalised forms of social relationships. (Kemmis, McTaggart & Nixon 2013, 12)

Therefore, the democratisation of knowledge, epistemic justice, and the promotion of a pluriversal world, or justice as a whole, are all examples of the challenges that the diverse and extended family of participatory approaches is aiming to overcome. Nevertheless, to critically engage with these practices, we need to analyse them and understand that not all practices and approaches might be directed to decolonise or democratise research in the way this book defends. Thus, the following chapter aims to clarify different traditions and goals within participatory research to uncover Western homogenising tendencies and their consequences. Doing so, we are able to highlight the pitfalls and shortcomings and advance towards decolonisation and social justice more broadly, whilst also defining an innovative participatory practice.

# References

Appiah, A. (1993). *In My Father's House: Africa in the Philosophy of Culture*. New York: Oxford University Press.

Berenstain, N. (2016). Epistemic exploitation. *Ergo, 3*(22), 569–590. https://doi.org/10.3998/ergo.12405314.0003.022.

Boidin, C., Cohen, J., & Grosfoguel, R. (2012). Introduction: From University to Pluriversity—A Decolonial Approach to the Present Crisis of Western Universities. *Human Architecture: Journal of the Sociology of Self-Knowledge, 10*(1), 1–6. https://scholarworks.umb.edu/humanarchitecture/vol10/iss1/2.

Bradbury, H. (ed.) (2015). *The SAGE Handbook of Action Research*. Thousand Oaks: Sage Publications.

Chilisa, B. (2012). *Indigenous Research Methodologies*. Los Angeles: Sage Publications.

Cooper, B., & Morrell, R. (eds) (2014). *Africa-Centred Knowledges: Crossing Fields and Worlds*. Woodbridge: Boydell & Brewer Ltd.

De Sousa Santos, B. (2010). *Descolonizar el saber, reinventar el poder*. Montevideo: Ediciones Trilce.

De Sousa Santos, B. (2014). *Epistemologies of the South: Justice against Epistemicide.* New York: Routledge. https://unescochair-cbrsr.org/pdf/resource/ Epistemologies_of_the_South.pdf.

Dussel, E. D. (2007). *Materiales para una política de la liberación.* Buenos Aires: Plaza y valdés España.

Escobar, A. (2007). Worlds and knowledges otherwise: The Latin American modernity/coloniality research program. *Cultural Studies, 21*(2-3), 179–210. https://doi.org/10.1080/09502380601162506.

Escobar, A. (2018). *Designs for the Pluriverse: Radical Interdependence, Autonomy, and the Making of Worlds.* Durham: Duke University Press.

Hlela, Z. (2018). Learning through the action of research: Reflections on an Afrocentric research design. *Community Development Journal, 53*(2), 375–392. https://doi.org/10.1093/cdj/bsw033.

Joseph, J. (2002). *Hegemony: A Realist Analysis.* New York: Routledge.

Kemmis, S., McTaggart, R., & Nixon, R. (2013). *The Action Research Planner: Doing Critical Participatory Action Research.* New South Wales: Springer Science & Business Media.

Mignolo, W. D. (2007). DELINKING: The rhetoric of modernity, the logic of coloniality and the grammar of de-coloniality. *Cultural Studies, 21*(2-3), 449–514. https://doi.org/10.1080/09502380601162647.

Mignolo, W. (2010). Cosmopolitanism and the de-colonial option. *Studies in Philosophy and Education, 29*(2), 111–127. https://doi.org/10.1007/ s11217-009-9163-1.

Mignolo, W. D., & Walsh, C. E. (2018). *On Decoloniality: Concepts, Analytics, Praxis.* Durham: Duke University Press.

Mbembe, J. A. (2001). *On the Postcolony* (Vol. 41). Berkeley: University of California Press.

Mbembe, J. A. (2015). Decolonizing knowledge and the question of the archive. Aula magistral proferida. Public lecture, Wits University (South Africa). https://wiser.wits.ac.za/system/files/Achille%20Mbembe%20-%20 Decolonizing%20Knowledge%20and%20the%20Question%20of%20the%20 Archive.pdf.

Parra-Romero, A. P. (2016). ¿ Por qué pensar un giro decolonial en el análisis de los conflictos socioambientales en América Latina? *Ecología Política, 51,* 15–20. https://www.ecologiapolitica.info/?p=6006.

Reason, P., & Bradbury, H. (2008). *The SAGE Handbook of Action Research: Participative Inquiry and Practice.* Los Angeles: Sage Publications.

Rowell, L. L., Bruce, C. D., Shosh, J. M., & Riel, M. M. (eds) (2017). *The Palgrave International Handbook of Action Research.* London: Palgrave Macmillan.

Smith, L. (1999). *Decolonizing Methodologies: Research and Indigenous Peoples.* London: Zed Books.

Soldatenko, G. (2015). A contribution toward the decolonization of philosophy: Asserting the coloniality of power in the study of non-western philosophical traditions. *Comparative and Continental Philosophy, 7*(2), 138–156. https://doi.org/10.1179/1757063815Z.00000000059.

Tamdgidi, M. H. (2012). Editor's note: To be of but not in the university. *Human Architecture: Journal of the Sociology of Self-Knowledge, 10*(1), 1. https://www.okcir.com/product/decolonizing-the-university-practicing-pluriversity/.

Wa Thiong'o, N. (1986). *Decolonizing the Mind.* London: James Currey.

Zibechi, R. (2015). *Descolonizar el pensamiento crítico y las prácticas emancipatorias.* Buenos Aires: Ediciones Desde Abajo.

# 3. Traditions and Limitations of Participatory Research

Power is the ability or capacity to do something or act in a particular way, whereas inequality is the lack of equality, the ability not to be treated fairly. These two concepts are very crucial elements in the university, they work hand-in-hand with one another. Whereby we have come to a point where when you do not have status or if you are not well-known by the management of the university, your issues or concerns will not be taken into account. It relates to who you are, what you are and how well you are connected to those people. This is what our country has become: 'status'.

When it comes to inequality it is a very critical issue in a sense that we as the students of the university, we are not treated equally, given the same opportunities and privileges. It plays a very vital role in the university because there is a big difference between white and black students, we are all not being given the same opportunities, leading to racism among other issues. Also, here, language discrimination plays a huge role, for example, last year accounting students wrote an auditing paper only to realise that the question paper on the Afrikaans side already contained the right answers.

What does that create?

It creates unfairness and unequal distribution of opportunities and privileges.

*Narratives on Social Injustices: Undergraduate Voices*, 201

## 3.1 Introduction

This chapter explores the complexities when investigating participatory approaches as a research field. Firstly, the chapter divides the field into four major research areas (industrial, development, Indigenous, and educational) in order to clarify the diverse foundational assumptions of different practices and their distinct theoretical grounds. Among the

 https://doi.org/10.11647/OBP.0273.03

research areas, the industrial branch represents the beginning of Action Research (hereafter AR), a term coined by Kurt Lewin (1946). Secondly, the development family adds a critical perspective to the initial AR practice. This family uses terminologies such as Participatory Research (hereafter PR) and Participatory Action Research (hereafter PAR) as a way to highlight that active and engaged participation lies at the core of these practices. In this section, various traditions are presented and their commitment to some of the decolonial aims is outlined, in addition to their focus on liberation and emancipatory-type theories. The third family, the Indigenous family, focuses on post-colonial theory. It is founded on the invisibility of Indigenous people, and their ways of understanding research and producing knowledge. And the final category, the educational family, is presented due to the educational focus of this book. This family is explored via the category of Educational Action Research (from now on EAR), and subcategories such as Action Science (AS), Action Learning (AL), Classroom Action Research (CAR), Action Learning Action Research (ALAR)/Participatory Action Learning Action Research (PALAR) and Critical Participatory Action Research (CPAR).

After the exploration of all these branches, a summary of the major challenges throughout the field is provided. The chapter investigates issues around individual/collective practices, the contested terms and application of participation in different practices, credibility and validity within the academic context, and the challenges arising from embracing diverse practices. This chapter focuses on the gaps between each of the four proposed branches and decoloniality, highlighting spaces where we might usefully introduce the Capabilities Approach as a theoretical frame. Thus, this chapter provides the starting point for a conceptualisation of participatory capabilities-based research, in order to resolve certain limitations of these four branches.

## 3.2 Introducing Participatory Approaches

Participatory approaches represent an extended family composed of methods, methodologies and research typologies, from the most conventional and academic frame to the most radical post-modernist-decolonial understanding of enquiry (Reason & Bradbury 2008;

Bradbury 2015; Rowell at al. 2016). This diversity of practices is reflected in the numerous terminologies used among the international literature in the field, highlighting different origins, aims and theoretical influences (Etmanski et al. 2014; Dick 2015; Higgins 2016). To provide some examples of these diverse typologies, the table below presents just a few terminologies.

Table 1: Typologies of participatory approaches.

| Participatory Action Research | Cooperative Enquiry | Soft System Approaches | Feminist Participatory Action Research |
|---|---|---|---|
| Action Research | Industrial Action Research | Participatory Research | Participatory Community Research |
| Educational Action Research | Action Science | Classroom Action Research | Community Based-Research |
| Participatory Rural Appraisal | Action Learning | Critical Participatory Action Research | Community-Based Participatory Research |
| Tribal Participatory Research | Constructionist Research | Participatory Learning and Action | Cooperative Research |
| Critical System Theory | PALAR (PAL and AR) | Participatory Indigenous knowledge Research | Visual Participatory Research |
| Participatory Design Research | Queering Participatory Design Research | Design-Based Research | Rapid Rural Appraisal |
| Participatory Rural Appraisal | Participatory Poverty Assessment | Appreciative Enquiry | Participatory Video |

The sample above shows that participatory approaches have been adapted to different fields and practices, creating specific tools for scholars that are committed to democratic values, social change, and social accountability in different ways (Reason & Bradbury 2008). For this reason, the present chapter aims to make an in-depth exploration of these typologies, highlighting some traditions and current challenges in order to provide the space for a capabilities-based typology.

First of all, the diversity highlighted above has mostly been embraced by scholars in the field in a positive way. Reason and Bradbury (2008), among others (Greenwood & Levin 2006; Dick & Greenwood 2015), honour and value all the different orientations, appreciating the richness and diversity of this wide family. Additionally, Chambers (2008) calls it *eclectic pluralism*, which is inclusive of its diversity, expressing that all participatory typologies must be complemented by 'mutual and critical reflective learning and personal responsibility for good practice' (2008, 331). Equally, Dick and Greenwood (2015) attest that 'being sectarian and narrow about the varieties of AR is not an option' (2015, 195). Nevertheless, although it seems positive to embrace all these typologies, it is true that not all of them act and are implemented in the same way, nor are their aims all equal. This fact might obstruct the way scholars in the field understand the different practices and traditions, impacting the mutual and reflective learning between them. For this reason, the following section attempts to undertake a critical analysis and to present a structure of traditions among participatory practices, in order to better understand their differences and commonalities and their role in decoloniality.

## 3.3 Participatory Approaches: An International Analysis

Action Research is the broadest term for naming this type of practice, although as the following sections will highlight, initial understandings of AR differ greatly, with current practices and debates about participation and community involvement. Countless terminologies can be found within the AR family, as mentioned above, and it is very difficult to track down a clear classification or definition in the literature.

In an attempt to historically organise influences over AR, Feldman (2017) proposes a classification based on three eras (Era 1, Era 2 and Era 3, see Feldman 2017) in the English-speaking world. This analysis, although helpful and inspiring, does not confront major complexities within the field, and makes the Spanish-speaking tradition, along with many other non-English speaking traditions, invisible. Therefore, to advance current classifications this chapter presents four research areas to be considered when referring to participatory approaches. These four areas structure the chapter, which considers their presentations and subcategories and concludes with limitations and possibilities for decoloniality and the democratisation of knowledge.

The four families are:

(1) the industrial family, where AR was born, which focuses on improving production processes and is strongly influenced by a positivist understanding of social change, implemented by cycles of reflection and action (Lewin 1946).

(2) The development family, which provides a more critical perspective in participation and epistemic debates and mostly focuses on community interventions and the voiceless (Fals-Borda & Rahman 1991).

(3) The Indigenous family, which is intimately linked with the development family, however, the Indigenous strand has acquired more radical perspectives.

(4) And finally, the educational family, which initially is the application of an industrial perspective to the improvement of professional educational practices (Noffke & Somekh 2009), but which is progressively being influenced by more critical perspectives such as Freireian pedagogy (Kemmis, McTaggart & Nixon 2013).

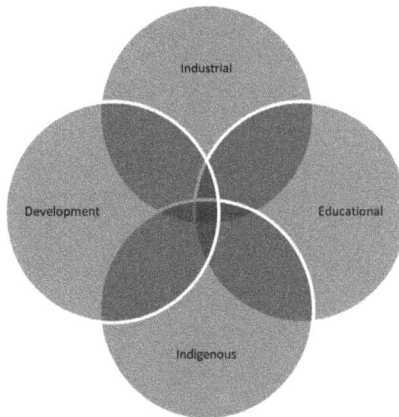

Figure 1: Participatory Families (image by the author, 2021).

Although the graphic seems to clearly divide these four areas, the categories can also be seen to overlap in terms of practices and foundational features. Nevertheless, some of them, such as the initial industrial family and the Indigenous family, possess irreconcilable theoretical features. To a certain extent, this complexity explains the current difficulties of classification and differentiation in the literature, which is camouflaged by an ethos of embracing the diverse and extended family of participatory approaches (Greenwood & Levin 2006; Dick & Greenwood 2015).

## 3.3.1 Industrial Family: Action Research

The industrial democracy movement refers to the first large-scale projects of AR (Greenwood & Levin 2006). Kurt Lewin was the first person to use the term AR, which dates back to 1934 (Adelman 1993).[1] Lewin was trained as a social psychologist and was interested in human behaviour, inter-group relations and social change (Lewin 1946). This led him, together with his students, to test factories and neighbourhoods in quasi-experimental studies, exploring the increased productivity that came about through inclusive participation instead of authoritarian management (Adelman 1993). For instance, an example of one of their studies is the case of the Harwood Factory in Virginia, where they explored how participation affected productivity and work absenteeism (Kristiansen & Blosch-Poulsen 2016). However, Lewin's studies were not only related to factories but also researched family habits and military efficiency. A particular example is his experiment conducting real-life research with the aim of achieving a particular goal in small groups, in this case, that of modifying family habits (Lewin 1947). Equally, Lewin conducted studies in the US, aiming to change food habits among American civilians and allowing the soldiers to get better quality meat, or worked with bomber squadrons in the Second World War, where the cycles of reflection and action are easily visible, with the process being repeated over and over again until the achievement of the goal (Kemmis, McTaggart & Nixon 2013).

---

1  Even though Lewin was the creator of the term 'Action Research' some authors (Gazda et al. 1997; Dash 1999) refer to Moreno as the methodological inventor of Action Research. J. L. Moreno was a group psychotherapist in 1914 and he applied action-oriented interventions for groups and inter-group therapies.

Lewin designed a research methodology which, through cycles of action and refection, could act as a catalyst for social change as a desirable aim, through a pragmatic and positivist frame of human behaviour. This positivist frame presumed that there were universal laws motivating human behaviour and, therefore, that it was a cause-effect problem. Generally, the researcher identifies the problem and implements the research until the behaviour in the population being researched changes. Lewin's research, especially in the early stages, aimed to change habits according to policy recommendations or the researcher's interest, with the participants' involvement going no further than their being changed in accordance with the researcher's desired outcome. This differs greatly from actual and/or critical understandings of AR.

According to Feldman (2017), the cycle of AR for Lewin was based on six steps.

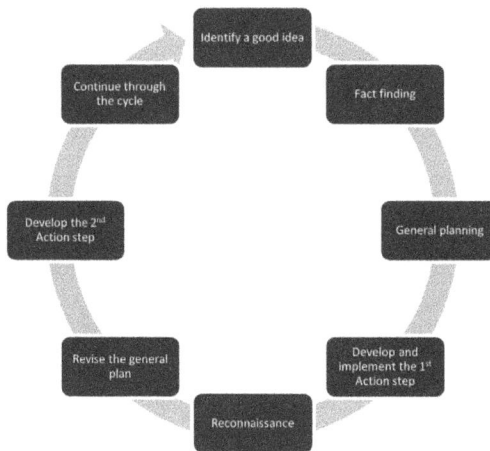

Figure 2: Diagram of Lewin's Action Cycle (image by the author, 2021, based on Fieldman 2017, 127).

Following these steps, the researcher acts as a catalyst for the desired behavioural change in the population.

Later in his career, Lewin also tried to democratise the research process by introducing into his research the participation of communities or groups excluded from his initial approach (Adelman 1993). However, there are challenges in how 'participation' is understood, due to Lewin's historical moment and his positivist scientific background. In Lewin's thought, participation was based on a superficial or instrumental enrolment or limited understanding of participation according to posterior practices (Kemmis, McTaggart & Retallick 2004). Problems were determined by experts, and participants were used to resolve the experts' concerns, such as changing eating habits to provide better pieces of meat for soldiers during the war, or reducing absenteeism in manufacturing for the benefit of the manufacturer's management.

Therefore, the scientific production and pragmatism underlying Lewin's notion of AR is clearly visible. As Adelman (1993) states, 'Action Research was the means of systemic enquiry for all participants in the quest for greater effectiveness through democratic participation' (Adelman 1993, 7). Nevertheless, that democratic participation was shaped by the circumstances of the time, and governed by authoritative and disciplinary models that were focused on increasing productivity. In general terms, his studies were generally more informed by a pragmatic and scientific positivist rigour than by an urge to expose abusive power relations within working environments or major ontological debates by unmasking an oppressive epistemic system. That is why Adelman (1993) corroborates:

> Lewin's ideas on democratic participation in the workplace did not include any critique of the wider society, particularly the range of economic relations between worker and employer, capital and labour. Indeed, a fair observation would be that although Lewin and his co-workers demonstrated the efficacy of action research for improving productivity, they did not develop conceptual structures that took explicit account of the power bases that define social roles and strongly influence the process of any change in the modes of production. (Adelman 1993, 10)

Therefore, although Lewin's approach attempted to increase democratic relations within the arduous and intricate industrial context after the Second World War in Europe, it was implemented as a means of advancing more productive industrial processes and more efficient solutions to social problems within a Western industrial context.

Nevertheless, after several decades of work, Lewin and his co-workers were able to classify four distinctive typologies according to the different practices, which evolved from their initial work (Adelman 1993). These typologies[2] were more varied, exposing not only the instrumental

---

2    For more information on the features of each of these categories, see Adelman (1993).

function of AR in increasing productivity, but also alternatives that have over the years become slightly different from the original AR type.

Today there is a broad range of definitions for AR, with a mixture of identifying features, which are at times contradictory, and originate from a wide range of discourses across participatory approaches from the 1930s until today. What is clear is that the initial understanding of AR seems now to be distant from current practices and restricted in its ability to advance decolonisation and democratise knowledge.

## 3.3.2 Development Family: Participatory Action Research and Participatory Research

In the 1960s 'participation' was added to AR, as an ideological sign of what came first: participation, not action. This second phase of AR is marked by enquiry implemented in developing contexts, such as Africa, Latin America and Asia (Kindom, Pain & Kesby 2007), all of which shared, to a greater or lesser extent, the desire for a different research practice (Brydom-Miller 2001). Enquiry was regarded as a toolkit that, when adequately supplied, could liberate the oppressed (Greenwood & Lewin 2006). Influenced by Freire's pedagogy, popular education and Orlando Fals Borda's awareness-building and liberating interventions, the practice of PAR spread across Colombia through Orlando Fals Borda, across Brazil through Freire, across Tanzania through Liisa, and across India through Tandon (Brydom-Miller 2001; Thiollent & Colette 2017). Furthermore, Rowell and Hong (2017) acknowledge that Fals Borda used PAR as a way to reverse the unequal politics of knowledge through the validation of popular episteme.

There is however no consensus on who proposed PAR and when the terminology was coined, but two practitioners are generally mentioned and proclaimed as its initiators within the PAR literature: Marja-Liisa, with her Jipemoyo project (Nyemba & Meyer 2017), and Orlando Fals Borda in Colombia, who popularised the term 'Investigacion Accion Participativa' (Thiollent & Colette 2017).

First, Dr Marja-Liisa Swantz attributes the creation of PAR to herself through her work in Tanzania, stating that:

> Somehow I actually wanted to create a different way of doing research and so I did not base it on specific theories but looked for ideas how to make people co-researchers and aware of the significance of their

own ways of conceiving ideas and making use of their resources of knowledge. (Nyemba & Meyer 2017, 4)

She especially refers to the Jipemoyo project as her first PAR project from 1975–79, which aimed to encourage inhabitants of Jipemoyo, in Tanzania, to resolve their problems with their own resources (Nyemba & Meyer 2017).

Secondly, Orlando Fals-Borda is recognised as the initiator of PAR[3] in Colombia, which was influenced by a Freireian ideology (Brydom-Miller 2001). These interventions were characterised by their aim for radical social change and emancipation (Kindon, Pain & Kesby 2007). PAR was a practice focused on the liberation of oppressed groups and classes, and the unlocking of deplorable injustices arising from the politics of knowledge (Fals Borda & Rahman 1991). He highlighted the relevance of 'empathetic engagement' understanding participants and researchers as 'sentipensantes'.[4] The principal aim of PAR was the combination of different knowledges supporting excluded groups or communities through investigative techniques (Rappaport 2017). According to Rappaport (2017), Fals Borda combined rigorous data collection with the participatory process, inviting the relevant community or group to determine the agenda, and making them the ultimate owners of the research outcomes, free to use them as a political tool. This was a 'dialogo de saberes',[5] a communal self-reflection process, combining 'academic and grassroots notions of research' (Rappaport 2017, 147). Furthermore, Rappaport (2017) states that Vasco Uribe, another contemporary PAR practitioner, considered the process differently, placing ideas at the core and seeing thinking as a research process. For Uribe, it was not necessary to collect data, systematically analyse it, and give it back to the community. For him the process of thinking together was a counter-hegemonic way of non-academic research.

Although different practices could present different theoretical and practical insights, this group was characterised by a critical perspective of participation, where participants' enrolment meant ownership of the

---

3  The literature presents different terminologies. While initially Orlando Fals-Borda referred to the methodology as Participatory Research (Fals-Borda & Rahman 1991), posterior publications situate equally Fals-Borda (Thiollent & Colette 2017) and Swantz (Nyemba & Meyer 2017) as the creators of Participatory Action Research.
4  'Thinking-feeling individuals'.
5  'Knowledge dialogue'.

process from the very beginning to the very end, combining different knowledges. The use of research was seen as an ideological weapon against homogenising trends and the use of practice as a catalyst for the liberation of the communities or individuals oppressed (Fals Borda & Rahman 1991). However, in the last thirty years, development studies have made extensive use of this family of participatory approaches, diversifying its implementation; thus, new terminologies have come onto the scene,[6] expanding and homogenising the types of practice applied (Cornwall & Jewkes 1995). This homogenisation has limited the potential of PAR as a counterhegemonic tool for participatory research practitioners (Santos, 2013).

### 3.3.3 Indigenous Family: Indigenous Research

Indigenous research is closely related to PAR practices, however, in this case, Indigenous practices focus on Indigenous communities and are strongly linked with post-colonial theories. Scholars from this Indigenous branch believe that science is a universal or objective representation of reality, and legitimises its own politics of truth (Soldatenko 2015). Thus, there were, and continue to be, many scholars who highlight the contradictions within modernism and its imperial project (Thaman 2003; Escobar 2007; De Sousa Santos 2014, Dussel 2007; Appiah 2010; Mbembe 2015; Diop 2010). Thaman (2003) states:

> Critical reflection on the philosophy of science and liberal education, as well as what passes for 'objective' truths, will reveal that our academic education is not culture-free and gender-neutral, nor does it occupy an ideologically neutral high ground because academic, scientific, and liberal beliefs and values, like all beliefs and values, are embedded in a particular cultural curriculum and agenda. (Thaman 2003, 6–7)

Therefore, authors claim that there is a need to include Indigenous knowledges and worldviews, as the perspectives of a historically excluded group, and for them to be promoted and recognised (Ninomiya & Pollock 2016). What they refer to as Indigenous knowledges are:

---

6    Southern Participatory Action Research, Participatory Community Development, Rural appraisal, Cooperative enquiry, Participatory Community Research, Community-Based Participatory Research, Tribal participatory Research, Rapid Rural Appraisal, Participatory Rural Appraisal, Participatory Poverty Assessment or Development Research (Greenwood & Levin 2006; Kindon, Pain & Kesby 2007).

> Understood as the common sense ideas and cultural knowledge of local peoples concerning the everyday realities of living. They encompass the cultural traditions, values, belief systems, and the world views that, in any Indigenous society, are imparted to the younger generation by community elders. (Semali & Kincheloe 2002, 1)

Indigenous knowledges represent the internal processes through which members of the community understand themselves and their surroundings, their beliefs, and history (Semali & Kincheloe 2002). Supporters of Indigenous research have presented an alternative paradigmatic position, which explains differences from the 'academic paradigm'. The Indigenous paradigm negates the academic assumption that knowledge is created individually and that it is owned by the researcher and the academic community (Chilisa 2012).

Thus, this emphasis on post-colonial studies aligns this Indigenous branch with decolonial challenges in academia, as discussed in the previous chapter. For instance, for Chilisa (2012) decolonisation is the process of co-researching through community ontologies and epistemologies, recognising the colonial object of study and applying its palliative 'recognition' and 'use of otherness'. Therefore, as Smith (1999) highlights, it is a matter of decolonising the process of research through the deconstruction of its own established tools, such as interviews, and substituting them for flexible methods or already accepted Indigenous methods that do not contradict Indigenous cosmovisions and worldviews. For Nnaemeka (2004), it is within the decolonisation process that we can start to talk about participation and real democracy, when Indigenous views, Indigenous ontologies, knowledge and values can come to the forefront and be experienced. And for Dei (2014), this process can only start with the recognition of space, of knowing 'otherwise', of the political, emotional and spiritual aspects of knowledge. As she claims, 'Central to Indigenous research are concepts of spirituality, spiritual knowing, the interface of body, mind, soul, and spirit, and the nexus of society, culture, and nature' (Dei 2014, 52). As Hlela (2018) highlights in the case of Southern Africa, we need to discover and rediscover 'the value of Ubuntu' (Hlela 2018, 4–5) in a constant and engaging dialogue. For her it is a question of historical justice and commitment towards Indigenous communities' future.

Further, ethical questions are substantial when using Indigenous participatory research, as Chilisa (2012) remarks. The researcher is a 'provocateur and transformative healer guided by the four Rs: accountable responsibility, respect, reciprocity, and rights and regulations of the researched, as well as roles and responsibilities of researchers as articulated in ethics guidelines and protocols of the former colonised, Indigenous people and the historically oppressed' (Chilisa 2012, 7). In this matter, Chilisa (2012) proposes four dimensions for Indigenous research,

1. It targets a local phenomenon instead of using extant theory from the West to identify and define a research issue

2. It is context-sensitive and creates locally relevant constructs, methods, and theories derived from local experiences and Indigenous Knowledge

3. It can be integrative, that is, combining Western and indigenous theories

4. In this most advanced form, its assumptions about what counts as reality, knowledge, and values in research are informed by an Indigenous research paradigm. The assumptions in an Indigenous paradigm guide the research process

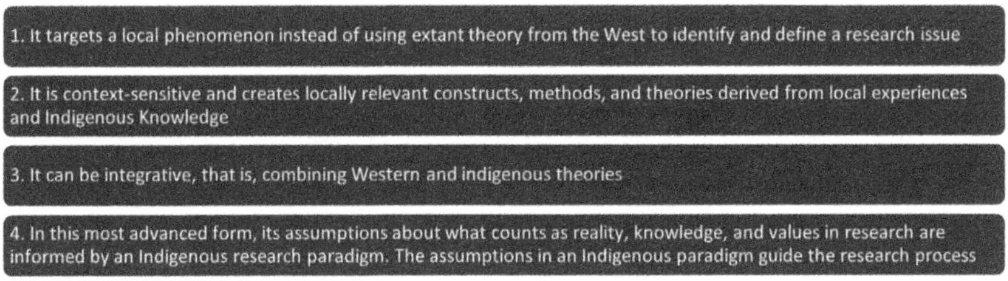

Figure 3: Four dimensions for Indigenous research (image by the author, 2021, based on Chilisa 2012, 13).

To conclude, Indigenous methodologies and research processes can be easily linked with PAR practices, however, their focus is slightly different as these practices are centred on Indigenous populations while PAR focuses on oppressed populations and communities. For this reason, Schroeder (2014) explains that Indigenous research is not the same as PAR, although Indigenous practitioners can use PAR as a methodology. It is, therefore, clear in this family that Indigenous research works towards the decolonisation of knowledge by widening the borders of the system, moving beyond a Eurocentric way of knowing (Dei 2014; Escobar 2007). However, the questions here is: can we operationalise decolonial research when we are not co-researching with Indigenous communities? What about experiential knowledge, intuitive, cultural or local knowledge coming from marginalised communities that are not necessarily Indigenous?

## 3.3.4 Educational Family: Educational Action Research

To conclude, the educational family offers a highly diverse field, which ranges from a more scientific approach, close to the European-Western perspective of AR, to a more radical perspective, situated close to the borders of a PAR practice. Thus, the following sections shall explore the varieties born of the need to accommodate distinct practices among educational practitioners.

The educational field nurtured the development of AR within pedagogy. In this area, AR is considered a learning process (McNiff & Whitehead 2002). According to the literature, Educational Action Research (EAR) accomplishes a different set of goals depending on the underlying theoretical background. It presents a diversity of practices among practitioners. All these varieties follow different guidelines, placing emphasis on different aspects and actors within the research. For instance, Action Science (AS) was born as an organisational/industrial strategy; however, it has been used to improve practices through collaboration and reflective dialogue among teachers (Argirys et al. 1985; Zuber-Skerrit, Fletcher & Kearny 2015). Conversely, Classroom Action Research (CAR) is mostly guided by teachers with the help of a professional researcher to explore and improve their own pedagogical practices (Somekh 2006; Whitehead 1991). The following sections will examine some of these EAR categories in order to provide a better overview of the different practices and applications of Educational Action Research.

## Educational Action Research as a Broad Category

As highlighted previously, AR has infiltrated the field of education, giving rise to the new category of Educational Action Research. EAR practitioners believe that AR involves a learning process: 'Action Research is always to do with learning, and learning is to do with education and growth' (McNiff & Whitehead 2002, 15). Furthermore, in the last twenty years, there has been an increasing interest in EAR across the Americas, Europe, Australia and Africa. Since the 1990s, interest has also grown in Asia and Eastern Europe (Noffke & Somekh 2009), and there is a flourishing academic literature on its application and theorisation (Carr and Kemmis 1986; Elliott 1991; McKernan 1991; Stenhouse 1975; McGrill & Beaty 1995 among others).

According to the literature, EAR aims to improve learning, teaching, curricula and administration within primary, secondary and tertiary educational institutions (Zuber-Skerritt, Fletcher & Kearney 2015; Altrichter et al. 1991). Moreover, it provides a link between those involved in educational institutions and movements seeking to bring about social change (Kemmis, McTaggart & Nixon 2013). As Kemmis, McTaggart and Nixon state 'they made the global, local and the personal, political' (Kemmis, McTaggart & Nixon 2013, 13).

Additionally, Kember (2000, 30) provides an explicit list of features which characterise the vision of EAR as a broad category. These are:

Table 2: Features of Educational Action Research (table based on Kember 2000, 30).

| |
|---|
| Project teams are composed of small groups who share a similar interest or concern. It is also possible for individuals to conduct AR projects within courses they teach. |
| The topic for the project is defined by the participants, to fit within the broad framework of investigating and improving some aspects of their own teaching. |
| Project groups meet regularly to report observations and critique their own practices. This discourse provides for the possibility of perspective transformation. |
| Projects proceed through cycles of planning, action, observation, and reflection. At least two cycles are normally necessary to implement and refine any innovatory practices. The time-scale for the cycles is consistent with the extended period necessary for perspective transformation. |
| Evidence of the effectiveness of teaching practices and their influence on student learning outcomes is gathered using interpretative methods. |
| The evidence gathered can be used to convince departmental colleagues, not originally participating in the project, that they too should change their practices and the curriculum. |
| Lessons learnt from the projects can be disseminated to a wider audience through publications. Participants are, therefore, eligible for rewards through the traditional value system of universities. |

As can be noted from the above features, in Educational Action Research, the staff of educational institutions are the main actors, and promote their own reflection and learning through their individual educational practices. Although nowadays there are varieties of EAR which also include students, academics tend to focus on teachers (secondary, primary), lecturers (tertiary) or university students of education (those who are training to teachers) (Carr & Kemmis 1986; Kember 2000). Two clear examples of this are visible in Carr and Kemmis (1986), when they state that EAR 'involves [educational] practitioners directly in theorising their own practice and revising their theories self-critically in the light of their practical consequences' (Carr & Kemmis 1986, 198), and Kember (2000), who gives teachers power over the research process:

> The topic is something of interest to the teacher so there is motivation for them to conduct the study. The topic can be some innovation they feel is worth introducing into their teaching. It can be a problem they want to solve or an issue they want to tackle. It can often be a concern that they have been aware of for some time, but which has lain dormant because they were unsure how to tackle it. (Kember 2000, 24–25)

Nevertheless, as previously discussed in relation to AR, the use of different practice discourses and traditions over the years has fostered an extensive variety of practices in EAR. Therefore, terms such as Classroom Action Research (CAR), Action Sciences (AS), Pedagogical Action Research (PAR), Action Learning (AL), Participatory Action Learning Action Research (PALAR) and Critical Participatory Action Research (CPAR) are becoming more and more common among EAR practitioners. In the following sections, I will explore these varied terms in order to develop a more informed perspective of the practices applied within education.

## Action Science

The first type reviewed in this section is Action Science. Action Science has mostly been used in organisations and management sciences, however, its application within educational institutions and educational practices makes it relevant for this section (Argyris et al. 1985). To a certain extent, this typology can be situated between the margins of Industrial Action Research and Educational Action Research.

AS was developed by Chris Argyris,[7] a student of Kurt Lewin who also was influenced by the work of John Dewey (Raelin 1997; Helskog 2014). In this typology, AS:

> Is a strategy for increasing the skills and confidence of individuals in groups to create any kind of organisation and to foster long-term

---

7    However, it can equally be attributed to his colleagues Schon, Putnam and McLain-Smith.

individual and group effectiveness. This strategy applies to any form of human relations, either organisational, group, or interpersonal contexts where individuals work on challenging tasks together.[8]

For AS the aim is to increase professional effectiveness by helping individuals in small groups,[9] improving practices through collaboration and reflective dialogue (Zuber-Skerritt, Fletcher & Kearney 2015). This is an organisational framework to improve practices that build systematically 'between academic organisational psychology and practical problems as they are experienced in organisations' (Kemmis, McTaggart & Nixon 2013, 10). Moreover, it pays attention to formal and professional knowledge-analysing gaps between theory and practice as a way to create new understanding and to change practices (Dash 1999). Therefore, this typology possesses a stronger link with initial approaches of AR from Lewin's tradition than other EAR practices, developing a systematic process of reflexivity individually or collectively with an organisational perspective.

## *Classroom Action Research*

Classroom Action Research (CAR) is a practice developed by teachers in their own classrooms, analysing their own practices with their students, mostly in the context of primary and secondary education (Somekh 2006). It usually involves an academic partner who helps the teacher to apply the research, collect data and reflect on how to improve their educational practice (Elliott 1991). Moreover, it mainly applies qualitative, interpretative modes of enquiry (Whitehead 1989). It consists of a practical exercise where theory and practice combine to displace 'living theory' or 'living one's educational values' (Dadds 1995; Goodnough 2008; Stenhouse 1975; Wells 2009). This typology seems to be the most widely used among practitioners in education, however, it has been criticised for not paying attention to the social and political aspects of educational institutions and their practices (Kemmis, McTaggart & Nixon 2013) as its focus tends to be on professional improvement and teaching efficiency.

---

8    See http://www.actionscience.com/actinq.htm#basic.
9    For more information see http://www.actionscience.com/actinq.htm#basic.

## Pedagogical Action Research

Norton (2009) proposes Pedagogical Action Research (PeAR) as a different methodology designed for an alternative educational context. He states:

> I want to consider briefly the history of the action research movement and show how being a practitioner doing action research in higher education is distinct from being a practitioner doing action research in other educational contexts. This is why I have coined the term pedagogical action research. (Norton 2009, 50)

Norton states that EAR might be of use to primary and secondary levels but is not of use to higher-education institutions. That is why he proposes Pedagogical Action Research (PeAR) as a specific typology for the higher-education context, due to its significant differences from other educational institutions. Norton highlights that PeAR 'refers to the principles of learning and teaching that occur at tertiary level' (Norton 2009, 59). Therefore, this practice is oriented to lecturers, creating a research process where professionals can systematically investigate their own teaching and learning, while also improving their practice and contributing to academic knowledge (Norton 2009).

According to Norton (2009), referring to the literature available in EAR, the purposes of PeAR are:

Table 3: Purposes of Pedagogical Action Research (table based on Norton 2009, 59-60).

| |
|---|
| A training for university academics in systematically analysing their own practice |
| A training for university academics in systematically analysing their research methods and expertise; an aid to reflective thinking which results in action |
| A support for professional efficacy |
| A way of challenging existing beliefs, concepts and theories in the scholarship of teaching and learning |
| A method of improving the student learning experience and their academic performance |
| A process that enables university academics to articulate their knowledge about learning and teaching |

| An approach that enables university academics to understand better the process of teaching and learning |
| A method of continuing professional development for university academics |
| A method of enhancing the quality of teaching and learning in universities |
| A method of inducting new professionals |
| An approach that helps university academics understand how practice is socially constructed and mediated |
| A process which can ameliorate the theory-practice gap in university learning referred to by Carr and Kemmis (1986) as 'praxis' |

Therefore, Norton's approach differs slightly from other EAR typologies, giving particular relevance to the context of higher education. However, his conceptualisation equally supports the idea of PeAR as a practice by educational professionals—university lecturers—for reflecting on their own pedagogy. Thus, it is a type of CAR, but one centred on higher-education institutions.

## Action Learning

Action Learning (AL) appeared in organisational contexts as a developmental innovation in the 1960s. This typology, along with Action Science, is situated on the border of the industrial and educational strands, however, its importance lies more in its formation of the foundational base for its educational successor ALAR/PALAR, which is explored in the following section.

Firstly, the term Action Learning was coined by Reg Revans, an academic professor of natural sciences, who transferred his attention to social sciences, and more specifically education, due to his interest in the role of non-experts in problem-solving (Pedler 2011). He criticised traditional approaches to management as unsuitable for solving problems in organisations (Kemmis, McTaggart & Nixon 2013). The aim of AL is:

> [The] improvement of human systems for the benefit of those who depend on them. Action learning is a pragmatic and moral philosophy based on a deeply humanistic view of human potential that commits us, via experiential learning, to address the intractable problems of organisations and societies. (Pedler 2011, 22)

In Revan's view, the aim underlying AL was to bring people together to learn from each other. For instance, this involved cultivating relationships between workers and their institutions, instil harmony and generate a positive method of conflict resolution (Dash 1999). According to Kemmis, McTaggart and Nixon (2013), the focal point of AL, in Revan's view, is organisation efficacy and efficiency. Although this focus is visible in his work and posterior academic publications, Revan also expressed a political commitment to a bottom-up approach to decision-making processes and organisational problem-solving (Revan, 2011).

Revan (2011) created an equation regarding processes of AL ($L = P + Q$), where L symbolises learning, P is programmed knowledge or the content of traditional instruction and Q is the questioning insight, derived from fresh questions and critical reflection. Pedler (2011) explains this equation by stating that Revan understood social problems differently to puzzles, and therefore there was no correct solution for social issues, just a compendium of possible choices, and thus Q was essential for new lines of thinking, action, and learning. Revan (2011) equally acknowledged that this learning process must be in small groups or 'sets' from the organisation, workplace or community which is under research. This equation and subsequent practices following AL were created to reflect critically on experiences and find a suitable action as an outcome of the shared learning experience (Zuber-Skerrit, Fletcher & Kearney 2015).

In the academic literature, AL seems to struggle to define the characteristics which distinguish it from AR. This is because of the absence of a definition from Revan (Pedler 2011) and the support of AL as an intrinsic personal/collective experience within AR (Kember 2000). According to Kember (2000), AR's relative popularity compared to AL lies in the former's non-existent literary proliferation, due to the unpublished nature of learning experiences, which are rarely shared among academics. Furthermore, McGill and Beaty (1995) acknowledge that both AR and AL share the same learning cycle, although AL does not necessarily apply a research process, so participants focus on their personal observations and reflections. They also highlight that while AR can be implemented by an individual, AL requires the involvement of a group (Kember 2000).

However, according to the literature, the two typologies are not as different as Kember (2000) or McGill and Beaty (1995) claim. Nowadays, there is not a single generally approved understanding of AR, nor is there a generally approved understanding of how to implement 'research' in AR or participatory approaches as a whole. As a result, scholars have already unified both terminologies into a sort of common ground, ALAR/PALAR, which is the next category.

## Action Learning and Action Research (Alar-Palar)

ALAR (Action Learning and Action Research) was originally proposed by Zuber-Skerritt (2001) as a practice which combined AL and AR. Nevertheless, in previous publications, Zuber-Skerritt (2011) has reconceptualised the term as PALAR, adding P (for 'participatory') to the original ALAR:

> ALAR has been extended to PALAR by adding and integrating the concept of participatory action research, mainly for achieving social justice for all, positive change and sustainable development in disadvantaged communities. (Zuber-Skerritt, Fletcher & Kearney 2015, 114)

Zuber-Skerritt and her colleagues have produced an extensive literature theorising and implementing PALAR (Zuber-Skerritt & Roche 2004; Zuber-Skerritt 2011; Kearney & Zuber-Skerritt 2012; Wood & Zuber-Skerritt 2013; Kearney, Wood & Zuber-Skerritt 2013; Zuber-Skerritt, Fletcher & Kearney 2015). They consider PALAR as more than a methodology, stating that it is more a way of living, working and being. It is a way of thinking influenced by values, philosophical assumptions, paradigms of learning, teaching and research (Zuber-Skerritt 2011). It advocates the 'philosophical and methodological assumptions about learning and knowledge creation' (Zuber-Skerritt, Fletcher & Kearny 2015, 107). PALAR is understood as a 'new vision of AR for professional learning in higher education and beyond' (Zuber-Skerritt, Fletcher & Kearney 2015, 10). They consider that it is applicable not only in an educational context, but also for individuals excluded from formal educational systems. They acknowledge that as a global community we need alternative epistemologies:

> We need to clarify what constitutes, in the widest sense, knowledge (including what is commonly recognised as scientific, conceptual, experiential, intuitive, local, Indigenous and cultural knowledge) and learning (including individual, collaborative, professional, organisational, critical and reflective learning). We need to understand how to facilitate the processes of learning and knowledge creation at all levels. (Zuber-Skerritt, Fletcher & Kearney 2015, 2)

Therefore, PALAR, and its predecessor ALAR, pay full attention to professional involvement in education, using a participatory practice as a means to reconstitute professionals' private and professional lives without excluding the external actors who do not take part in formal educational systems. This perspective opens up a more flexible and holistic approach to educational practices, which have traditionally been influenced by the industrial family and its focus on professional improvement in educational institutions. PALAR gives emphasis to the social and temporal context in which educational institutions are situated, as well as advancing some of the critiques proposed by the PAR or IR families.

## *Critical Participatory Action Research*

The last but not the least, category, is Critical Participatory Action Research (CPAR). It shares common characteristics with PALAR practices, due to its similar approach to participation and critical commitment to social issues, social change, and social justice. Nevertheless, CPAR was born out of a different theoretical framework, with different authors further developing it over the last thirty years (Kemmis 2008).

Carr and Kemmis (1986) conceptualised the term of Emancipatory Action Research (EmAR) during the 1980s. However, this conceptualisation was further theorised by these same academics together with other staff members at Deakin University in Australia, who collectively coined the term of Critical Participatory Action Research in the 1980s and 1990s. This typology was designed as an academic resource for students and published under the titles of *The Action Research Planner* and *The Action Research Reader* in 1988. CPAR emerged from the Deakin academics' dissatisfaction with CAR, which, according to them, did not present a critical perspective regarding the relationship between education and social change (Kemmis, McTaggart & Nixon 2013). They used CPAR as a means of advancing social justice and participants' emancipation from a critical theoretical perspective. They presented a distinction between Technical, Practical and Critical Action Research, selecting the critical line to determine their methodology (Carr & Kemmis 1986; 2005; Kemmis & McTaggart 2000; Zuber-Skerritt, Fletcher & Kearney 2015).

Additionally, the theoretical background of CPAR differs from other educational typologies. The group of scholars framed their methodology according to Habermas's thinking, which made the theorisation and practices slightly different. CPAR has a strong commitment to participation, a critical approach to social phenomena, and seeks to highlight disempowerment and injustices brought about by industrial societies (Kemmis & McTaggart 2000). It focuses on the revitalisation of the public sphere and the decolonisation of the life-world. It looks for alternatives to recreate *vivencias*,[10] and deconstructs those social systems that usually regard humans as institutionalised (Kemmis 2008). The approach provides a more comprehensive human perspective, exploring and acknowledging human life. CPAR regards participatory practice not only as an inclusive instrument, applicable to educational institutions and professionals, but also as a nexus with other AR collectives, building alliances with social movements (Kemmis 2008).

In brief, the feature that distinguishes it from other educational approaches is its strong positionality regarding who gets involved in the research project and how, which is also supported by some PAR practitioners (Fals-Bordan & Rahman 1991). They sustain the idea that participants do not need the explicit intervention of academic practitioners, and that participants are able to conduct research for themselves due to their 'insider' status and that, as insiders, they enjoy certain advantages when researching their own context (Kemmis, McTaggart & Nixon 2013). Moreover, this practice, like PALAR, also challenges the traditional practices of EAR, highlighting some of the decolonial issues discussed in the development and Indigenous categories. However, although it is important to understand traditions and their position in relation to decoloniality, it is perhaps even

---

10  *Vivencias* is the Spanish term for 'lived experiences'.

more important to understand their operationalisation and resulting limitations.

## 3.4 General Challenges within the Operationalisation of Participatory Approaches

Despite differences among categories, there are several challenges within the overarching category of participatory approaches that require attention due to the strong influence of Western science and the alignment of participatory practices with this discipline. The first complexities arise from the debate regarding the individual or collective practice of participatory approaches. The individual use of participatory practices refers to when a researcher enquires into her or his own practice as an Action Research process. In this individual area of AR, living theory exerts a huge influence on today's practices as part of educational strategies (Whitehead & McNiff 2006). This practice constitutes an individual reflection of a professional practitioner about her or his educational influence. On this matter, Adelman (1993) has heavily criticised the use of AR as an individual practice, citing Somekh and Schon as the major proponents of the idea. Adelman (1993) considers that individual uses of AR signal a departure from Lewing's original understanding of AR as a collective democratic process or posterior conceptualisation challenging an individual aspect of academic research (Chilisa 2012). Nevertheless, current academic literature continues to use Action Research as a process that can be developed individually, even if this might reproduce and uncritically accept the feature of knowledge as a private/individual entity, as assigned by Western science (Reason & Bradbury 2008; Chilisa, 2012).

On the other hand, the collective use of participatory practices seems to be a major source of disagreement among scholars. This disagreement arises from the diverse interpretation of 'participation' and the many levels of enrolment possible among practices and fields of application (Webb 1996; Hayward, Simpsons & Wood 2004; Cornwall 2003; Vaughn et al. 2016). Santos (2013, 499) rightly highlights that 'because different ideologies inform (P)AR discourse and practices, these parentheses also indicate that participation is regarded as a problematic term that presupposes different ideas of participation'. Equally, on this matter,

Thiollent and Colette (2017) question the fact that some scholars working in this field attribute little value to active participation. They critique scholars' superficial understanding of participant involvement and poor critical perspectives on what participatory practices aim for and fight against. This is connected to the abuse or misuse of participatory practices (White 1996; Higgins 2016) or the ambiguity resulting from the use of different terminologies (Balakrishnan & Claiborne 2016). All of these issues are summarised well in the following quote:

> The term participation has various meanings, forms, types, degrees, and intensity. It is sometimes confused with other terms such as 'collaboration' or 'cooperation'. Moreover, the term is also used rhetorically and in political or ideological discourse. We should note that the term participation or the adjectives 'participant' or 'participatory' are often associated with research or investigation as if it were easy to characterise – yet, in actuality, the research may or may not be participatory. (Thiollent & Colette 2017, 169)

The fact that scholars use this rhetoric does not automatically mean that their practices are participatory in nature, as Thiollent and Colette (2017) emphasise. Some scholars relate with the success of certain practices to their level of participation, and there are a significant number of practitioners who support the full participation of the co-researcher as an essential aspect of participatory approaches (Rowel et al. 2017; Wick & Reason 2009 among others). However, it is not clear to what extent these claims are purely theoretical or have been applied in practice. As Cornwall and Jewkes (1995) state:

> Participatory research is theoretically situated at the collegiate level[11] [Community full ownership] of participation. Scrutiny of practice reveals that this level is rarely if ever, achieved. Much of what passes as participatory research goes no further than contracting people[12] into projects which are entirely scientist-led, designed and managed [...] In many cases, people participate in a process which lies outside their ultimate control. Researchers continue to set the agendas and take responsibility for analysis and representation of outcomes. (1995, 1669)

---

11  Collegiate level involves full participation. The local people have control over the process in a process of mutual learning (Cornwall & Jewkes, 1995)

12  The contractual level of participation refers to when: 'people are contracted into the projects of researchers to take part in their enquiries or experiments' (Cornwall & Jewkes, 1995, p.1669).

Therefore, although there is an extended use of participation in research practices, the use of this and other terminologies might not actually refer to full participation, but conversely, may denote partial participation, as the extended use of participatory methods in academia.

Unfortunately, these challenges to full participation arise in a research field which accepts the diversity and heterogeneity of practices. What is clear is that the increase of participatory research in academic literature has ended up standardising and homogenising practices along Eurocentric lines (Vaughn et al. 2016; Thiollent & Colette 2017). 'Participatory' often means an engaging method following steps one, two and three for the researchers to collect data. These are what I here refer to as 'Western participatory trends'. Clearly, what many participatory approaches bring to the debate is the nature of science and the philosophical tensions between schools of thought, which is significant for the reconsideration of colonial issues in the present. Moreover, in this matter, Higgins (2016) acknowledges that participatory approaches have 'degenerated into a cure that may be worse than the disease' (2016, 1), exposing that the very idea that participatory approaches exist is mystifying, and distracts from the deep challenges that they present.

Regardless, all of these typologies perform distinctive functions and practices, and their accomplishments under different theoretical frames still make them valid. This heterogeneity of theoretical assumptions positions the different branches of participatory approaches as incommensurable. However, this issue can be overcome when we evaluate these practices in terms of their contribution to solving colonial issues and to promoting democratic practices in a particular way, as this book does.

# 3.5 Conclusion

This chapter has provided an exhaustive analysis of participatory approaches. Firstly, it has classified four research areas that are not static, but fluid. This structure has contributed to a clearer understanding of the foundational pillars of various typologies. By revealing some of the more relevant categories, and discussing their commonalities and divergences, we have established a better perspective on participatory issues and debates.

Let us reflect briefly on the categories analysed. Firstly, the industrial category seems to perpetuate many of the critiques of the hegemonic system. It defines the AR process as a rational process of thinking. AR focuses on efficiency and social change in a desirable way for the researcher, who is able to identify any issues. It promotes a vision of a community or group of individuals that need help from an expert to change, which is problematic from a decolonial perspective. This pragmatic view limits the potential of such practices to challenge some of the colonial issues highlighted in previous chapters. With this observation, I am not denying the use of AR in this way, but I am highlighting its internal limitations with regard to certain colonial challenges. For instance, AR does not consider the multiplicity of knowledge systems or the involvement of participants in all stages of the research process, as participation is mostly limited to a contractual manner. Furthermore, management theories, which are rooted in post-Enlightenment European thinking, limit understandings of industries, organisations and human relations outside of Western societies.

Secondly, although there is a critical strand within the educational category, the majority of practices seem to approach the issue individually, from an industrial perspective, as, for instance, evident in the extended use of projects in which teachers reflect on how to improve their pedagogies. Again, this practice is not bad per se, and should continue to be implemented to achieve its own particular aims, i.e. the research of pedagogical practices. However, just as this study is highlighting colonial issues, these types of practice (like conventional research processes) instrumentalise the participants to achieve a desirable outcome or to better understand a phenomenon in order to change it. Moreover, the educational category, in general, seems to pay little attention to the connection of educational institutions with society more broadly, or to their role in the resolution and advancement of social justice as a political and ideological tool from the dominant system (Freire 1972). This excludes two particular typologies, CPAR and PALAR, which I will explore below as part of the development category, given that they are situated in the margins between both education and development.

The Indigenous category makes a relevant and adequate critique of the Western system and its impact on communities. Nonetheless, this perspective can be seen at times to focus too greatly on Indigenous Peoples, neglecting other knowledge systems in the process. This is not the case for all scholars and practices of this group. However, it is most definitely a widespread approach among scholars in this group.

Finally, the development category presents a powerful critique of the hegemonic system of domination and a strong defence of epistemic justice. However, although the development category claims the need for full participation, this does not mean that their actual practices involve communities or individuals as agents of the process, as previously highlighted (Cornwall & Jewkes 1995). Homogenising tendencies definitely constrain the potential of PAR. Further, the development category is mostly based on Western theories that might misdirect their potential towards decoloniality. For instance, scholars use complete theories, instead of approaches able to accommodate cultural specificities for cultural translation. This might be the case for CPAR, or other theories related to ALAR/PALAR (living theory, experiential learning theory or hope theory), typologies that, although not necessarily in the development family, are situated in the margin between educational and development practices.

All these limitations provide a need for the introduction of an alternative framework that, although in this investigation applied to the educational context, does not overlook society at large, and can be used both within and outside of educational institutions. Moreover, this alternative framework needs to be conceptualised in line with decolonial critiques so as to provide a flexible ontological approach that is able to accommodate different epistemic systems. This is the Capabilities Approach.

Therefore, in order to overcome these challenges within participatory approaches, it is necessary to explore how this debate is in conversation with the Capabilities Approach. We must ask how a capabilitarian participatory practice can be informed by this decolonial perspective to advance current limitations in the field, and to orient our practice towards a genuine democratisation of knowledge. Thus, the following chapter aims to provide a justification of how the Capabilities Approach is aligned with decoloniality and Southern perspectives, as part of a pluriversal and decolonial vision to theoretically orient our participatory practices. It will explore how the Capabilities Approach, being ontologically incomplete and epistemically diverse, can provide a more adequate theoretical foundation for the decolonial aim of participatory practices as a way to overcome hegemonic, homogenising and Western participatory trends.

# References

Adelman, C. (1993). Kurt Lewin and the origins of action research. *Educational Action Research, 1*(1), 7–24. https://doi.org/10.1080/0965079930010102.

Altrichter, H., Kemmis, S., McTaggart, R., & Zuber-Skerritt, O. (1991). Defining, confining or refining action research? In O. Zuber-Skerritt (ed.). *Action Research for Change and Development* (pp. 3–9). Aldershot: Gower Publishing Company.

Appiah, K. (2010). Europe upside down: Fallacies of the new Afrocentrism. In R. R. Grinker, S. C. Lubkeemann and C. B. Steiner (eds). *Perspectives on Africa: A Reader in Culture, History and Representation* (pp. 48–54). Oxford: Wiley-Blackwell.

Argyris, C., Putnam, R., & Smith, D. M. (1985). *Action Science: Concepts Methods and Skills for Research and Intervention* (Vol. 13). San Francisco: Jossey-Bass Inc Pub.

Balakrishnan, V., & Claiborne, L. (2016). Participatory action research in culturally complex societies: opportunities and challenges. *Educational Action Research, 25*(2), 185–202. http://dx.doi.org/10.1080/09650792.2016.1206480.

Bradbury, H. (ed.) (2015). *The SAGE Handbook of Action Research*. Thousand Oaks: Sage Publications.

Brydon-Miller, M. (2001). Education, research, and action: Theory and methods of participatory action research. In D. L. Tolmon and M. Brydom-Miller (eds). *From Subjects to Subjectivities: A Handbook of Interpretive and Participatory Methods* (pp. 76–89). New York: New York University Press.

Carr, W., & Kemmis, S. (1986). *Becoming Critical: Knowing through Action Research*. Geelong: Deakin University.

Carr, W., & Kemmis, S. (2005). Staying critical. *Educational Action Research, 13*(3), 347–358. https://www.tandfonline.com/doi/abs/10.1080/09650790500200296.

Cornwall, A. (2003). Whose voices? Whose choices? Reflections on gender and participatory development. *World Development, 31*(8), 1325–1342. https://doi.org/10.1016/S0305-750X(03)00086-X.

Cornwall, A., & Jewkes, R. (1995). What is participatory research? *Social Science & Medicine, 41*(12), 1667–1676. https://doi.org/10.1016/0277-9536(95)00127-S.

Chambers, R. (2008) PRA, PLA and pluralism: Practice and theory. In P. Reason and H. Bradbury (eds). *The SAGE Handbook of Action Research* (pp. 297–318). London: Sage Publications.

Chilisa, B. (2012). *Indigenous Research Methodologies*. Los Angeles: Sage Publications.

Dadds, M. (1995). *Passionate Enquiry and School Development: A Story about Teacher Action Research*. London: Routledge.

Dash, D. P. (1999). Current debates in action research. *Systemic Practice and Action Research, 12*(5), 457–492. https://link.springer.com/article/10.102 3/A:1022465506555.

De Sousa Santos, B. (2014). *Epistemologies of the South: Justice against Epistemicide*. New York: Routledge. https://unescochair-cbrsr.org/pdf/resource/ Epistemologies_of_the_South.pdf.

Dei, G. J. S. (2014). Indigenizing the school curriculum. In G. Emeagwali and G. J. D Dei (eds). *African Indigenous Knowledge and the Disciplines* (pp. 165–180). Leiden: Brill (Sense Publishers).

Dick, B. (2015). Reflections on the Sage Encyclopedia of Action Research and what it says about action research and its methodologies. *Action Research, 13*(4), 431–444. https://doi.org/10.1177%2F1476750315573593.

Dick, B., & Greenwood, D. J. (2015). Theory and method: Why action research does not separate them. *Action Research, 13*(2), 194–197. https://doi.org/10.1 177%2F1476750315573594.

Diop, C. A. (2010). The meaning of our work. In R. R Grinker, S. C. Lubkemann and C. B. Steiner. *Perspectives on Africa: A Reader in Culture, History and Representation*. (pp. 44–47). Oxford: Wiley-Blackwell.

Dussel, E. D. (2007). *Materiales para una política de la liberación*. Madrid: Plaza y valdés Editores.

Elliott, J. (1991). *Action Research for Educational Change*. Buckingham: Open University Press.

Escobar, A. (2007). Worlds and knowledges otherwise: The Latin American modernity/coloniality research program. *Cultural Studies, 21*(2-3), 179–210. http://dx.doi.org/10.1080/09502380601162506.

Etmanski, C., Hall, B. L., & Dawson, T. (eds) (2014). *Learning and Teaching Community-Based Research: Linking Pedagogy to Practice*. Toronto: University of Toronto Press.

Fals-Borda, F., & Rahman, M. A. (1991). Action and knowledge breaking the monopoly with participatory action-research. New York: Apex Press.

Feldman, A. (2017). An emergent history of educational action research in the English-speaking world. In Rowell L., Bruce C., Shosh J., Riel M. (eds). *The Palgrave International Handbook of Action Research* (pp. 125–145). New York: Palgrave Macmillan US. https://doi.org/10.1057/978-1-137-40523-4_8.

Freire, P. (1972). *Pedagogy of the Oppressed*. Harmondsworth: Penguin.

Gazda, G. M., Kipper, D. A., and Treadwell, T. W. (1997). A message from the executive editors. *International Journal of Action Methods: Psychodrama, Skill Training, and Role Playing, 50*(1), 3.

Goodnough, K. (2008). Dealing with messiness and uncertainty in practitioner research: The nature of participatory action research. *Canadian Journal of Education, 31*(2), 431.

Greenwood, D. J., & Levin, M. (2006). *Introduction to Action Research: Social Research for Social Change*. Thousand Oaks: Sage Publications.

Hayward, C., Simpson, L., & Wood, L. (2004). Still left out in the cold: Problematising participatory research and development. *Sociologia Ruralis, 44*(1), 95–108. https://doi.org/10.1111/j.1467-9523.2004.00264.x.

Helskog, G. H. (2014). Justifying action research. *Educational action research, 22*(1), 4–20. https://doi.org/10.1080/09650792.2013.856769.

Higgins, C. (2016). The promise, pitfalls, and persistent challenge of action research. *Ethics and Education, 11*(2), 230–239. https://doi.org/10.1080/174 49642.2016.1185831.

Hlela, Z. (2018). Learning through the action of research: reflections on an Afrocentric research design. *Community Development Journal, 53*(2), 375–392. https://doi.org/10.1093/cdj/bsw033.

Kearney, J., & Zuber-Skerritt, O. (2012). From learning organization to learning community: Sustainability through lifelong learning. *The Learning Organization, 19*(5), 400–413. https://doi.org/10.1108/09696471211239703.

Kearney, J. F., Wood, L., & Zuber-Skerritt, O. D. (2013). Community–university partnerships using participatory action learning and action research (PALAR). *Gateways: International Journal of Community Research and Engagment, 6*, 113–130. https://doi.org/10.5130/ijcre.v6i1.3105.

Kember, D. (2000). *Action Learning and Action Research: Improving the Quality of Teaching and Learning*. London: Routledge.

Kemmis, S. (2008). Critical theory and participatory action research. In Reason, P., and Bradbury, H. (eds). *The SAGE Handbook of Action Research: Participative Inquiry and Practice*, 2 (pp. 121–138). London: Sage Publications.

Kemmis, S., & McTaggart, R. (2000). Participatory action research. In N. Denzin & Y. Lincoln (eds). *The SAGE Handbook of Qualitative Research* (pp. 559–603). Thousand Oaks: Sage Publications.

Kemmis, S., McTaggart, R., & Nixon, R. (2013). *The Action Research Planner: Doing Critical Participatory Action Research*. Singapore: Springer Science & Business Media. https://doi.org/10.1007/978-981-4560-67-2.

Kemmis, S., McTaggart, R., & Retallick, J. (2004). *The Action Research Planner*. Karachi: Aga Khan University, Institute for Educational Development. https://doi.org/10.1007/978-981-4560-67-2.

Kindon, S., Pain, R., & Kesby, M. (eds) (2007). *Participatory Action Research Approaches and Methods: Connecting People, Participation and Place*. London: Routledge.

Kristiansen, M., & Bloch-Poulsen, J. (2016). Participatory hierarchies: A challenge in organisational Action Research. *International Journal of Action Research, 12*(2), 144.

Lewin, K. (1946). Action research and minority problems. *Journal of Social Issues, 2*(4), 34–46.

Lewin, K. (1947). Frontiers in group dynamics II. Channels of group life; social planning and action research. *Human Relations, 1*(2), 143–153.

Mbembe, A. (2015). Decolonizing knowledge and the question of the archive. [Paper presentation] *Public lectures Wits Insitute for Social and Economic Research (WISER) University of Witwatersrand, Johannesburg (South Africa)*. https://wiser.wits.ac.za/sites/default/files/private/Achille%20 Mbembe%20-%20Decolonizing%20Knowledge%20and%20the%20 Question%20of%20the%20Archive.pdf.

McGrill, I., & Beaty, L. (1995). *Action Learning: A Guide for Profeessional, Management and Educational Development*. London: Kogan Page.

McKernan, J., (1991). *Curriculum Action Research. A Handbook of Methods and Resources for the Reflective Practitioner*. London: Kogan Page.

McNiff, J. & Whitehead, J. (2002). *Action Research: Principles and Practice*. London: Routledge Falmer.

Neumann, J. E. (2005). Kurt Lewin at the Tavistock Institute. *Educational action research, 13*(1), 119–136. https://doi.org/10.1080/09650790500200271.

Ninomiya, M. E. M., & Pollock, N. J. (2017). Reconciling community-based Indigenous research and academic practices: Knowing principles is not always enough. *Social Science & Medicine, 172*: 28–36. https://doi.org/10.1016/j.socscimed.2016.11.007.

Noffke, S. E., & Somekh, B. (eds) (2009). *The SAGE Handbook of Educational Action Research*. London: Sage Publications.

Norton, L. S. (2009). *Action Research in Teaching and Learning: A Practical Guide to Conducting Pedagogical Research in Universities*. New York: Routledge.

Nnaemeka, O. (2004). Nego-feminism: Theorizing, practicing, and pruning Africa's way. *Signs: Journal of Women in Culture and Society, 29*(2), 357–385. http://www.jstor.org/stable/10.1086/378553?origin=JSTOR-pdf.

Nyemba, F., & Mayer, M. (2017). Exploring the roots of participatory action research: An interview with Dr Marja-Liisa Swantz. *Action Research*, 16(3), 319–338. https://doi.org/10.1177%2F1476750316684003.

Pedler, M. (2011). *Action Learning in Practice*. New York: Gower Publishing, Ltd.

Rappaport, J. (2017). Participation and the work of the imagination: A Colombian retrospective. In Rowell, L. L., Bruce, C. D., Shosh, J. M. and Riel M. M. *The*

*Palgrave International Handbook of Action Research* (pp. 147–159). New York: Palgrave Macmillan US.

Raelin, J. A. (1997). A model of work-based learning. *Organization Science, 8*(6), 563–578. https://doi.org/10.1287/orsc.8.6.563.

Reason, P., & Bradbury, H. (2008). *The SAGE Handbook of Action Research: Participative Inquiry and Practice.* London: Sage Publications.

Revans, R. (2011). *ABC of Action Learning.* New York: Gower Publishing, Ltd.

Rowell, L. L., Bruce, C. D., Shosh, J. M., & Riel, M. M. (eds) (2017). *The Palgrave International Handbook of Action Research.* London: Palgrave Macmillan.

Rowell, L. L., & Hong, E. (2017). Knowledge democracy and action research: Pathways for the twenty-first century. In Rowell, L. L., Bruce C. D., Shosh J. M. and Riel M. M. *The Palgrave International Handbook of Action Research* (pp. 63–83). New York: Palgrave Macmillan US.

Santos, D. (2013). (Participatory) action research and the political realm. *Counterpoints, 354*, 492–513.

Schroeder, H. (2014). Governing access and allocation in the Anthropocene. *Global Environmental Change, 26*, A1–A3. https://doi.org/10.1016/j.gloenvcha.2014.04.017.

Semali, L. M., & Kincheloe, J. L. (2002). *What is Indigenous Knowledge? Voices from the Academy.* New York: Routledge.

Soldatenko, G. (2015). A contribution toward the decolonization of philosophy: Asserting the coloniality of power in the study of non-western philosophical traditions. *Comparative and continental philosophy, 7*(2), 138–156. https://doi.org/10.1179/1757063815Z.00000000059.

Somekh, B. (2006). Constructing intercultural knowledge and understanding through collaborative action research. *Teachers and teaching: theory and practice, 12*(1), 87–106. https://doi.org/10.1080/13450600500365460.

Stenhouse, L. (1975). *An Introduction to Curriculum Research and Development.* London: Heinemann Educational Publishers.

Tandon, R., Hall, B., Lepore, W., & Singh, W. (2016). *Training the Next Generation of Community-Based Researchers: A Guide for Trainers.* Victoria: PRIA & University of Victoria.

Thaman, K. H. (2003). Decolonizing Pacific studies: Indigenous perspectives, knowledge, and wisdom in higher education. *The Contemporary Pacific, 15*(1), 1–17. http://hdl.handle.net/10125/13690.

Thiollent, M., & Colette, M. M. (2017). Action research and participatory research in Brazil. In Rowell, Bruce, Shosh & Riel (ed.). *The Palgrave International Handbook of Action Research* (pp. 161–176). Los Angeles: Palgrave Macmillan.

Vaughn, L. M., Jacquez, F., Lindquist-Grantz, R., Parsons, A., & Melink, K. (2016). Immigrants as research partners: A review of immigrants in community-based participatory research (CBPR). *Journal of Immigrant and Minority Health,* 19(6) 1457–1468. https://doi.org/10.1007/s10903-016-0474-3.

Webb, G. (1996). Theories of staff development: Development and understanding. *The International Journal for Academic Development, 1*(1), 63–69. https://doi.org/10.1080/1360144960010107.

Wells, G. (2009). Dialogic inquiry as collaborative action research. In Noffke, S. E. and Somekh, B. (eds). *The SAGE Handbook of Educational Action Research* (pp. 50–61). London: Sage Publications.

Wicks, P. G., & Reason, P. (2009). Initiating action research: Challenges and paradoxes of opening communicative space. In Noffke, S. E. and Somekh, B. (eds). *The SAGE Handbook of Educational Action Research* (pp. 243–262). London: Sage Publications.

Wood, L., & Zuber-Skerrit, O. (2013). PALAR as a methodology for community engagement by faculties of education. *South African Journal of Education, 33*(4), 1–15.

White, S. C. (1996). Depoliticising development: the uses and abuses of participation. *Development in Practice, 6*(1), 6–15. https://doi.org/10.1080/0 961452961000157564.

Whitehead, J. (1989). Creating a living educational theory from questions of the kind, 'How do I improve my practice?'. *Cambridge Journal of Education, 19*(1), 41–52. https://doi.org/10.1080/0305764890190106.

Whitehead, J. (1991). *How Do I Improve My Professional Practice as an Academic and Educational Manager? A Dialectical Analysis of an Individual's Educational Development and a Basis for Socially Orientated Action Research.* Uunpublished doctoral dissertation, University of Bath, UK. http://people.bath.ac.uk/edsajw/bk93/8wc90.Pdf.

Whitehead, J., & McNiff, J. (2006). *Action Research: Living Theory.* London: Sage Publications.

Zuber-Skerrit, O. (2001). Action learning and action research: paradigm, praxis and programs. In Sankara, S., Dick, B. and Passsfield, R. (eds). *Effective Change Management through Action Research and Action Learning: Concepts, Perspectives, Processes and Applications* (pp. 1–20). Lismore: Southern Cross University Press.

Zuber-Skerrit, O. (2011). *Action Leadership: Towards a Participatory Paradigm* (Vol. 6). Dordrecht: Springer Science & Business Media.

Zuber-Skerrit, O., Fletcher, M., & Kearney, J. (2015). Professional Learning in Higher Education and Communities: Towards a New Vision for Action Research. London: Springer.

Zuber-Skerrit, O., & Roche, V. (2004). A constructivist model for evaluating postgraduate supervision: a case study. *Quality Assurance in Education, 12*(2), 82–93. http://dx.doi.org/10.1108/09684880410536459.

# 4. Democratising Participatory Research: A Capabilitarian Conceptualisation

We live in a society where some people are more equal than others. One gender is better than the other. One sex group is better than the others. One skin colour is better than others. One religion, background, even how you look, some people who look a certain way are taken as more beautiful than the other ones.

Power is the mother of all oppressors. People oppress the opposite group. Because they want power. They want to become dominant so they belittle the other group to feel power.

All these things that we are oppressed by are things we don't choose to be. But what do these groups do for power?

Children are raped, people are unfairly dismissed, and blood is spilled all over because you are different to your oppressor. All because the other group wants you to die in silence.

When will it all come to an end?

When will our land be a safe place where you would want to raise your child?

When will our land be a safe place to be black?

When will our land be a safe place to leave our grandmothers at home so we can work without fear that they will be raped?

When will it be okay not to be straight?

When will it be okay to follow any religion you want?

When will we be completely free?

*Narratives on Social Injustices: Undergraduate Voices*, 2018

 https://doi.org/10.11647/OBP.0273.04

# 4.1 Introduction

This chapter poses the question of how, if coloniality is central for participatory practices, we can resolve the field's limitations and controversies? For this reason, the chapter introduces the Capabilities Approach, linking its foundational elements with those of decolonial debates. This section aims to illustrate the current commonalities between both positions and the potential of the Capabilities Approach to fill some of the limitations in the field of participatory practices. To this end, the chapter uses an open-ended version of the Capabilities Approach defended by Amartya Sen (1999; 2009).

Furthermore, the chapter continues to conceptualise Democratic Capabilities Research (DCR) through five open-ended principles that accommodate the variety of practices and implementations needed to democratise participatory research from a combined decolonial, capabilities and Southern perspective. This perspective is flexible and contextually related—thus, open-ended—as is the view of the Capabilities Approach supported in this chapter.

# 4.2 The Capabilities Approach and Decoloniality: A Possible Bond Despite Discrepancies

Despite the global influence of human development from positivist perspectives, the Capabilities Approach (the foundational formulation of human development) presents a radical shift from traditional tendencies. While Western intellectual currents opt for aggregation and universal formulas, which align with the modernist and imperialist modus operandi, the Capabilities Approach calls for stakeholder engagement (Sen 1999; Spreafico 2016). It brings the individual to the fore, with a strong sense of democracy and diversity of voices (Sen 1999). It displaces the technocratic analysis/solution, and represents a unique, singular perspective among all those available. Nevertheless, this vision of the CA is not always channeled towards its grassroots potential.

Therefore, this section highlights the importance of the Capabilities Approach as a means of balancing Western thinking with Southern epistemic systems. It develops a theoretical space that is incomplete, and therefore able to accommodate contexts that are essentially different from Western and Eurocentric societies. This theoretical contribution is relevant and necessary after the previous chapters. Thus, the following sections argue, without being dogmatic, that the Capabilities Approach sustains an ontologically incomplete positionality than enables it to embrace different cultural specificities. It provides a diversified epistemic space that is capable of accommodating a more robust understanding of participation from a decolonial perspective of justice in education, and of challenging homogenising participatory tendencies, even if this might involve foundational reconsideration of this approach.

## 4.2.1 A Capabilities Overview

Firstly, to elaborate on some of the major elements of the Capabilities Approach, the work of Amartya Sen mainly focuses on outlining an approach that might provide better ways to evaluate human development. Sen (1999) criticises previous theorists, because their evaluative frameworks are incomplete; for instance, exclusively focusing on economic features such as GDP. Thus, he introduces a new way to look at human development that relies on an evaluative space that is determined by the freedoms that people enjoy; a space that is people-centred and multidimensional (Sen 1999, 2009).

For Sen, freedom is the basis of development, not just as an end, but also as a principal means to that end (Sen 1999). The development aim is to remove the 'unfreedoms' that 'leave people with few choices and little opportunity of exercising their reasoned agency' (Sen 1999, xii). It refers to the real freedoms that people have to be and to do the things that they have reason to value (Sen 2009). This is why, if we want to evaluate an individual's well-being, we must pay attention to their effective freedoms/capabilities (Robeyns 2005; Nussbaum 2011).

Capabilities thus, are the real opportunities people have to live the life they have reason to value or to be the person they want to be (Sen 1999, 2009; Nussbaum 2011) and functionings are the beings and doings that can be achieved through their capabilities (Sen 1999, 2009). Sen criticises approaches which focus on outcomes (functionings) because they have little information about real people's lives (Sen 1999), even though they are also a necessary detail for evaluating human development. For instance, the fact that two students succeed at university and both obtain their degrees actually says very little about their experiences during the process. If we consider that one of the students comes from a middle-class family while the other is from an Indigenous community, both may well obtain their degrees, but their experience, and the process by which they have done so, is completely different. Therefore, two similar outcomes, in this case obtaining a degree, can differ greatly from the capabilities they enjoy and the process towards achievement. The same scenario applies when we talk about institutions of knowledge production. For instance, there might be two research centres, one in the Global North and another in the Global South, and both secure funds for their research project. This says very little about their freedoms and the process to acquire those funds. While Global South institutions might experience many unfreedoms, having to overcome their epistemic marginalisation in order to win that funding, Global North institutions will manage much more easily because of their epistemic advantage in the global knowledge system (Walker & Martinez-Vargas 2020). Thus, the process and the capabilities, real freedoms that are available during that process, provide important information for determining someone's well-being in an evaluative and prospective framework of human development.

On the other hand, the Capabilities Approach does not ignore the context in which people are positioned and how this affects their available options and preferences. Firstly, it conceptualises three different conversion factors that interact in our opportunities and freedoms, either by enhancing or constraining them. These are social, personal and environmental conversion factors (Sen 1999; Robeyns 2005). Personal conversion factors refer to those personal features related to the individual's body. Thus, they are physical or mental disabilities, psychomotor skills or metabolism (Robeyns 2005). For instance, a student with limited mobility will need more resources than a person with no mobility disability in order to attend classes in a university, which has not implemented a plan to remove architectural barriers. Social conversion factors are those linked to our social context; they may be gender practices, social norms, hierarchies or government policies. All of these play a crucial role in the performance of our opportunities. Thus, a person who has been born in a country where democratic values are powerful will have more opportunities to achieve participation in their political sphere than someone who is born in a dictatorship, where opportunities for participation and public reasoning are low. The last of the conversion factors are environmental conversion factors, which refer to public provisions, good climate and infrastructural facilities (Robeyns 2005). For instance, the installation of lighting on a street can affect the capability of free movement of a woman walking at night in a country where security is an issue.

Due to the specific context used in this book and its decolonial and Southern perspective, these conversion factors might not correspond with the experiences and cosmovisions of many in the South. That is why, in this book, I propose a merged category, a Southern and decolonial category that I have named 'Colonial Conversion Factors'. The main argument for defending this unique conversion factor is to provide the visibility needed to address colonial effects on individuals' freedoms for good and bad. It acknowledges Southern collectivist and critical cosmovisions that do not separate individuals from collectives and their social conditions (Tutu 1999). Hence, colonial conversion factors are neutral factors formed by historical events that shape the lives of many today and they are not divided among collective and individual levels. Any individual limitation or advantage is determined by the combination of social, historical and environmental circumstances. Thus, individual conversion factors are challenged by decolonial thought, as it presumes a 'normalcy' standard that categorises individuals as separate from their social and political contexts. It ignores the fact that critical disability theory deconstructs individual impairments as socially developed (Ndlovu 2021) as well as psychological, psychiatric profiling (Foucault 2013) and educational opportunities (Rosen-Velasquez 2016). Thus, individual and social advantages and disadvantages to exercise their freedoms are intertwined. As Ndlovu (2021, 73) attests, 'The process and the criteria used in the categorisation and naming of individuals and groups are a form of dehumanisation, because normalcy is a concept that cannot be universalised: It is a subjective and contextual phenomenon'. Therefore, social, environmental and individual 'normal' standards are determined by the political and social contexts. That is why colonial conversion factors confer huge advantages on those that were part of the powerful colonial system in the past and that continue to be part of its neo-colonial and Western system in the present. The colonial system allows them to fit into the 'normalcy' and 'human being' zone.

Hence, in many ways colonial conversion factors affect populations and historically oppressed communities in the Global South. The point is to highlight that colonial conversion factors are important for an understanding of social and political challenges in the Global South and in a context such as South Africa. Further, it is necessary for scholars in the Global North to acknowledge them, if we want to start questioning the ways in which epistemic injustices are understood and reproduced. Certainly, the type of oppression that are experienced in the Global South are not the same as those in the Global North. We need to acknowledge and differentiate these types of oppression through our theoretical foundations, by conceptualising terms that better represent and reflect these varied experiences and cosmovisions. Challenging traditional concepts and their theorisations is foundational to decolonial and epistemological resistances. However, I will come back to these concepts in other parts of the book, exploring their conceptualisation and its effects on valued capabilities in the empirical chapters (Chapters Five, Six and Seven).

Another important element of the Capabilities Approach is agency. In this area, Crocker (2008) says that individuals are affected by the daily dynamics of life and the ways in which we act in the world, co-opted by major forces and not as full agents. That is why he states (2008, 156157) that:

> a person is an agent with respect to action x just in case she (1) decides for herself rather than someone or something else forcing the decision to do x; (2) bases her decisions on reasons, such as the pursuit of goals; (3) performs or has a role in performing x; and (4) thereby brings about or contributes to the bringing about of change in the world.

Therefore, the point is not to achieve a perfect exercise of our agency, but rather to try, in each of the four components, to achieve it to the maximum, despite the circumstances surrounding us. The aim is to overcome passivity and rather promote the full, or much fuller, exercise of our agency, i.e. acting 'consciously, on purpose and for a purpose' (Crocker 2008, 157).

Nevertheless, the Capabilities Approach is not only a prospective and evaluative framework through which to assess human development and well-being. Beyond that, it represents an incomplete idea of justice. Generally, social justice seems to be as ambiguous as the term 'participatory', and perhaps even more so (Buchanan & Mathieu 1986). It is a term whose definition has historically been ascribed to the few elites able to influence its understanding (Capeheart & Milovanovic 2007). Moreover, it has become a highly contested idea that differs according to individuals and place. Sen (2009) claims that there is a need to identify unfair situations through an evaluative framework in order to take action against them. However, this identification is not based on a dichotomous frame, but as a continuum, where situations can be assessed as more or less according to the individual capabilities evaluation. Moreover, Sen (2009) addresses questions such as how to enhance justice or remove injustices rather than resolve the question of what justice is, or how a perfectly just society would look, and how that might differ according to time and place. The use of capabilities as a means of assessing individuals and detecting shortfalls is a sufficient way to promote an open-ended version of justice, which does not aim to build itself as a complete theory of justice. It is not a question of building a justice theory, but of allowing partial justices to understand one another in a plural world.

Hence, moving beyond a transcendental institutionalism is precisely what the Capabilities Approach contributes to debates on justice. The Capabilities Approach connects justice 'with the way people's lives go, and not merely with the nature of the institutions surrounding them' (Sen 2009, x). These implications are far-reaching for participatory approaches and decolonial ideas. The introduction of a capabilities-based participatory research not only pays attention to the diverse lives the members have reason to value, but equally uses the processes as a catalyst of member's freedoms. However, these ideas will be developed in the following section. Firstly, we will investigate the commonalities between the Capabilities Approach and the decolonial debate.

## 4.2.2 An Incomplete Theoretical Foundation

The potential contribution of the Capabilities Approach to decoloniality and to participatory approaches lies in its incompleteness and non-universalist perspective. Frequently, Eurocentric theories tend to orient participatory practices and conceptualisations of participation. Nevertheless, this vision of theory as universal and totalising is deeply rooted in the Enlightenment period as part of the Eurocentric-modern project (Mignolo 2007). This is why scholars have, for several decades, been pointing out that knowledge is contextual and should be assessed according to the place and time whence it emerges, and should then be connected globally throughout epistemic system networks (De Sousa Santos, 2014).

All of this has created fruitful debates. It has certainly brought about a shift in the means of theorising, especially in the field of social sciences. For instance, Hoffmann and Metz say that 'theory cannot provide a pre-defined, absolute set of procedures' (2017, 2). Thus, flexible approaches are required, 'incomplete theories' that can act as a space in which to translate different cultural assumptions (De Sousa Santos 2006a). Similarly, De Sousa Santos (2006a) says:

> Knowledge as emancipation does not pretend to build itself as a big theory but as a translation theory that can convert in the epistemological base of the emancipatory practices, being these practices finite, incomplete and thus only sustainable if it is able to be incorporated into networks. (2006a, 30)

In this incompleteness, the Capabilities Approach, in its more flexible and open perspective as presented by Amartya Sen (1999; 2009), is a suitable and appropriate partial theory. It can be a translation tool to promote decoloniality and recognition of other epistemologies and worldviews. Moreover, it frames participatory practices according to a group's specificities and respects their own cultural frameworks. This can be achieved through the Capabilities Approach's notion of 'positional objectivity' (Sen 2004), which recognises the varying views of different actors situated in the social fabric. 'Positional objectivity is both objective and relative to the position of the observer' (Bonvin, Laruffa & Rosenstein 2017, 7). It challenges positivist views, arguing that an objective position and a relative position are both necessary and substantial.

Indeed, although the terminology is slightly different, the decolonial debate advocates the very same idea. Dussel (2007) argues that what has to be promoted through a pluriverse is a 'subjectivity of intersubjectivities'—in the sense of an incomplete positionality that needs a compendium of subjectivities—in the same way that Sen promotes the diversification and inclusion of 'positional objectivities'. Bonvin, Laruffa and Rosenstein argue that:

> The issue, then, is not to create the conditions allowing people to abstract themselves from their own interest and situations, but also give equal weight to all existing positional objectivities, which requires overcoming the material, symbolic and cognitive barriers identified. (Bonvin et al. 2017, 8)

Nevertheless, the democratic potential of the Capabilities Approach is jeopardised when arguing for a universalisation of capabilities or a universal conception of well-being. This reverses its foundational incompleteness into a universal theory of justice. Within the CA, a group of scholars supports the universalisation of capabilities, with the creation of a global capabilities list (Nussbaum 2011). Without diminishing its relevance and importance in such complex times of injustice and global inequalities, it perhaps simplifies the colonial challenge of Global South societies ignoring the power that certain societies exercise over others.

This position might impede the agency of individuals to decide their relevant capabilities in their own time and context. It might decrease the democratic potential, or freeze the context and time that greatly influences capabilities choices in a constantly changing reality. Sen supports a partial onto-epistemological incompleteness, which is well described in the following quote:

> Pure theory, Sen contends 'Cannot freeze' a list of capabilities for all societies for all times to come, irrespective of what the citizens come to understand and value. That would not only be a denial of the reach of democracy, but also a misunderstanding of what a pure theory can do. (Hoffman & Metz 2017, 2)

Therefore, the potential of the Capabilities Approach as a decolonial tool lies in its understanding, from an emancipatory perspective, that is its being able to acknowledge and recognise the diversity of lives that different people have reason to value, including the knowledges they value (Sen 1999). As Watene (2016, 287) claims, 'the approach recognises that culture is a constitutive part of well-being and a constructive factor in how life is valued'. Thus, the Capabilities Approach avoids the claim of universalism, inasmuch as it is able to locate and provide the space for an imperfect pluriverse. Bonvin et al. (2017) agree that the idea of 'reason to value' for Sen transcends the universalistic misrepresentation of rationality from deliberative theorists. The incompleteness of the approach is a means of avoiding parochialism, but equally of broadening the notions of rational public debate and democracy beyond their Western definitions. Hence, Sen's approach provides a more adequate platform to sustain cross-cultural and participatory dialogue, whilst leaving the diverse reasons and values open through the centrality of agency in his approach (Watene 2016).

Another key point to argue regarding the Capabilities Approach and its potential contribution to decoloniality is its individual focus, the individual person being the final entity but also being able to decide which freedoms are important and relevant. Whilst this individualism has been conceptualised as an anthropocentric understanding, Robeyns (2005) has defended it as an ethical or methodological individualism, which differs from an ontological individualism. In the case of the Capabilities Approach, ethical individualism situates the person as the moral unit but does not restrict reality to a person's view, due to the substantial position of democracy and public scrutiny. This debate is especially relevant in its introduction to participatory approaches and ecologies of knowledge, due to the anthropocentric Western perspective of life (Zaffaroni 2012). First, scholars advocating decoloniality maintain that cultures, like groups, are not homogeneous (Dussel 2007). They stress the need to understand the individualities that compose a particular group (Dussel 2007; De Sousa Santos 2010; Mignolo 2007), an aspect which the Capabilities Approach is able to capture. And secondly, the 'anthropocentric fear' with regard to the Capabilities Approach is unjustified, provided that the approach is incomplete and therefore, flexible enough to transcend the individual as the unique capabilities-deserving entity or the focus of attention for capabilities. For instance, D'Amato (2020) has eloquently explored this in his article 'Collectivist Capabilitarianism'. Furthermore, another option could be to provide animals or rivers with capabilities, which is already an ongoing topic of debate in the capabilities literature (Nussbaum 2017; Kramm 2020). As mentioned above, the Capabilities Approach is an incomplete theoretical foundation which can be revised and complemented to better adjust it to our specific context and ontological positions, even if it needs further revisions and reconceptualisations of its fundamental elements. Moreover, there have been many debates about collective capabilities (Ibrahim 2006; Rosignoli 2019) and structures of living together that explore the interrelation between individuals and their capabilities, adjusting the approach to more collective frameworks (Deneulin 2006). Certainly, this does not mean that the Capabilities Approach is intrinsically suited to a decolonial perspective, but rather that the approach is open enough to re-work and accommodate different cosmologies. As Watene (2016, 294) eloquently confirms in his discussion of Maori cosmovisions, 'while Sen's theory cannot fully appreciate Maori values that are not grounded in human freedom, his theory is open to them', however, 'rethinking capability theories and looking for spaces beyond the capability approach are required to make development conversations truly inclusive and truly global'.

On the other hand, capabilities can be defended as being aligned with decolonial ideas, due to the concept of 'diatopical hermeneutics' defended by De Sousa Santos (2006b; 2010). To bring about the ecology of knowledges, it is necessary to make use of what Santos (2006a; 2015) has called a 'Diatopical hermeneutics', which is the practice of dialogue where different knowledges can be translated into a something comprehensible to others. It is partly a theory of translation, which makes cultures and local cosmovisions understandable to each other. The role of a diatopical hermeneutic is not only to translate local worldviews but also to look for 'isomorphic' issues and their different responses to it. It provides the assumption that all cultures are incomplete and relative,[1] and therefore that all of them can gain from being in translation with each other (De Sousa Santos 2010). Sen (1999) equally sustains this idea, when he defines democracy as the inclusion of as many positional objectivities as possible (Bonvin et al. 2017). In this case, capabilities can be used as part of diatopical hermeneutics, providing the space to translate between different cultures, and diverse means of human flourishing, well-being, and human development. Capabilities can look for isomorphic elements among diverse cultures, and act as a link for them to understand each other in a space of democratic dialogue, as the following chapters will demonstrate.

All of the above situates the Capabilities Approach in a similar perspective on justice, while the decolonial debate calls for the removal of historical injustices through the conservation and promotion of

---

1    The use of the word 'relative' does not claim for a philosophical posture of cultural relativism. De Sousa Santos himself states that cultural relativism is an erroneous positionality, just like cultural universalism (De Sousa Santos 2010).

diversity in the world, throughout the pluriverse project. The Capabilities Approach fosters the expansion of the freedoms that people need in order to lead different lives, not only in terms of basic resources but also the mere consideration of open spaces for diverse individuals' and groups' valuable lives (Sen 2009).

Thus, to conclude, the table below summarises the different elements discussed in this section, detailing the commonalities between the Capabilities Approach and decoloniality.

Table 4: Comparing Decoloniality and the Capabilities Approach.

|  | Decoloniality | Capabilities Approach |
|---|---|---|
| Theoretical space | (Non-universalism) Partial theory: Ontologically incomplete and epistemologically diverse. | Incomplete theory — Approach: As a cultural translation theory. Ontologically open and able to accommodate epistemic diversity reworking central elements and ideas of this approach. |
| Voices | Subjectivities of intersubjectivities. | Positional objectivities. |
| Individualism/ Anthropocentrism | Pay attention to individuals that compose groups, but equally oppressed groups and entities that are beyond humans (beyond anthropocentrism). | Moral individualism. Flexible enough to reconsider humans as the only capabilities deserving attention. |
| Democracy | Non Western-institutionalised. Democracy, participation as central. | Acknowledge the Western appropriation and imposition of democratic institutions. Consider democracy in a broad sense, as inclusion of voices from different positionalities. |

| Diversity | Universe to be transformed into a pluriverse, which highlights and promotes diverse knowledges and cosmovisions. Allows individuals to live out of the hegemonic mono-culture.<br><br>Promotion of ecology of knowledges. | Development as the expansion of freedoms that different individuals have reason to value (doings and beings). Promoting different lives that individuals have reason to value. |
|---|---|---|
| Units for cultural translation | Diatopic hermeneutic. | Capabilities. |
| Justice | Onto-epistemological justice, removing hegemonic structures that do not allow diverse people to lead different lives and recognise diverse knowledges. | Removal of unfreedoms and promotion of the different lives diverse individuals have reason to value.<br><br>Pay attention to processes and outcomes. |

Therefore, this section has corroborated that even with foundational limitations the Capabilities Approach can be aligned with decolonial ideas, when certain aspects of this approach are reconsidered. Firstly, it presents an open-ended, onto-epistemological position that embraces a diversity of perspectives. This is framed in an incomplete theoretical foundation for decoloniality. This position does not acquire a radical positionality, as has been true of certain decolonial perspectives. It does not deny the richness of the European tradition or the relevance of Western knowledge, but positions it on an equal footing with other traditions, and displaces its superiority. For instance, it does not deny universal capabilities lists but reminds us that capabilities choices and conceptualisations are culturally related; and they require global discussions, especially with communities in the Global South if they are to be considered global (rather than universal). Secondly, democracy is approached broadly, including many voices in a horizontal dialogue.

This is especially relevant with the use of participatory approaches that include processes of knowledge production much more than a classified and reduced group of individuals selected by an institution in a hierarchic system. It not only represents the inclusion of diverse voices, but also the representation and validation of other knowledge systems and cosmovisions in order to enhance our democratic spaces. Thirdly, the ecology of knowledges is compatible with the Capabilities Approach as the latter is able to value other lives that different individuals have reason to value, and therefore, other knowledge systems. This section has claimed that capabilities can be used as a multi-cultural translation tool, helping us to look for isomorphic elements in different cosmologies. This does not mean unifying these elements, but rather looking within the cultural specificities for elements that are not the same, but that retain symbolic similarities. This section has concluded that both the Capabilities Approach and decoloniality sustain the preservation of our Global South diversity as a way to achieve social justice. It has also claimed that the issue is not only related to resource inequalities, but also to historical structures of oppression, such as colonial conversion factors. Thus, multidimensional oppressions hinder different peoples from living the lives that they, diverse individuals in the South and North, have reason to value in different places and times (Sen 1999).

## 4.3 Conceptualising a Capabilities-Based Research Process

Participatory approaches are of interest in the area of human development and the Capabilities Approach. Whilst the combination of both fields is a relatively recent phenomenon, more scholars are becoming interested in this approach, due to its participatory nature and the centrality of public scrutiny and democracy as instruments to enhance people's freedoms.

Some scholars, mostly from development studies, have explored theoretical debates between participatory approaches and the Capabilities Approach (Biggeri & Anich 2009; Clark, Biggeri & Frediani 2019; Duraiappah et al. 2005; Frediani 2006; 2007; 2010; Mink 2016; Negrini 2009; Pellisery & Bergh 2007; Robeyns 2006). Others have used participatory methods and methodologies in educational studies (Boni & Millan 2015; Boni & Walker 2016; Fertig 2012; Heather 2014; Lizzio & Wilson 2004; Ley 2013; Vanderkinderen & Rose 2014), or community projects (Conradie 2013a; Conradie 2013b; Conradie & Robeyns 2013; Lavelle-Wijohn 2017; Mazigo 2017). In addition, some studies have focused on its application in environmental projects (Simpson 2018; Simpson & Basta 2018) or children's projects (Del Moral-Espin, Perez-Garcia & Galvez-Munoz 2017), among others.

However, there are three main challenges and a clear gap in the publications linking the Capabilities Approach and participatory approaches. Firstly, there is very limited literature about the interrelation of participatory approaches and the Capabilities Approach, which is especially deficient in the Southern and decolonial areas of research. The literature mostly focuses on development studies and the application of participatory methods. The use of participatory methodologies is residual, and almost non-existent. And, finally, there seems to be a diversity of terminologies in use among the community of scholars using participatory practices—Action Research, Participatory Action Research or Indigenous Research. However, despite the flourishing of new terminologies in the field of participatory approaches, this community has not agreed or attempted to understand or conceptualise their practices as informed and theorised under the Capabilities Approach, nor indeed through a decolonial lens.

Therefore, after exploring the limitations within the field of participatory approaches in Chapter Three, highlighting inconsistencies regarding participation and the need to move towards more critical and decolonial participatory approaches, this chapter conceptualises Democratic Capabilities Research (DCR). DCR acts as a capabilitarian theoretical ground, considering weaknesses within the participatory field. This tool is deliberately incomplete (Sen 1999) so it can be adapted to different research fields and contexts in debates of decoloniality and epistemic justice. Equally, it embraces the most critical commonalities between the diverse participatory families previously displayed, contributing to the extended family of participatory approaches. It adds a more suitable theoretical frame from a Southern perspective that moves beyond totalising theories and Western perspectives, as a way to understand justice broadly.

To explore the constitutive elements of Democratic Capabilities Research more deeply, and to answer the question of why these elements—'Democratic' and 'Capabilities'—were chosen above others, the following section will highlight each of them through a capabilities lens. It links these concepts with decolonial and participatory debates, highlighting the theoretical and practical advantages of using this incomplete theoretical ground.

## 4.3.1 Democratic Capabilities Research

To understand DCR as a practice, firstly, it seems relevant to clarify the main elements of the Capabilities Approach within this proposed participatory research. DCR arises from two main terminologies within the Capabilities Approach, i.e. 'Democracy' and 'Capabilities'. Sen (2009) clearly states in his preface to *The Idea of Justice*:

> Democracy is assessed in terms of public reasoning, which leads to an understanding of democracy as 'government by discussion'. But democracy must also be seen more generally in terms of the capacity to enrich reasoned engagement through enhancing informational availability and the feasibility of interactive discussions. Democracy has to be judged not just by the institutions that formally exist but by the extent to which different voices from diverse sections of the people can actually be heard. (2009, xii-xiii)

In this introduction, Sen (2009) not only provides a different perspective of democracy through the extended representative democratic system (Isakhan & Stockwell 2011; Bonvin, Laruffa & Rosenstein 2017) but equally dismantles the Eurocentric creation and appropriation of democracy. Sen (2009) highlights the erroneous dilemmas between groups, which argue for the imposition of democracy in non-Western territories, and groups, which argue against a Western-centric imposition of democracy. By framing democracy as public reasoning, it becomes much more than a Western creation, and represents elements found in different civilisations and time periods across history (Sen 2009). Therefore, if democracy is the platform for public discussion by individuals, as opposed to exclusively powerful and well-established institutions, these discussions should embrace all of the dimensions and cosmovisions prevailing in the world beyond regional and institutionalised logics. It is about promoting an alternative way to advance an inclusive system of pluriversal progress. Bonvin et al. (2017) clarify Sen's notion of democracy, stating that:

> The normative implication is that democratic processes should include as many positional objectivities as possible. Indeed, the more such

viewpoints are included and considered, the more collective decisions will be objectively informed. In this perspective, effective democratic participation is justified on epistemological grounds, as a prerequisite to reach informed decisions. It is not based simply on the normative superiority of collective discussion or public debate over unilateral imposition, but on the epistemological necessity to include all relevant information into the collective decision-making processes. (Bonvin et al. 2017, 8)

Therefore, the Capabilities Approach is able to promote a heterogeneous epistemic foundation, according to which it is no longer only one valid type of knowledge, but the promotion of a democratic dimension, which must be composed of different voices. As Bonvin et al. (2017) state:

The Capabilities Approach calls for re-politicising the production of knowledge—in contrast to contemporary tendencies that reduce the process of policy formulation to a technical matter based on scientific evidence. (2017, 11)

Thus, a participatory research project like DCR must include a conceptualisation of democracy, such as the one above, understanding the need to promote the diversification of voices and the enhancement of inclusivity within processes of knowledge creation.

On the other hand, capabilities are the real freedoms that a person enjoys (Sen 1999). They are 'the substantive freedoms he or she enjoys to lead the kind of life he or she has reason to value' (Sen 1999, 87). Thus, capabilities represent all those freedoms to do and to become the person that different individuals and collectives want to be, but equally to be able to lead their lives in the way they have reason to value (Sen 1999). Furthermore, this includes being able to live under a different cosmovision or being able to value one's communal/cultural knowledge system. Therefore, capabilities are an incomplete unit of analysis, which can embrace a diversity of ways of living and respect Southern perspectives.

## 4.3.2 Contributions of a Capabilities-Based Perspective to Participatory Approaches

Despite the two main elements of the Capabilities Approach composing this DCR practice informed by decolonial debates, we must also explore this incomplete framework's contribution to participatory approaches.

The decolonial debate and its Southern positionality calls for more inclusive means of knowledge production, and more flexible epistemic and ontological/cosmological frameworks. The use of participatory research is one way to overcome the Western-centric boundaries within higher-education institutions. However, these practices are at times pervasively used to mimic the very colonial logics they condemn, contributing towards the homogenisation of the field instead of its diversification. On the other hand, the Capabilities Approach can be a useful theoretical framework for understanding the implications of Western traditions in our work as participatory practitioners. In doing so, we are reinforcing the theoretical foundation of participatory practices from a Global South perspective and reversing some of the actual limitations, overcoming colonial challenges for justice and the democratisation of knowledge.

## *Why Democratic and Not Participatory?*

'Participation' or 'participatory' is a highly contested word, as discussed in previous chapters (Hayward, Simpson & Wood 2004; Webb 1996; Frediani 2015). The divergent understandings of 'participation' represent an intricate theoretical space that is overestimated, with the aim of providing more or less space for an individual's participation. Sen (1999; 2009) states that whilst individuals might participate in national elections, voting once every four years, this does not equate to democracy in a broad sense. It can be said that participation is one necessary component of democracy, but is not democracy in itself, or democracy in a broad sense, as the Capabilities Approach presents it. Do we want to create participatory spaces of knowledge production? Or do we want to create democratic spaces of knowledge production?

The term 'democracy', from a capabilities perspective, focuses on the micro-politics of everyday life, acting according to what we want to do and be from a critical perspective, taking conscious decisions over our political affairs and expressing them through our conscious agency (Sen 1999; Crocker 2008). Public interaction through dialogue is a necessary precondition of this aim, which requires us to accommodate as many perspectives (positional objectivities) as possible (Sen 1999), or an ecology of knowledges (De Sousa Santos 2014). This is especially important, whether we approach participation in knowledge production through our own traditional frameworks, or offer space for more democratic knowledge creation, which extends beyond simple participation. Democracy represents a wider methodological understanding of participation. When individuals share a democratic space, members of the group are doing more than participating in something. They are creating a new intellectual space, which did not exist before they got together. They are raising their voices and knowledge in different ways and forms. Thus, democracy understood through a capabilities framework provides a wider-reaching concept, whose adequacy may be evaluated according to the voices being heard (positional objectivities) and scrutinised publicly.

This concept, thus, avoids current ambiguities in the use of participation, expanding its meaning from an instrumental idea to a communal dialogue. Participation is a component of democracy, thus democracy acquires a more solid normative meaning through the Capabilities Approach. It is not enough merely to involve individuals in the process of research; it is a necessary step forward to reverse the structures of power over the spaces of knowledge creation, returning democratic elements such as ecologies of knowledge (De Sousa Santos 2014). It is not only a question of participation, but also of more inclusive democratic knowledge networks, which can connect, particularly with the voiceless, beyond the individual academic research endeavour.

## *Why Capabilities and Not Action?*

Equally, in participatory approaches and due to the dominant logics and practices of production and efficiency, most participatory projects—especially those focused on AR practices—are expected to have a tangible outcome which impacts the context and/or participants in different ways. One example of this might be behavioural changes in a community, which were explored in Chapter Three. This instrumental perspective can diminish a more critical perspective of such practices, narrowing the focus to a part of the whole. Certainly, a problematic and paternalistic approach is reproduced when researchers force community change under their own logics and assumptions. But what about communities' own aspirations of change? What about the collective impact on research members during our joint work? And the impact on the lives that they, as individuals and groups, have reason to value independently of our research agendas?

This is well illustrated by the Capabilities Approach, as in the example displayed above. If we pay attention to, for instance, educational outcomes in terms of a qualification certificate, we miss the inequalities in the process of achievement, the freedoms that different individuals and groups have to reach a certain outcome. We can observe the same oversight in participatory practices, due to their pedagogical relevance. What about the freedoms that diverse individuals and the group enjoy and/or enhance during a participatory practice? What about enhancing the freedoms valued by oppressed groups and disadvantaged groups? Which capabilities are valuable for those individuals/groups, and is the participatory process able to expand them or not? These questions shift our attention from the concrete collective action expected by the researcher, as in traditional participatory projects, to the impact on the lives the participants have reason to value, having taken into consideration their context, cosmovisions and preferred ways of living.

Therefore, when groups are implementing participatory research projects, it is important to pay attention to the participants' valuable capabilities , the potential choices that the process enhances and/or constrains. Equally important are the functionings and tangible research outcomes for the individuals/group involved. DCR, thus switches 'Action' to 'Capabilities',[2] providing an alternative view for exploring collaborative research, which pays attention not only to the tangible outcomes desired by the researcher, but also to the co-researchers' and communities' valued freedoms.

In conclusion, the Capabilities Approach as a framework can greatly contribute to the theorisation and operationalisation of participatory practices. It provides an incomplete framework able to accommodate the challenges that participatory approaches must face in the twenty-first century in an increasingly complex and homogenising landscape. To do so, it redirects the knowledge creation process to the co-researchers' valuable lives, providing the evaluative and normative foundation to enhance their capabilities. It maintains a democratic space in which to

---

2    'Capabilities' are the real freedoms people have to be and to do the things they have reason to value, what people are able to do and to be (Sen 1999; Robeyns 2017).

share and enhance valuable capabilities and knowledges for the lives that the co-researchers involved have reason to value.

## 4.3.3 Foundational Principles

The following section justifies the foundational elements of this proposed DCR process, clarifying the challenges, when theoretical implications are brought down to earth, as real practices. Thus, Democratic Capabilities Research is here presented as a practical insight for imperfectly achieving and protecting communites' epistemic freedoms. It is necessary to recognise the incompleteness of the tool and to add it to the current compendium of participatory tools being used in efforts for justice according to a particular Southern understanding. Democratic Capabilities Research presents a participative research process as a pedagogical space, which is flexible enough to embrace different worldviews and knowledges through a critical analysis of the valuable freedoms of the team members, thus presenting a Southern viewpoint. Equally, it cannot be considered as a method, which follows one, two or three specific steps, or as a simple data collection tool, nor can it be considered a methodology. It is a tool, which should be developed in each individual context as a full research process by co-researchers.

The following paragraphs highlight some of the practical implications of DCR. These key points are still in the process of being defined and refined and therefore are not complete or final. As already mentioned, the DCR project is only possible within wide networks of individuals who are connected by the shared aim of improving or creating differently. These principles are informed by the decolonial debate, participatory approaches and the Capabilities Approach. Hence, these principles have been assimilated into a coherent DCR framework to provide an alternative viewpoint capable of democratising participatory research while respecting its contextualisation. According to this conceptualisation, there are five original DCR foundational principles. These are not exhaustive but are intended to provide points of resistance that we might be able to navigate as researchers in academia:

- **Injustice as an initial issue:** Injustice/s should be the foundational issue/s, which means that 'injustice' is not framed by the 'facilitator', but embraces a multiplicity of understandings of injustice according to the members involved, respecting cultural and context-based cosmovisions. This is the open-ended epistemological level, opening up to other cosmologies and bringing together a group of individuals and their knowledge systems in order to investigate an injustice that affects them and other individuals and therefore, which they have good reasons to research. The facilitator is here an ally to prompt and sustain collective agency, and their role is not to determine the research agenda of the group.

- **Internal and external epistemic diversity**[3] (**ecology of knowledges**): In the sense of the promotion of the ecology of knowledges throughout the research process. This involves validating knowledge systems that are traditionally excluded and bringing them to the research process, in the way that is required by the team and the particular circumstances of the project. Hence, it involves including knowledges such as, but not limited to, scientific, conceptual, experiential, intuitive, local, Indigenous, cultural, spiritual and/or popular. The facilitator here has a substantial responsibility to demystify hegemonic knowledge, but also to discuss and create platforms for the assessment of other knowledge systems.

- **The voiceless as knowledge creators:** DCR is a space of democratic (to the extent that this is possible) knowledge creation for the excluded. The participants involved represent collectives excluded from 'validated knowledge production processes', which does not mean that they do not create knowledge in their own frameworks or use validated sources of knowledge. They are epistemic agents, but the point is to bring their epistemic materials to the validated knowledge system and to reduce their epistemic marginalisation and obstructions within the hegemonic system.

---

3    See Chapter Seven for more information.

- **Uncertain horizon:** This involves flexibility in the sense that DCR is not a business plan, nor a sterile methodological intervention. Therefore, it is desirable to promote and conserve an 'uncertain horizon' able to transform what comes next through the constant democratic dialogue and decision-making of the research group. This approach seems especially difficult in scientific contexts, which are flooded with endless bureaucracy, efficiency drives, and results-orientated projects. These issues underscore the urgency and imperative need for the approach to discuss and debate every step taken by the research team.

- **DCR as a platform to expand/achieve the participants' capabilities:** Capabilities expansion and achievement is placed under a critical lens; the facilitator should collectively investigate and promote the expansion of the capabilities that are deemed valuable for the members during the research project. This capabilities enhancement cannot be evaluated with an external checklist, but through an individual and collective exploration of the valued capabilities of the members of the group. This orients the practice towards the identified valued capabilities, as well as assessing the process by evaluating the extent to which these capabilities and related functionings have been expanded and achieved.

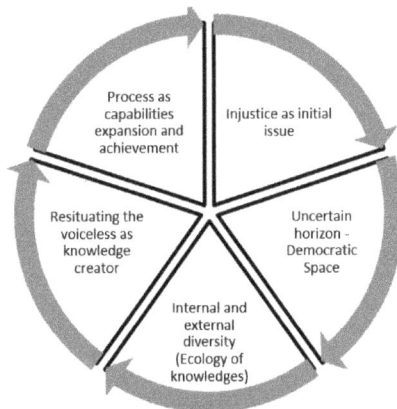

Figure 4: Principles of Democratic Capabilities Research (image by the author, 2021).

DCR does not represent a linear approach to research, nor does it constrain its 'partial phases' into timeframes. Spaces are complex and, therefore—in a DCR practice—a few phases can be implemented at the same time, some stages can be repeated at various points in the research, and so on. DCR not only represents an approach to research, it is a framework within which to understand a research process in itself. DCR is not separate from the daily life of the members; real life and DCR are in constant conversation as a space of questioning, reflection and learning. Therefore, DCR goes beyond a conventional research process, and it offers a way of co-constructing sense together, co-building reality and co-creating pluriversal knowledge imperfectly and within complex and convoluted social and political spaces of power, in which the group and the facilitators are situated.

# References

Biggeri, M., & Anich, R. (2009). The deprivation of street children in Kampala: Can the capability approach and participatory methods unlock a new perspective in research and decision making? *Mondes en Développement*, 2, 73–93. https://doi.org/10.3917/med.146.0073.

Boni, A., & Millán, G. F. (2015). Action-research using participatory video: A learning experience in San Lorenzo, Castellón, Spain. *Commons. Revista de Comunicación y Ciudadanía Digital*, 5(1), 119–138. https://doi.org/10.25267/commons.2016.v5.i1.06.

Boni, A., & Walker, M. (2016). *Universities and Global Human Development: Theoretical and Empirical Insights for Social Change*. London: Routledge.

Bonvin, J. M., Laruffa, F., & Rosenstein, E. (2017). Towards a critical sociology of democracy: The potential of the capability approach. *Critical Sociology*, 44, 953–968. https://doi.org/10.1177%2F0896920517701273.

Buchanan, A., & Mathieu, D. (1986). Philosophy and justice. In Cohen (ed.). *Justice* (pp. 11–45). Boston: Springer US.

Capeheart, L., & Milovanovic, D. (2007). *Social Justice: Theories, Issues, and Movements*. London: Rutgers University Press.

Clark, D. A., Biggeri, M., & Frediani, A. A. (eds) (2019). *The Capability Approach, Empowerment and Participation: Concepts, Methods and Applications*. London: Springer.

Conradie, I. (2013a). *Aspirations and Capabilities: The Design and Analysis of an Action Research Project in Khayelitsha, Cape Town*. Unpublished doctoral dissertation, University of Western Cape, South Africa.

Conradie, I. (2013b). Can deliberate efforts to realise aspirations increase capabilities? A South African case study. *Oxford Development Studies, 41*(2), 189–219. https://doi.org/10.1080/13600818.2013.790949.

Conradie, I., & Robeyns, I. (2013). Aspirations and human development interventions. *Journal of Human Development and Capabilities, 14*(4), 559–580. https://doi.org/10.1080/19452829.2013.827637.

Chilisa, B. (2012). *Indigenous Research Methodologies.* Los Angeles: Sage Publications.

Connell, R. (2014). Using southern theory: Decolonizing social thought in theory, research and application. *Planning Theory, 13*(2), 210–223. https://doi.org/10.1177%2F1473095213499216.

Crocker, D. A. (2008). *Ethics of Global Development: Agency, Capability, and Deliberative Democracy.* Cambridge, MA: Cambridge University Press.

D'Amato, C. (2020). Collectivist capabilitarianism. *Journal of Human Development and Capabilities, 21*(2), 105–120. https://doi.org/10.1080/19452829.2020.1732 887.

Davis, J. M. (2007). Rethinking the architecture: An action researcher's resolution to writing and presenting their thesis. *Action Research, 5*(2), 181–198. https://doi.org/10.1177%2F1476750307077322.

Del Moral-Espin, L., Perez-Garcia, A. & Galvez-Munoz, L. (2017). Una buena vida: Definiendo las capacidades relevantes para el bienestar desde las voces de niños y niñas. *Sociedad e infancias, revistas científicas complutenses, 1,* 203–237. https://doi.org/10.5209/SOCI.55932.

Deneulin, S. 2006. *The Capability Approach and the Praxis of Development.* Basingstoke: Palgrave Macmillan.

Dussel, E. D. (2007). Materiales para una política de la liberación. Madrid: Plaza y valdés España.

De Rond, M., & Miller, A. N. (2005). Publish or perish: Bane or boon of academic life? *Journal of Management Inquiry, 14*(4), 321–329. https://doi.org/10.1177 %2F1056492605276850.

De Sousa Santos, B. (2006a). *La universidad popular del siglo XXI.* Lima: Fondo Editorial de la Facultad de Ciencias Sociales-UNMSM.

De Sousa Santos, B. (2006b). *Conocer desde el Sur: Para una cultura política emancipatoria.* Mexico City: Fondo Editorial de la Facultad de Ciencias Sociales—UNMSM.

De Sousa Santos, B. (2010). *Descolonizar el saber, reinventar el poder.* Montevideo: Ediciones Trilce.

De Sousa Santos, B. (2014). *Epistemologies of the South: Justice against Epistemicide.* New York: Routledge. https://unescochair-cbrsr.org/pdf/resource/ Epistemologies_of_the_South.pdf.

Duraiappah, A. K., Roddy, P., & Parry, J. E. (2005). *Have Participatory Approaches Increased Capabilities?* Winnipeg: International Institute for Sustainable Development. https://www.iisd.org/pdf/2005/economics_participatory_approaches.pdf.

Fertig, M. (2012). *The Relationship between the Capability Approach and Action Research in the Context of Primary School Leadership in Ghana.* Paper presented at the annual conference of the HDCA, 5–7 September 2012, Jakarta.

Frediani, A. A. (2006). *Participatory Methods and the Capabilities Approach: HDCA Introductory Briefing Note.* https://hd-ca.org/publications/participatory-methods-and-the-capability-approach.

Frediani, A. A. (2007). *Participatory Research Methods and Capability Approach: Researching Dimensions of Housing.* Oxford: Oxford Brookes University.

Frediani, A. A. (2010) *Participation: From Tyranny to Human Development? Participatory Capabilities in Development Planning.* Paper presented at the 7th annual conference of the HDCA, 21-23 September 2010, Amman, Jordan. https://hd-ca.org/publications/participation-from-tyranny-to-human-development-participatory-capabilities-in-development-planning.

Frediani, A. A. (2015). *'Participatory Capabilities' in Development Practice: The Bartlett Development Planning Unit, 121.* DPU working paper no 178. http://www.masterhdfs.org/masterHDFS/wp-content/uploads/2014/05/1.-Frediani-2015-%E2%80%98Participatory-Capabilities%E2%80%99-in-Development-Practice.pdf.

Foucault, M. (2013). *History of Madness.* London: Routledge.

Hayward, C., Simpson, L., & Wood, L. (2004). Still left out in the cold: Problematising participatory research and development. *Sociologia Ruralis,* 44(1), 95108. https://doi.org/10.1111/j.1467-9523.2004.00264.x.

Heron, J., & Reason, P. (1997). A participatory inquiry paradigm. *Qualitative Inquiry,* 3(3), 274–294. https://doi.org/10.1177%2F107780049700300302.

Heather, J. K. (2014). *The Upwards Spiral Using Participatory Action Research to Define, Evaluate and Take Action in Regards to Education for a Culture of Peace in Nicaragua.* Paper presented at the annual conference of the HDCA, 2–5 September 2014, Athens, Greece.

Hoffmann, N., & Metz, T. (2017). What can the capabilities approach learn from an Ubuntu ethic? A relational approach to development theory. *World Development,* 97, 153–164. https://doi.org/10.1016/j.worlddev.2017.04.010.

Ibrahim, S. S. (2006). From individual to collective capabilities: The capability approach as a conceptual framework for self-help. *Journal of Human Development,* 7(3), 397–416. http://dx.doi.org/10.1080/14649880600815982.

Isakhan, B., & Stockwell, S. (eds) (2011). *The Secret History of Democracy.* London: Palgrave Macmillan.

Kramm, M. (2020). When a river becomes a person. *Journal of Human Development and Capabilities, 21*(4), 307–319. https://doi.org/10.1080/19452829.2020.1801 610.

Lavelle-Wijohn, E. (2017). *Brain Injury Whānau Action Project (BIWAP): Increasing the capabilities of families of adults with brain injury to live their lives in the ways they have reason to value.* Unpublished doctoral dissertation, Auckland University of Technology, Australia.

Ley, T. (2013). *The Added Value of Analyzing Participation in a Capability Perspective.* Final Conceptual Report: 'Inequality, disadvantage, social innovation and participation'. SocIEtY EU-CP (ed.), 63–85.

Lincoln, Y. S., Lynham, S. A., & Guba, E. G. (2011). Paradigmatic controversies, contradictions, and emerging confluences, revisited. In Denzin & Lincoln (eds). *The SAGE Handbook of Qualitative Research,* 4 (pp. 97–128). Thousand Oaks: Sage Publications.

Lizzio, A., & Wilson, K. (2004). Action learning in higher education: An investigation of its potential to develop professional capability. *Studies in Higher Education, 29*(4), 469–488. https://doi.org/10.1080/030750704200023 6371.

Mazigo, A. F. (2017). Promoting social innovation through action research: Evidence from an empirical study in the fisheries sector of Ukerewe district in Tanzania. *Journal of Human Development and Capabilities, 18*(2), 239–257. https://doi.org/10.1080/19452829.2016.1256276.

Mink, A. (2016). *What is Capability Driven Design and Why Use It?* http://www.design4wellbeing.info/.

Mignolo, W. D. (2007). DELINKING: The rhetoric of modernity, the logic of coloniality and the grammar of de-coloniality. *Cultural Studies, 21*(2-3), 449–514. https://doi.org/10.1080/09502380601162647.

Ndlovu, S. (2021). Humanness and ableism: Construction and deconstruction of disability. In Steyn & Mpofu (eds). *Decolonising the Human: Reflections from Africa on Difference and Oppression.* Johannesburg: Wits University Press.

Negrini, M. (2009). *Parents at Play: Participation and Empowerment in Arts-Based Development Research in Two Communities of Peru.* Paper presented at the 6th annual conference of the HDCA, 10–12 September 2009, Lima, Peru.

Ninomiya, M. E. M., & Pollock, N. J. (2016). Reconciling community-based Indigenous research and academic practices: Knowing principles is not always enough. *Social Science & Medicine, 172,* 28–36. https://doi.org/10.1016/j.socscimed.2016.11.007.

Nussbaum, M. C. (2011). *Creating Capabilities: The Human Development Approach.* Cambridge: Harvard University Press.

Nussbaum, M. C. (2017). Human capabilities and animal lives: conflict, wonder, law: A symposium. *Journal of Human Development and Capabilities, 18*(3), 317–321. https://doi.org/10.1080/19452829.2017.1342382.

Pellissery, S., & Bergh, S. I. (2007). Adapting the capability approach to explain the effects of participatory development programs: Case studies from India and Morocco. *Journal of Human Development, 8*(2), 283–302. https://doi.org/10.1080/14649880701371174.

Reason, P., & Bradbury, H. (2008). *The SAGE Handbook of Action Research: Participative Inquiry and Practice.* Los Angeles: Sage Publications.

Robeyns, I. (2005). The capability approach: A theoretical survey. *Journal of Human Development, 6*(1), 93–117. https://doi.org/10.1080/146498805200034266.

Robeyns, I. (2006). The capability approach in practice. *Journal of Political Philosophy, 14*(3), 351–376. https://doi.org/10.1111/j.1467-9760.2006.00263.x.

Robeyns, I. (2017). Robeyns, I. (2017). *Wellbeing, Freedom and Social Justice: The Capability Approach Re-examined.* Cambridge: Open Book Publishers.

Rosen-Velasquez, E. (2016). Dropouts as delinkers from the modern/colonial world system. In Grosfoguel, Hermandez & Rosen-Velasquez (eds). *Decolonizing the Westernized University: Interventions in Philosophy of Education from Within and Without.* Durham: Lexington Books.

Rosignoli, F. (2019). Categorizing collective capabilities. *Partecipazione e conflitto, 11*(3), 813–837. http://dx.doi.org/10.1285/i20356609v11i3p813.

Sen, A. (1999). *Development as Freedom.* New York: Random House.

Sen, A. (2004). Dialogue capabilities, lists, and public reason: Continuing the conversation. *Feminist Economics, 10*(3), 77–80. http://dx.doi.org/10.1080/1354570042000315163.

Sen, A. (2009). *The Idea of Justice.* Cambridge, MA: Belknap.

Simpson, N. P. (2018). Applying the capability approach to enhance the conceptualization of well-being in environmental assessment. *Journal of Human Development and Capabilities, 19*(3), 133. https://doi.org/10.1080/19452829.2018.1469118.

Simpson, N. P., & Basta, C. (2018). Sufficiently capable for effective participation in environmental impact assessment? *Environmental Impact Assessment Review, 70*, 57–70. https://doi.org/10.1016/j.eiar.2018.03.004.

Spreafico, A. (2016). *Measurement Literature Review.* Miratho working paper 2016/1. http://www.miratho.com/resources/Miratho%20Working%20Paper%202016_1_Measurement%20literature%20review.pdf.

Schroeder, H. (2014). Governing access and allocation in the Anthropocene. *Global Environmental Change, 26*, A1A3. https://doi.org/10.1016/j.gloenvcha.2014.04.017.

Smith, L. T. (2013). *Decolonizing Methodologies: Research and Indigenous Peoples.* London: Zed Books.

Tutu, D. (1999). *No Future without Forgiveness.* New York: Doubleday.

Vandekinderen, C. & Roose, R. (2014). *A common framework for participative research in local youth policy from a capability perspective.* Conceptual Guide for the Participative Research Report from Social Innovation-Empowering the young for the common good project (SocIEtY project) Bielefeld: society-youth.eu.

Vaughn, L. M., Jacquez, F., Lindquist-Grantz, R., Parsons, A., & Melink, K. (2016). Immigrants as research partners: A review of immigrants in community-based participatory research (CBPR). *Journal of Immigrant and Minority Health,* 19(6), 1457–1468. https://doi.org/10.1007/s10903-016-0474-3.

Walker, M., & Martinez-Vargas, C. (2020). Epistemic governance and the colonial epistemic structure: Towards epistemic humility and transformed South-North relations. *Critical Studies in Education,* forthcoming, 1–16. https://doi.org/10.1080/17508487.2020.1778052.

Watene, K. (2016). Valuing nature: Māori philosophy and the capability approach. *Oxford Development Studies,* 44(3), 287–296. https://doi.org/10.1080/13600818.2015.1124077.

Webb, G. (1996). Theories of staff development: Development and understanding. *The International Journal for Academic Development,* 1(1), 63–69. https://doi.org/10.1080/1360144960010107.

Yassi, A., Spiegel, J. B., Lockhart, K., Fels, L., Boydell, K., & Marcuse, J. (2016). Ethics in community-university-artist partnered research: Tensions, contradictions and gaps identified in an 'Arts for social change' project. *Journal of Academic Ethics,* 14(3), 199–220. https://doi.org/10.1007/s10805-016-9257-7.

Zaffaroni, E. R. (2012). *La Pachamama y el humano.* Buenos Aires: Ediciones Madres de Plaza de Mayo.

# 5. Co-Researchers' Valued Capabilities

My story is different because it speaks on the basis of my personal narrative, which I have developed over the two and a half years of having been a university student. My narrative also touches on the years of my life prior to the University of the Free State. How I have made sense of my world as a black individual in a post-apartheid/so-called democratic country, how I make sense of the world as a gay man in a homophobic and queerphobic space and finally how I make sense of the world in a capitalist/economically oppressive and corrupt system as a poor human being.

Power and inequalities have always been and remain a part of my daily life at the university. I have recently learnt that in the examination of inequalities, it is crucial that I equally evaluate my own position of privilege which might directly or indirectly cause me to be powerful and therefore, oppressive to others through my actions. I have been oppressed all of my life. I have been a victim of the abuse of power that was used to make me believe that I was less than and obviously less than all human beings. I will take you through the experiences mentioned above in which power and inequalities were dominant in my personal life as a black, gay, poor, and relatively oppressed person who is now a student of governance and political transformation at the University of the Free State. Due to the fact that this is a collaborative book; I will not be too long in explaining much about my life before university.

A series of my early childhood memories involve my uncle constantly beating up on me and very aggressively telling me to act like a boy, because that is what I am. This to me was not always clear, I did not always understand what it meant but I could tell that I acted a bit different, maybe a lot different from my brother and I preferred to play with my mother's bags and wore my sister's clothes. I was around three or four years old. My uncle would beat the hell out of me to such an extent that I could tell that my mother was in more pain than I was. Although my uncle died around that time, over the years I have met many of his duplicates. I have met him many times that I can recall. I see him in the

 https://doi.org/10.11647/OBP.0273.05

people who, in my everyday life make it a point to communicate it to me that my sexuality is unacceptable. I met him in kids and teachers in school who would remind me that I needed to act a certain way because I was just a bit too soft for a boy and my association with the girls was just disgusting. I met him in my grandmother who would call me all names under the sky, which taught me that in actual fact, I was gay and that wherever I go in life men will always beat me up, because I am not man enough. To cut the long story short, I still meet him every day in homophobic, angry, ignorant people who are so convinced that my sexuality is of a sinful nature.

University for me has not always been a transformative space, but I appreciate the movements and the eagerness to fight for what we, as the students, believe in. It was events such as the protest that followed immediately after Shimla Park and Fees Must Fall that encouraged me to act upon my own conditions about my sexuality. I started engaging in many conversations with queer bodies, trans, gay, lesbian, etc., most of which I had met in student activism for (falls) and protests against racial oppression that we had experienced here.

In all of those encounters, I gauged a necessity to start vocalising our own experiences as far as our sexualities and bodies were on the line during the protest whilst even in spaces of activism, we remained victims of queerphobia and hatred from our cis heterosexual counterparts. There was not much confidence in me, although I understood the need to start speaking about the problems. Through a student movement that had been established to vocalise black student voices, we could create a fully operational structure on which we could rely to speak about race issues. We discussed at one of the movement's meetings that we needed to start to vocalise all sorts of injustices including those imposed on the LGBTQI community. The aim was to create the space to be inclusive and, if at all, not oppressive in any way. I do not speak on LGBTQI issues because it is enjoyable but because it is my duty to create that consciousness and expose the norms we have been socialised to adhere to as society.

University should be a transformative space where we are able to stand for something and literally when we leave this place we need to leave with ultra-perspectives. University as they say is a microcosm of the extended society but if we start to inject a sense of positive influence and challenge the myths we have been told about other people, and if we start to channel our minds for change at this very stage, then we will not have to worry about corrective rape or the escalating statistics of the killing of queer people in our country.

Nevertheless. I most certainly am proud of the progress that the country has made. I could not imagine not having access to facilities and intuitions by virtue of being black, for instance. It is perhaps a blessing and a curse to be living in a democratic country, more than merely a curse, or is it really? And is it as democratic as we claim?

Political power at the current moment is held by very selfish, greedy and power-hungry patriarchs. The economy, which also translates to opportunities for black people to make a stable, decent income, and issues such as land are still held in the very same hands. There are still loopholes in many of the county's policies in regard to the latter. Privilege and power instruments prevail in the hands of the fortunate. I live in a country where even though we had made improvements here and there, I am exposed to many perspectives of the scope of economic (freedoms) and economic liberations. One is my hometown, where the positionality of young people remains hopeless. The problematics range from the lack of the establishment of opportunities and giving youth the instruments to create opportunities and income in the form of skills development. The irony of this opinion though is, of course the breathtaking statistics of unemployed graduates in townships like Umlazi. Which makes me wonder what the future holds.

I equally am exposed to a part of the country where some of my classmates come from massively rich, middle-class backgrounds with a solid private education. We can argue the obvious; ours is a weak and flawed education system but that gives no mercy when I have to compete academically at university level. Does that not also guarantee that I cannot be certain about quickly finishing my degree on time and get a well-paying job, move to a better class community and finally money?

Money is a huge part of my life in university. My very being on campus requires a certain amount of payment per year. But I want to reflect on the subjugation of black, poor students to the lack of funding. My story is not representative of the entire black, poor student majority but we certainly do share sentiments when it comes to the subject.

My story begins when I found out that I had been accepted to the University of the Free State but the person who told me this exciting news told me I had not qualified for financial aid. I discussed this with my aunt who offered to make a few basic payments from the investments she had made over the years. I took a bus the following day from Durban to Bloemfontein, with a few thousands; a few for registration, a few for rent and less than a thousand to start my life. I had made it a mission of mine to get here and find whoever was responsible for financial aid and beg them to give me money to study. In my first few months, I relied on my aunt (the sole breadwinner) for money. Fine. But I mean, it was quite a load for her as she had to support three other people in my family who were also at institutions of higher learning. So, I still needed aid. I was told to attend classes in the meantime and not worry about fees. I remember getting a call from my biological mother who is unemployed to just return home and see what I could do with my life after she had broken the news that my aunt had lost her job in February, after my arrival in Bloemfontein in January. At that time there was no other person to help me out with regards to paying for me. My life was too expensive, I was away from home and I had no idea where I was going to get money to pay for my studies. The following day, I went and looked for the SRC offices and met a girl who did not promise anything but said she would try to get me funding. We struggled together as I went to her office. She called people every day in higher offices on my behalf asking for funding without success.

I struggled with funding throughout the course of my first year and nothing was working. I had a diary that I had gotten during registration that had all the contact details of the rectorate and the SRC. I started to email all of these people repeating my story on every single email, basically begging for funding. I sent everyone and I was either getting negative feedback or no feedback at all. I contacted companies, organisations, and people that I had Googled and that too was unsuccessful. Later that year (2015) I received another call from home that would change the rest of my life. My cousin had called to tell me that my aunt passed away. Of all the devastation I had gone through fighting to be at school and being determined not to leave Bloemfontein, it all seemed to have been a waste of time. I suffered from depression from both the loss of a loved one and the fact that I had absolutely no money to go on. I survived the rest of the year staying in a residence that I had found on the assistance of Mosa Leteane and the then Dean of Student Affairs, Cornelia Faasen. I finally received funding from the university in 2016 for both my first year and my second year, after a very long time of begging and struggling. Financial aid came through after that and saved the day.

My story is not really special but it is a story that does two things. Firstly, it reflects on the sense of urgency that is needed to ensure that funding models are implemented to address the issue of deregistration and the number of students who drop out every year due to the funding obstacle. It also brings light to the level of trauma and depression that we end up having to suffer within this space. Honestly, we are not fine and generally students are not okay mentally, not even because of academics, but with all the challenges that are entangled around having to survive university. We can further argue that depression is not recognised by the university as a disease that many students suffer. In many cases, I sat and imagined that perhaps life would be fine if I had gone home and did not have to deal with my funding and personal problems due to our social inequalities.

*Narratives on Social Injustices: Undergraduate Voices*, 2018

# 5.1 Introduction

This chapter is centred around the debate on the universalisation of capabilities—the creation of universal capabilities for all (Nussbaum 2011)—in relation to the evidence that arose from the DCR case study developed in South Africa. Firstly, using a prospective application of the Capabilities Approach, the chapter argues the need to identify the valued capabilities of a group of co-researchers before undertaking participatory practices such as DCR. The analysis is made by exploring the valued capabilities for the twelve student co-researchers in the case study, incorporating the fluid aspect of capabilities and presenting the four central capabilities for this group: Epistemic, Ubuntu, Human Recognition and Self-Development capabilities.

Furthermore, as the argument is to highlight the importance of contextual capability choices, instead of a universal list, Nussbaum's central capabilities (2011) are used to compare and understand their differences. Thus, the chapter argues that despite the contribution made by this universal list to the field of human development, we still have good reason to scrutinise it, as many cultural and contextual specificities—Southern perspectives—can be lost in such aggregations, thereby missing the grassroots potential of the Capabilities Approach. For instance, the Ubuntu capability identified in this group exposes current understandings of care and support from the Global South that in its Western form limits a contextual vision of this freedom. Further, by investigating these contextual factors we can appreciate how colonial conversion factors activate insurgent capabilities against oppressions of basic freedoms.

The final section of the chapter focuses on the actual prospective frame designed by the facilitator prior to the participatory project in this DCR case study. The frame highlights the strategies drafted according to the most valuable capabilities among the group of participants. Moreover, the actual application of these strategies is presented in a tabulated summary to show how the author—as facilitator—applied the different recommendations from the prospective plan during the DCR project.

## 5.2 The Capabilities Approach as a Prospective Frame

The Capabilities Approach can be used not only as an evaluative frame, but also as a prospective approach. Comim, Qizilbash and Alkire (2008) claim that:

> A prospective application of the Capabilities Approach, in contrast [to the evaluative application], is a working set of the policies, activities and recommendations that are considered, at any given time, most likely to generate considerable capability expansion—together with the processes by which these policies/activities/recommendations are generated and the contexts in which they will be more likely to deliver these benefits. (2008, 30)

Therefore, a prospective application of the Capabilities Approach to our participatory practice can provide us with a set of recommendations for enhancing capabilities expansion in our research team. In this case I am not expecting this prospective perspective to answer the question of how and why capabilities are being expanded, but rather to produce a set of group-related recommendations prior to our participatory project. Using the Capabilities Approach as a prospective guide for our DCR participatory practices, we ask what capabilities are valuable for this research team, and what strategies can be designed prior to our participatory project in order to enhance them. Once again, citing Comim et al. (2008), the aim of this prospective approach is to find 'which prospective recommendations could or should arise from the Capability Approach' (2008, 32). However, these affirmations lead us to pose other questions, such as whether these recommendations are based on capabilities? And if so, which capabilities? Are we to use a pre-designed capabilities list or not? And why? Therefore, before addressing the details from the DCR project, I will argue for the use of a contextual capabilities list in order to enhance the use of the Capabilities Approach under a prospective frame prior to our participatory DCR project.

## 5.3 Preparing Our DCR Project as Facilitators: Precooked or Home-Cooked Capabilities?

As the questions above have highlighted, one of the main questions to consider after having proposed this prospective use of the CA for our

DCR projects is what the focus of our analysis is. Also, if we are using capabilities, which capabilities shall we use? A pre-designed list or a contextual list?

Pre-designed capabilities lists are available within the capabilities literature. Some of them focus on a specific context (Walker 2006) and others are more generic, such as Nussbaum's central capabilities list (Nussbaum 2011). Nevertheless, building from the argument put forward as part of our Southern location, we have good reasons to design our own contextual list in order to offer contextual recommendations for our DCR participatory practice. Indeed, Spreafico (2016) argues that despite the time-consuming and elevated cost of some participatory practices:

> Deliberative or participatory exercises are more coherent with the Capabilities Approach as put forwards by Sen (1999). It requires engaging representative samples of stakeholders as reflexive agents in order to capture their considerations over which capabilities matter most. (2016, 10)

Our Southern perspective requires this open-ended version of the Capability Approach (Sen 1999). As Hoffmann and Metz clearly state, in Sen's version of the Capabilities Approach, 'capabilities cannot freeze a list of capabilities for all societies, for all times to come, irrespective of what the citizens come to understand and value' (Hoffmann & Metz 2017, 2). In addition, in line with Bonvin, Laruffa, and Rosenstein (2017), the idea of 'reason to value' for Sen transcends the universalistic misrepresentation of rationality. Therefore, from both perspectives what we need within the Capabilities Approach literature is a more dynamic model which is capable of embracing our cultural and contextual specificities, beyond Western and Northern universal aggregations, which are overwhelmingly applied in the field. Therefore, to further elaborate on these ideas, in the following section I explore the group capabilities list from the DCR co-researchers, in comparison with Nussbaum's capabilities list. The chapter argues that, despite there being some commonalities between these valuable capabilities and elements from Nussbaum, some elements are missing or are presented from different perspectives, and Nussbaum's list appears not to be incommensurable. Consequently, a Southern analysis could greatly expand our available information about what exactly these capabilities mean for this specific group in the context and time in which they were explored, and why. Moreover, it substantially helps us in the subsequent process of designing our prospective capability plan and fulfilling the fifth principle of DCR, as enhancing valued capabilities.

### 5.3.1 Understanding DCR Co-Researchers' Valuable Capabilities as Dynamic and Contextual

Prior to the DCR participatory project, I conducted individual interviews (of two to three hours) with each of the potential participants. This first interview aimed to identify the valuable capabilities for these students at that time. Hence, although I explored their life stories, much of the interview was focused on their valued capabilities at the moment we spoke, and why they were important for them. Following the individual interview, I dedicated time to designing an individual capabilities list for each of them, basically by giving each valuable capability a title, followed by a brief definition. Moreover, I met with each of the participants again in order to jointly discuss their individual list, in case any changes were required. As a final step, I aggregated all the individual lists into a single common list and this was discussed several times during the course of the DCR participatory project, being more an iterative mutual development than a conventional collection of data.

Despite the difficulties involved in drawing them all together, due to the differences in their lives, some definite categories arose from this process, giving rise to six general valuable capabilities among the members. Table 5 presents the outcome of this iterative analysis of capabilities preferences among the members, highlighting exactly which capabilities were most important for them.

Among the twelve participants, a total of six valuable capabilities were detected: (1) Self-determination, (2) Epistemic,[1] (3) Human Recognition, (4) Ubuntu, (5) Health and (6) Free Time and Leisure. However, various questions can arise from looking at this table, for instance, why these capabilities and not others? Or, why was health only deemed valuable by three of the participants?

---

1   This capability was initially named as 'knowledge and Learning capability' but subsequently changed to 'Epistemic Capability'

Table 5: Co-researchers' valued capabilities.

| VALUED CAPABILITIES | Self-Development | Epistemic | Human Recognition | Ubuntu | Health | Free Time and Leisure |
|---|---|---|---|---|---|---|
| Kungawo | X | X | X | X | | |
| Minenhle | X | X | X | X | | |
| Khayone | X | X | X | X | | |
| Amahle | X | X | X | X | X | |
| Siyabonga | | X | X | X | X | X |
| Lethabo | X | X | | X | X | |
| Karabo | X | X | X | X | | |
| Bokamoso | X | X | X | X | | |
| Rethabile | X | X | | X | | |
| Thato | X | X | X | X | | |
| Iminathi | | X | X | X | | X |
| Lesedi | X | X | X | X | | |
| | 10 | 12 | 10 | 12 | 3 | 2 |

To a certain extent, this identification and analysis focused on capabilities that they valued highly at a specific time, as opposed to a generic perspective. This reduced the list and made it more focused. It missed out some essential capabilities due to them being valued to a lesser degree at that time, or due to adaptive preferences interacting with their choices (Teschl & Comim 2005). Therefore, in cases like this study, we can observe what I call active capabilities—capabilities that are highly relevant at the time and in the context in which the person is assessing her or his choices. The intention here is not to create a static and permanent selection, but rather to detect those capabilities that are relevant during the period that the team works together.

Hence, all these capabilities preferences seem to be located inside a continuum from 'more active' (highly relevant) to 'less active' (less relevant). The entire continuum is divided by a threshold that allows the capabilities to become visible when identifying them. For instance, in the top part, we can discern the capabilities that were visible at the time of our discussions. These capabilities are relevant due to the circumstances in their lives—different conversion factors—which affected their choices. In the DCR group, Self-Development, Epistemic, and Ubuntu capabilities were closely related to the age and the situation, as these were undergraduate students working towards their future in South Africa. These freedoms were crucial in allowing them to lead their life in the way they wanted, especially because of the many conversion factors jeopardising them (Sen 1999). Human recognition was mostly linked to colonial conversion factors, in terms of racial structures, which activated or increased the value of this capability for many of them, as the text excerpts at the beginning of each chapter clearly show and the following sections will corroborate.

In contrast to the active space, the threshold, or the passive area, can indicate capabilities that are less important due to the circumstances surrounding the individual—for instance, the context helping them to easily achieve this capability—or due to adaptive preferences (Teschl & Comim 2005). Although all the capabilities identified in this table are open to a more thorough analysis from a capabilities perspective, I here focus only on those classified above the threshold. This is sufficient for our purposes as the process allows us to easily identify the capabilities active at the time of our DCR participatory project in order to design the prospective plan and orient our DCR project towards their valued capabilities. Nevertheless, it is relevant to highlight the insurgent character of some of these capabilities, as seen in those marked in black.

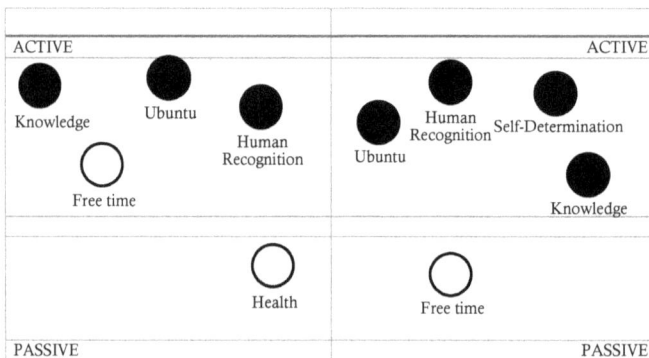

Figure 5: Dynamic and Contextual model of valuable capabilities (image by the author, 2021).

To differentiate between those simply valued or highly valued capabilities within the active space, I use the term 'Insurgent capabilities'. They are central capabilities for these students, however, they are jeopardised by the surrounding conditions. For instance, their Human Recognition is negatively affected by racial structures in South Africa, and their Epistemic capability is constantly negated due to the challenges they face in order to access higher-education institutions in the country and to belong to the hegemonic epistemic system. We can say, then, that insurgent capabilities become active as a response to systemic marginalisation—colonial conversion factors—that characterise the lives of many in a Global South context at specific moments. As the storyteller of the excerpted account opening this chapter said, it concerns how I make sense of the oppressive world in which I live and to which I am subjected:

> How I have made sense of my world as a black individual in a post-apartheid/so-called democratic country, how I make sense of the world as a gay man in a homophobic and queerphobic space; and finally how I make sense of the world in a capitalist/economically oppressive and corrupt system as a poor human being.

My reasoned perception of the world and the oppressive structures surrounding me determine my capabilities choices at a specific moment. These choices are not unaltered or intrinsic choices, but rather insurgent choices against an oppressive system that denies my most fundamental humanity and the freedoms associated with it, for instance, the freedom of being recognised as a worthy member of the society in which I live. Although this book aims to present many experiences and capabilities choices, we can say that the overwhelming majority of the group experienced this bias in one way or another, as the coming chapters will illustrate. Even in the best-case scenario, that of being a black, middle-class student on campus, does not totally exonerate you from the negative influence of colonial conversion factors over your freedoms in this context. Thus, insurgent capabilities are better able to explain capabilities' fluid scenarios, preserving the changing dimension of preferences and valued capabilities.

Insurgent capabilities will therefore be related to what are known as adaptive preferences. However, although adaptive preferences might cause adaptations in a negative way, constraining aspirations and preferences, we can argue that the same extreme deprivation can cause insurgent adaptations against that same oppression (Watts 2009). While the latter talks about the absence of certain choices and thus capability limitations to choose what to value due to persistent deprivation, the former refers to the enhancement of the value of certain central capabilities as a reaction to highly oppressive systems, even if their available choices are fairly obstructed. Hence, even when Sen claims:

> Unfavourable social and economic circumstances as well as lifelong habituation to adverse environment might induce people to accept current negative situations. (Teschl & Comim 2005, 230)

This inducement towards acceptance seems to misrepresent what these students would, and do, ultimately choose as valuable in their lives, despite the adverse circumstances. What they have reason to value in a specific moment has much to do with their lived experiences. Further, their repetitive experiences of oppression are able to enhance the value of certain capabilities, as insurgent capabilities in order to overcome contextual 'unfreedoms'. Insurgent capabilities not only support this flexible understanding of capabilities and reaction towards structures of oppression, but also the agentic aspects that play a part when deciding about valued capabilities amidst obstructive circumstances, especially in contexts such as the Global South.

Therefore, coming back to Figure 5, by understanding valued capabilities as situated along a continuum, we can acknowledge the incompleteness of the analysis in terms of choices being adapted or enhanced to the individual's circumstances. These circumstances are constantly moving and impacting students' preferences, as these insurgent capabilities have shown. However, at the same time, we can simplify the complex process of selecting valuable capabilities, by taking into account adaptations or resistances, and focusing on those that are situated in the active area of each individual, as main valued capabilities.

Hence, this framework provides a pragmatic approach, a fluid scenario to easily access categories as active and/or insurgent capabilities for designing the prospective structure of our participatory practices, as will be presented in the following section. In order to do this, what is required is not a precise appraisal of whether these or other capabilities are valuable for a specific individual forever, irrespective of what occurs in her or his life. What is worth exploring for this case are recommendations (general strategies) to enhance some of the capabilities identified as central at the time of the analysis through the DCR participatory project. This is even more valid when certain capabilities are identified as insurgent, or as essential for the group of participants, due to their reiterated and sustained marginalisation as a result of colonial conversion factors.

## 5.3.2 Comparing Co-Researchers' Valuable Capabilities with Nussbaum's Central Capabilities

This analysis classifies capabilities according to different degrees, which makes capabilities more dependent on the particular circumstances and lives of the individuals, and even more so with insurgent capabilities as reactions to oppressive systems. From a capabilities perspective, scholars may ask why we do not use a pre-designed list, such as Nussbaum's capabilities list.[2] This decision would simplify our work and be extremely time-efficient. However, there are very good reasons to pay attention to the specificities of our participatory groups, due to the fact that a single list might not be suitable for all contexts and all cases (Hoffmann & Metz 2017). In this matter, Nussbaum acknowledges that her formulation of central capabilities is abstract in order to facilitate its translation to contextual implementation (Nussbaum 2011).[3] Nevertheless, it is not only its level of abstraction and intended universalisation, but its own categories, the Western cosmovision underlying them, and their incommensurability, that makes it inadequate for other contexts and situations in the Global South.

---

2    Nussbaum's capabilities list has been chosen for its pretension to be universal, because the argument of this study is to acknowledge the cultural differences among capabilities preferences and conceptualisations. To a certain degree, this study could have employed a particular capabilities list, such as some proposed in the area of higher education (see Walker 2006; Wilson-Strydom 2016, among others). Nevertheless, our argument seeks to highlight the inconsistencies of using a universal list, such as Nussbaum's list, above and beyond other contextually related lists, and the importance of agency in capabilities choices.

3    Nussbaum's perspective on the Capabilities Approach is slightly different from that of Amartya Sen. The aim of her intellectual project is the creation of a universal theory, and therefore a universal capabilities list, that can operationalise these capabilities as rights for all human beings.

Hence, in order to illustrate these limitations, this section compares Nussbaum's capabilities with the co-researchers' identified capabilities. The text will then highlight the potential of capabilities to be used as a cultural translation (De Sousa Santos 2014). Capabilities are dependent on the context, culture and moment of life of the individuals. Therefore, they are not static, but rather dynamic, and can be compared with other capabilities lists created in other contexts.

## Epistemic Capability

Although it seems simplistic to reduce twelve different understandings of the epistemic capability into one single meaning, there are some fundamental ideas that are common to the group of co-researchers. There were two main ways in which this capability was important for them. Firstly, as an end, mostly related to better understanding and epistemic contribution to the world and the challenges surrounding them. Secondly, as a means to achieve (mainly) financial freedom. Therefore, two contextual claims can be made regarding these two important ways of considering this epistemic capability as dynamic and contextual.

Although both the ends and the means can be related and interwoven, the emphasis on using processes of learning and diverse sources of knowledge to better understand their context and expand their informational basis to make better choices is substantial for this group. Numerous colonial conversion factors that these students experience would not affect other undergraduate students in an affluent European country to the same extent, nor would their understanding of this capability be equal. For these students it is of paramount importance to be able to reason critically and think about the circumstances and the injustices surrounding them as receivers, but also as contributors, of epistemic materials (Fricker 2015). It is also clear that their hermeneutical marginalisation due to colonial conversion factors makes this epistemic capability even more relevant for them, as an insurgent capability. In many cases they are the first generation in their families to access higher-education institutions in the country (Goetze 2018; Mathebula 2019). For them, these colonial conversion factors induce them to an epistemic exploitation, as explained by Berenstain (2016, 572):

The exploitative nature of epistemic exploitation derives from several of its features. These include the opportunity costs associated with the labour of educating the oppressor, the double bind that marginalised people find themselves in when faced with the demand to educate, and the default sceptical responses from the privileged when the marginalised do acquiesce and fulfil their demands.

As the story opening this chapter told us, the decision to become an activist in LGBTQI organised groups on campus is not prompted by leisure, but by an urgent obligation or a demand to educate others. Hence, the enhancement of their knowledge is a necessity, rather than merely an option for this group, due to their epistemic marginalisation. It is an insurgent capability.

Furthermore, this capability seems to have a direct connection with access to resources, especially in terms of job access. Financial freedoms are hugely affected by generations of epistemic marginalisation in South Africa. While three of the twelve students enjoyed a relatively good financial situation, nine of them did not. Nevertheless, they all felt that it was important and necessary to succeed in their undergraduate programmes in order to access a dignified job and achieve financial stability for themselves and their loved ones. To a certain extent, these students had a really clear understanding of how the skills and learning they acquired during their higher education would be able to provide for their families, extended families, friends in need, and for their future selves. For instance, it would be difficult to see this situation in a 2021 Swedish context, in the sense that the individuals' enjoyment of capabilities would not be the same, nor would the conversion factors that impeded their expansion and therefore the reasons to value that specific capability. Hence, although money is considered here not as a capability, but a resource, this good is intimately related to the students' epistemic capability. Thus, for them, the epistemic capability acts as a fertile (Nussbaum 2011; Wolff & De-Shalit 2007) and insurgent capability providing access to resources and reducing the negative effects of colonial conversion factors on their and their loved ones' freedoms. It is a necessary capability for undertaking their Ubuntu and family responsibilities, or what is commonly known as 'black taxes' (Mhlongo 2019).[4]

On the other hand, when comparing this valuable capability for the co-researchers to Nussbaum's capabilities list, although some similarities can be found, they can by no means be regarded to be the same. The epistemic capability in this group could be linked to one of Nussbaum's central capabilities, the capability of sense, imagination and thought. Sense, imagination, and thought is defined by Nussbaum (2011) as:

> **Being able to use the senses, to imagine, think and reason**—and to do these things in a 'truly human' way, **a way informed and cultivated by an adequate education,** including, but by no means limited to, literacy and basic mathematical and scientific training. ~~Being able to use imagination and thought in connection with experiencing and producing works and events of one's own choice, religious, literary, musical, and so forth. Being able to use one's mind in ways protected by guarantees of freedom of expression with respect to both political and artistic speech, and freedom of religious exercise. Being able to have pleasurable experiences and to avoid non-beneficial pain.~~ (Nussbaum 2011, 53. Bold and strikethrough in original)

Only the parts that refer to the epistemic capability of the group are marked in bold. In this case, the second part of this capability (which is struck through) falls into the category of human recognition capability of this group, rather than epistemic capability (see the section titled 'Human Recognition Capability' below). Moreover, there is an instrumental value of human recognition capability for this group that is missed by Nussbaum's classification. We can also problematise the notion of 'adequate education' used by Nussbaum. Adequate for whom? And where? Are we talking about Western educational standards?

In this case, an appropriate definition for this epistemic capability as defined by this group will be:

> Being able to use the senses, to imagine, think, reason and share our knowledge with others and to do these things in a way informed and cultivated by a fair and less oppressive education. This must include

---

4   'Black taxes' is a highly debated concept in South Africa and refers to an individual responsibility to contribute to the economic and social freedoms of one's community, when one overcomes their own financial challenges, usually because other members of the community helped them to achieve this end. (For more information see Mhlongo 2019).

our informal African knowledge systems and fair access to our formal Western education system. Being able to use these knowledges and use them to advance economic and other freedoms for our loved ones and for us.

Hence, as presented above, for these students, success in higher education and acquisition of knowledge and skills that can help them to achieve financial freedom through employment is extremely important, not only for their own lives, but also for their ability to help others. The context of where they live leads them to closely connect knowledge with financial and other essential freedoms, and to regard it as a collective way of understanding epistemic freedoms. Moreover, knowledge for them is more than simply learning in Eurocentric institutions. It is a question of accessing these Eurocentric institutions, but also contributing to them with their own knowledge and their own learning about their knowledge systems, always in fair conditions, due to the relevance of colonial conversion factors. Therefore, although a few of Nussbaum's elements are present in this case, others can be related to the DCR group's epistemic capability through different capabilities from her list, whereas others are missing entirely.

## *Ubuntu Capability*

Ubuntu is perhaps the most interesting case among the capabilities discussed in this section. Twelve of the students valued Ubuntu in terms of helping or supporting others and being helped or supported. However, this Ubuntu perspective went beyond the idea of support, help or affiliation. For them, this capability was framed to some extent by the African metaphysical assumption that '[a] person is a person through other persons' (Du Toit 2004). This concept, which may in some ways be romanticised and exoticised, profoundly shapes this particular understanding of this capability as a way of living with others. For this group, the capability of Ubuntu meant or represented a particular ontological position in which reality is conceptualised through our human interactions by highlighting the importance of 'we' over 'I' (Migheli 2017). As Hoffmann and Metz acknowledge, Ubuntu is the idea that 'we cannot survive on our own, that we are vulnerable creatures in need of others to exist and to become who we are' (2017,

5). Certainly for these students, Ubuntu is central in their lives because they were born in South Africa after apartheid and have experienced the consequences of many colonial conversion factors in their freedoms and the freedoms of those they love. Promoting Ubuntu is the only way to overcome their colonial marginalisation (Gade 2011). This not only expands or contextualises this capability in comparison with Nussbaum's list, but also expands our cultural understanding of its impact on other capabilities, as we have seen in the previous discussion of epistemic capability. It is a question not only of acquiring knowledge and contributing to the pool of shared knowledge, but also of using these epistemic materials to help others and to better our societies and living conditions as oppressed collectives.

For this case, two of Nussbaum's capabilities can be considered to fall under the category of Ubuntu; namely those of emotions and affiliation (but only the first point). Nussbaum defines the central capability of emotions as:

> Being able to have attachments to things and people outside ourselves; to love those who love and care for us, to grieve at their absence; in general, to love, to grieve, to experience longing, gratitude, and justified anger. Not having one's emotional development blighted by fear and anxiety. (Supporting this capability means supporting forms of human association that can be shown to be crucial in their development). (2011, 54)

Equally, she defines affiliation—only the first point—as:

> Being able to live with and towards others, to recognise and show concern for other humans, to engage in various forms of social interaction; to be able to imagine the situation of another. ~~Protecting this capability means protecting institutions that constitute and nourish such forms of affiliation, and also protecting the freedom of assembly and political speech.~~ (2011, 54. Bold and strikethrough in original)

Therefore, in this case, we would need to aggregate two of the capabilities from Nussbaum's list. However, we would still be lacking the cultural understanding of affiliation and connection with other human beings, mediated by the strong ontological position of Ubuntu. Accordingly, this not only requires us to consider it as important to be affiliated with and assertive to others, but also to be able to understand reality as a continuous interaction between humans—a fully relational reality. Thus, a relational perception of reality merges institutions and agents, focusing only on humans and their actions to improve and positively influence the lives of others. A definition for this group is:

> Being able to live with and towards others, to recognise our intrinsic connections with other human beings and our inseparable condition. Being able to love, care for and help others despite the difficult circumstances, just as we are loved cared for and helped by others to pursue our aspirations.

This cooperative and culturally related perspective might clash with many of the conceptualisations of capabilities produced or influenced by scholars from the Global North, thus influencing our framing of this and other capabilities, as many scholars have claimed (D'Amato 2020; Dejaeghere 2020, among others). Nevertheless, this perspective does not call for another universal way of understanding this or other capabilities, but requires us to recognise the relevance of contextual and cultural features in the way we conceptualise valuable capabilities, such as this Ubuntu capability. Capabilities are our decolonial epistemic foundation and therefore the space for cultural translation. However, this translation cannot be achieved if we do not investigate our diverse and plural cultural spaces and contexts. Furthermore, what we can definitely affirm is that this Ubuntu capability is an insurgent and central capability for these students, given how it has impacted the conceptualisation of other capabilities presented in the list. Moreover, it is a central way to overcome students' colonial conversion factors and their associated marginalisation (Le Grange 2012).

## *Human Recognition Capability*

Human recognition emerged as one of the most highly valued capabilities within the group. Nevertheless, this capability was closely linked to colonial conversion factors concerning their context and how these influenced each of their lives, as can be seen in the chapter's opening stories relating to issues of racism, gender inequalities or economic challenges. Most of the students' lives are marked by colonial conditions, which shape what they value. These students' human recognition capability refers to the minimum recognition a human being deserves in order to become a respected and dignified human being in their society. The students repeatedly report experiencing discrimination against themselves and in a manner that relegates them to sub-human status. As the author of the story opening this chapter highlights, 'I have been a victim of the abuse of power that was used to make me believe that I was less than, and obviously less than all human beings'. As Mpofu and Steyn (2021, 3) eloquently affirm 'the fight for liberation as a form of social justice is also a struggle for the recovery of denied and lost humanity'.

In many forms, the absence of human recognition enhances its importance, and disables active political participation in a variety of ways. Further, it seems that human recognition, in this case, was linked with voice and political participation, whereas in Nussbaum's case it is not. Two different capabilities from Nussbaum's list are needed in order to frame the human recognition capability for this group. One of these is the capability of affiliation—but only the second point:

> Having the social bases of self-respect and non-humiliation; being able to be treated as a dignified being whose worth is equal to that of others. This entails provisions of non-discrimination on the basis of race, sex, sexual orientation, ethnicity, caste, religion, national origin, and species. (2011, 54)

The second is the capability of having control over one's environment—but only the political part:

> Being able to participate effectively in political choices that govern one's life; having the right of political participation, protections of free speech and association. (2011, 54)

In the DCR case, control over one's environment (political) was not a separate capability from affiliation (second point). Moreover, using affiliation as the concept that summarises the capability seems to miss the central point in this group, where affiliation is related to Ubuntu capability. Therefore, human recognition is able to embrace the freedom of being recognised and consequently able to participate in political spheres. It means being identified as a worthy member of that group and therefore connecting with others in equal conditions through fair participation. Thus, the DCR capability would look like this:

> Being able to treat and be treated as a dignified human being whose worth is equal to that of your oppressor, being able to be recognised by others, and not experience dehumanisation due to your race, sex, sexual orientation, ethnicity, religion and so on. Not having your

essential opportunities to function as a genuine and worthy human being diminished. Being able to participate as actively as others in more privileged positions and to help others to participate and become recognised members despite the unequal colonial structures.

Certainly, the exclusion of many communities in South Africa during apartheid has marked these group-valued capabilities, with their historic past highlighting the importance of better status and dignity but also that of others. Again, this is not only about them achieving or enhancing this capability, but helping others to achieve it, as the Ubuntu capability has shown. It is also important to bear in mind that the capabilities, as conceptualised for these students, are capabilities against a system of oppression; they are capabilities as insurgency, not as the promotion or enhancement of well-being. That is why it is important to use the terms colonial conversion factors and insurgent capabilities in this context, whilst also highlighting that is not about a general aim for equality. It is rather an aim to become equal to their oppressors and the more privileged classes who previously denied them and their community fundamental freedoms and their intrinsic humanity.

## *Self-Development Capability*

Equally, self-development is a valued capability for the group due to historical conditions. In many ways, their aspirations and personal projects are impacted by colonial conversion factors that prevent them from becoming who they want to be. For instance, in many cases these students did not access university the first time that they applied due to their incapacity to pay their fees or to afford the expensive student life. Equally, in many cases they did not access their primary degree choice, and had to decide which degree to study according to the bursaries available to them. Their personal projects are mediated by the little freedoms they enjoy, due to their past (Walker & Mathebula 2019).

Thus, although the capability of practical reason on Nussbaum's list can be associated with this group's valuable capability, the self-development capability is broader and at the same time more specific for this group. Nussbaum defines practical reason as:

Being able to form a conception of the good and to engage in critical reflection about the planning of one's life (This entails protection for the liberty of conscience and religious observance). (Nussbaum 2011, 54)

For this group, self-development needs to be rephrased in a more detailed manner as resistance against hegemony:

> Being able to collectively form a conception of the good through your community life, cultural learning, and experiences, besides institutional impositions, to lead your context-valued lives. Being able to do so in a reflective way, critically assessing the social stereotypes and labels that surround your community and you due to your historical past and cultural heritage. Being able to make active decisions about your life in order to lead it in the way your community have reason to value and to help others to do the same. Being able to do so with acceptance, resilience, and optimism due to repetitive adverse conditions for your loved ones and for you. Being able to understand the diverse factors that impede your community and you from leading your valued lives, and to create new collective forms of resistance.

This definition highlights that, beyond the generic understanding given by Nussbaum, there are actually three main constitutive elements for this capability in this case. First, being able to reflect collectively and critically about the life you want to lead, understanding the colonial factors surrounding you, and learning from your life experiences and culture. Second, being able to make decisions that directly enable you to lead the life you want to despite your colonial marginalisation. And third, to do so with acceptance, resilience and optimism. The first point may simply be an expansion of Nussbaum's conceptualisation, however, the second is more focused on the freedom to make decisions, to take action for one's personal project and those of others, as well as on insurgency against colonial structures of oppression. Moreover, the third is culturally focused, in the sense of acting with a specific perspective, as defined by the students with an optimistic and positive attitude, but also collectively. In brief, as well as in other capabilities, self-development requires the incorporation of other cultural elements such as Ubuntu principles, in order to better represent the perspectives and context of this group.

### 5.3.3 Defending a Contextual Capabilities List for Our DCR Participatory Projects

In summary, Nussbaum's central capabilities list can be used to explore whether our group's preferences match them (or not), and perhaps to further understand 'passive' capabilities for a more detailed or precise way of analysing valuable capabilities. This is due to the fact that capabilities—as argued in Chapter Four—can be used as part of diatopic hermeneutics[5] (De Sousa Santos 2006a, 2006b, 2014). Hence, capabilities can be used as an incomplete epistemic foundation for translating different cultures, e.g. in the case of the Ubuntu capability and its comparison with Nussbaum's capabilities of affiliation or emotions. This does not aim to unify. Conversely, it is more a question of looking for isomorphic elements—elements that are similar or different and can explain their meaning—as I do in this section. Which elements relate to one another, and which do not? Moreover, this analysis expands our informational basis for each capability and incorporates different cultural and contextual specificities that are missed when using universal lists. For instance, we might appreciate the insurgent components or the importance of Ubuntu capability influencing other central capabilities, or being commensurable and interconnected.

Table 6: Comparison of Nussbaum's capabilities list vs the DCR group's valued capabilities.

| NUSSBAUM'S CENTRAL CAPABILITIES | DCR GROUP'S VALUABLE CAPABILITIES |
|---|---|
| Sense, imagination, and thought  Control over one's environment (material) | Epistemic  (As an end and instrumental to financial and other substantial freedoms, collective perspective) |
| Emotions  Affiliation (1) | Ubuntu  (*Ubuntu* togetherness perspective) |
| Control over one's environment (Political)  Affiliation (2) | Human recognition  (Respect and voice/participation overcoming oppression) |
| Practical reason | Self-Development  (Resilience and positive attitude) |

5    See Chapter Three for more information.

Therefore, although there are similar elements between the two lists, as highlighted in this section and summarised in Table 6, there are some specificities that can be lost if we design our prospective plan according to a general list. The aim of this approach is to develop our prospective framework, but also to advance more contextually-based capabilities that acknowledge the richness and relevance of Southern perspectives beyond global aggregations.

## 5.4 DCR: Theory in Practice

After the identification and selection of valued capabilities, the next step is to understand how a prospective framework can be designed. How did this specific framework for the DCR project look, and how was it implemented? The first section here explores the DCR framework, which is divided into three categories: (1) valuable capabilities, (2) main consideration for that specific capability, and (3) strategies to be implemented during the project.

### 5.4.1 DCR Facilitator Framework

Of the six capabilities that arose from the data, only the capabilities that were relevant for six or more of the members were selected to construct the prospective framework of the project. The prospective capabilities plan was built over three categories in a deductive thinking process. First, the principal capabilities for the strategy—those considered as highly important by six or more members of the group—were selected. Second, these capabilities were divided into the main considerations the students made when referring to them, i.e., in terms of the main constitutive elements that arose from the main capability. And third, specific strategies that might enhance or 'imperfectly' achieve that freedom throughout the process were considered. These strategies were especially guided toward actions that the researcher—the facilitator— could realistically undertake when working with a DCR group. Hence, Table 7 presents the detailed prospective framework for the DCR project according to the co-researchers' valued capabilities.

Table 7: DCR case study prospective framework.

| CAPABILITY | MAIN CONSIDERATIONS | STRATEGY |
| --- | --- | --- |
| **1. EPISTEMIC** | 1.1. Formal knowledge | 1.1.1. To provide spaces to explore together how scientific/Western knowledge is produced. |
| | | 1.1.2. To use the project to enhance useful skills for their academic degrees. |
| | 1.2. Employability (Financial access) | 1.2.1. To provide training in skills that might assist their prospects of employment. |
| | | 1.2.2. To provide proof of participation at the end of the project. |
| | 1.3. African knowledge systems | 1.3.1. To give value to other types of knowledges. |
| | | 1.3.2. To use spaces in the project to apply these knowledges in relation to others and understand their unequal relations. |
| | | 1.3.3. To provide spaces to share our multi-epistemic knowledge among different groups and to be active receivers of these knowledges. |
| **2. HUMAN RECOGNITION** | 2.1. Respect | 2.1.1. To balance colonial logics and power structures within the group, enabling the participation of all the members. |
| | | 2.1.2. To value every intervention knowing the positionality from where it comes and to use the project as a space to assess these opinions together with respect and love as receivers and givers of epistemic materials despite the social inequalities underlying the group. |
| | 2.2. Voice/Participation | 2.2.1. To use positive reinforcement for those who tend to participate less. |
| | | 2.2.2. To distribute roles of responsibility to those participants who are less active. |
| | | 2.2.3. To create spaces to discuss our different levels of participation and why this happens within the group, due to our localised social positions and power structures within the group. |

| 4. SELF-DEVELOPMENT | 3. UBUNTU |  |
|---|---|---|
| | | 3.1. Networks (Emotional support) |
| 4.1. Critical thinking | 3.2. Networks (Information) | 3.1.1. To meet with the members outside of the project, in order to create spaces for mutual understanding, friendships and emotional support beyond the project meetings. |
| | | 3.1.2. To allow conversations about personal challenges to be taken into account for the group and to work together towards helping others. |
| 4.1.1. To avoid simplistic explanations or the presentation of one unique perspective. | 3.2.1. To use alternative communication channels (besides our group meetings) as a way for the members of the group to connect with each other and share information and useful networks. | |
| 4.1.2. To allow and foster different perspectives, in order to assess them together. | | |

This table is a practical example of how a prospective pedagogical plan can be designed for a DCR project. This plan can be a key document for the project and be further discussed with the participants beyond the facilitator's role. Further, it provides guidance for the facilitator in order to enhance co-researchers' valued capabilities, treating the research as a process for capabilities expansion and establishing the threshold by which to assess the process during and after the participatory project.

# 5.5 Conclusion

This chapter aimed to explore how a prospective perspective of the Capability Approach can be applied to our DCR practices, arguing that it actually has substantial benefits and orients our practices towards the collective aims of the co-researchers when situated in the Global South. The first section was dedicated to exploring what a prospective approach within the Capabilities Approach actually is. This perspective presented an analysis of capabilities that can provide us with a set of specific recommendations for implementing our DCR participatory project. Further, the DCR project would be closely related to the co-researchers, following DCR principle number five. However, the second and third sections highlighted some methodological questions. When deciding about capabilities, we need to clarify whether we want to use a pre-designed capabilities list from the literature or whether we want to use our own elaborated list. The latter was defended by comparing the DCR valuable capabilities with Nussbaum's central capabilities list. Furthermore, this has provided evidence showing that although we can look for isomorphic elements—elements that are not necessarily the same, but similar—we still add value with our specific list, especially by highlighting insurgent capabilities and local cosmovisions through the category of Ubuntu.

The final part of the chapter focused on the actual prospective framework designed for this DCR participatory project. First, it clarified how this list of capabilities emerged from the data and the steps taken to reach this outcome. And finally, the prospective plan was presented in a table with three levels: valued capabilities, the main considerations, and strategies for each consideration.

# References

Berenstain, N. (2016). Epistemic exploitation. *Ergo, 3*(22), 569–590. https://doi.org/10.3998/ergo.12405314.0003.022.

Bonvin, J. M., Laruffa, F., & Rosenstein, E. (2017). Towards a critical sociology of democracy: The potential of the capability approach. *Critical Sociology, 44,* 953–968. https://doi.org/10.1177%2F0896920517701273.

Comim, F., Qizilbash, M., & Alkire, S. (eds) (2008). *The Capability Approach: Concepts, Measures and Applications.* Cambridge: Cambridge University Press.

D'Amato, C. (2020). Collectivist capabilitarianism. *Journal of Human Development and Capabilities, 21*(2), 105–120. https://doi.org/10.1080/19452829.2020.1732887.

Dejaeghere, J. G. (2020). Reconceptualizing educational capabilities: A relational capability theory for redressing inequalities. *Journal of Human Development and Capabilities, 21*(1), 17–35. https://doi.org/10.1080/19452829.2019.1677576.

De Sousa Santos, B. (2006a). *La universidad popular del siglo XXI.* Lima: Fondo Editorial de la Facultad de Ciencias Sociales — UNMSM.

De Sousa Santos, B. (2006b). *Conocer desde el Sur: Para una cultura política emancipatoria.* Mexico City: Fondo Editorial de la Facultad de Ciencias Sociales — UNMSM.

De Sousa Santos, B. (2014). *Epistemologies of the South: Justice against Epistemicide.* New York: Routledge. https://unescochair-cbrsr.org/pdf/resource/Epistemologies_of_the_South.pdf.

Du Toit, C. W. (2004). *The Integrity of the Human Person in an African Context: Perspectives from Science and Religion.* Pretoria: Research Institute for Theology and Religion/UNISA Press.

Fricker, M. (2015). Epistemic contribution as a central human capability. In George Hull (ed.). *The Equal Society: Essays on Equality in Theory and Practice* (pp. 73–90). Lanham: Lexington Books. https://rowman.com/ISBN/9781498515719/.

Gade, C. B. (2011). The historical development of the written discourses on Ubuntu. *South African Journal of Philosophy, 30*(3), 303–329. https://doi.org/10.4314/sajpem.v30i3.69578.

Goetze, T. S. (2018). Hermeneutical dissent and the species of hermeneutical injustice. *Hypatia, 33*(1), 73–90. https://doi.org/10.1111/hypa.12384.

Hoffmann, N., & Metz, T. (2017). What can the capabilities approach learn from an Ubuntu ethic? A relational approach to development theory. *World Development, 97,* 153–164. https://doi.org/10.1016/j.worlddev.2017.04.010.

Le Grange, L. 2012. Ubuntu as an architectonic capability. *Indilinga: African Journal of Indigenous Knowledge Systems, 11*(2), 139–145. https://www.ajol.info/index.php/indilinga/article/view/125874.

Mathebula, M. (2019). Recognising poor black youth from rural communities in South Africa as epistemic. *Critical Studies, 7*(1) 64–81. https://doi.org/10.14426/cristal.v7i1.181.

Migheli, M. (2017). Ubuntu and social capital: A strong relationship and a possible instrument of socio-economic development. *Cambridge Journal of Economics, 41*, 1213–1235. https://doi.org/10.1093/cje/bew070.

Mhlongo, N. (2019). *Black Tax: Burden or Ubuntu?* Johannesburg: Jonathan Ball Publishers.

Mpofu, W., & Steyn, M. (2021). The trouble with the human. In Steyn, M. & Mpofu, W. (eds). *Decolonising the Human: Reflections from Africa on Difference and Oppression.* Johannesburg: Wits University Press.

Nussbaum, M. C. (2011). *Creating Capabilities: The Human Development Approach.* Cambridge: Harvard University Press.

Sen, A. (1999). *Development as Freedom.* New York: Random House.

Sen, A. (2009). *The Idea of Justice.* Cambridge, MA: Belknap.

Spreafico, A. (2016). *Measurement Literature Review.* Miratho working paper 2016/1. http://www.miratho.com/resources/Miratho%20Working%20Paper%202016_1_Measurement%20literature%20review.pdf.

Teschl, M., & Comim, F. (2005). Adaptive preferences and capabilities: Some preliminary conceptual explorations. *Review of Social Economy, 63*(2), 229–247. https://doi.org/10.1080/00346760500130374.

Walker, M. (2006). *Higher Education Pedagogies.* London: McGraw-Hill.

Walker, M., & Mathebula, M. (2019). Low-income rural youth migrating to urban universities in South Africa: Opportunities and inequalities. *Compare, 50*(8), 1193–1209. https://doi.org/10.1080/03057925.2019.1587705.

Watts, M. (2009). Sen and the art of motorcycle maintenance: Adaptive preferences and higher education. *Studies in Philosophy and Education, 28*(5), 425–436. https://doi.org/10.1007/s11217-009-9127-5.

Wilson-Strydom, M. (2016). A capabilities list for equitable transitions to university: A top-down and bottom-up approach. *Journal of Human Development and Capabilities, 17*(2), 145–160. https://doi.org/10.1080/19452829.2014.991280.

Wolff, J., & De-Shalit, A. (2007). *Disadvantage.* London: Oxford University Press.

# 6. The South African DCR Project: Undergraduates as Researchers

Senzeni na?

Kwenzeka kanjani ukuthi kube nomehluko omukhulu kangaka phakathi kwabantu bemibala eyahlukahlukene? Ithi ngiphinde. Kwenzeka kanjani ukuthi umbala (OWODWA) kube yinto eyenza ukuthi mangidlula ngasemotweni yomuntu anyuse amafasitela akhe, abe nemoto engaziyo ukuthi kuyoba iphupho ngize ngiqede ukukhokhela isikweleti sokufunda, ngisize futhi nasekhaya.

Angiboni ukuthi kumina nalaba abafana nami ukuba nezingcindezi ngenxa yokungazi ukuthi ikhona imali yokuqeda esikoleni yinto enjengokuphefumula, kodwa kaze abelungu bayacabanga ngazo lezinkinga ngesinye isikhathi, akufani. Akufani.

Angiqondi ukuthi losizi luyophela nini. Kwanzima ukuphila bengaboni iziphambano esizithwele, bengaboni ukuqina okudingakalayo ukuze sikwazi ukuqhubeka nsuku zonke. Bengaboni ukuthi ukuba mnyama akuyinto yesikhumba sami kuphela kodwa futhi yinto yempilo yami yonke. Akekho umuntu othanda ukuphila elokishini, othanda ukuphila ngamagranti, othanda ukungazi ukuthi ukudla okulandelayo kuzophumaphi, ongazi ukuthi ingane yakhe mhla iyobamba itoho emayini iyobuya neziphi izifo ngenxa yokufuna ukubeka ukudla etafuleni.

Akekho umuntu othanda ukusebenza umlungwini impilo yakhe yonke kodwa uma eseneminyaka engamashumi ayisikhombisa angabi nesenti lokuveza akwenzile.

Angiqondi ukuthi njengelizwe siqhubeka kanjani nsuku zonke senze sengathi lezinkinga ziyonyamalala noma singenzi lutho ukuzishintsha. Angiqondi ukuthi abelungu ababuboni kanjani lobuhlungu esiphila nabo abangasoze babubone. Angiqondi ukuthi kutheni bamangala uma sitoyitoya sengathi sifuna okuningi kakhulu. Sifuna impilo ephilekayo, qha!

Let's never let the fire burn out, as long as the burden remains.

*Narratives on Social Injustices: Undergraduate Voices*, 2018

https://doi.org/10.11647/OBP.0273.06

# 6.1 Introduction

This chapter explores the DCR process undertaken by twelve undergraduate students at the University of the Free State in 2017. Various sources of data are displayed here, such as the second and third phases of interviews, reports on participant observation and my individual journal. The text not only provides a comprehensive account of the activities carried out by the group, but also highlights the collaborative decision-making during the process, together with the platform for the ecology of knowledges and expansion of their valued capabilities. First of all, a total of nine official workshops took place between March and October 2017.

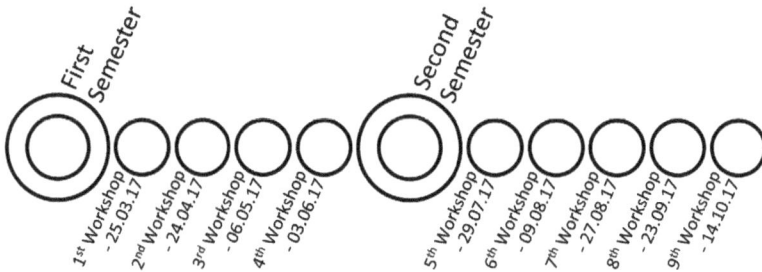

Figure 6: Workshop schedule (image by the author, 2021).

The team usually met once a month although at times it was more than once, as in the sixth and seventh workshops or during our informal meetings, which are displayed in the last section of the chapter. Except for the first workshop and part of the second, which were designed by the facilitator, all the meetings closed by collaboratively discussing the agenda for the following day. This meant that the members were actively involved in the creation and implementation of the process from the very beginning of the project.

The working periods were variable although most took place from 9 a.m. to 5 p.m. The group usually had breakfast together, normally at 8 a.m., and a break for lunch at around 12:30 p.m., together with small breaks in between. These periods were mostly used for informal conversations amongst the members of the group. Some days were especially significant, and the group stayed talking until late after the workshops had concluded, and some days we even went home together. The form of compensation was discussed and agreed by the group during the first workshop. Moreover, due to the nature of the project and the need to access online information, members who did not have a personal laptop were lent one for the duration of the project. In total, seven of the twelve members enjoyed the use of a laptop during the project.

Furthermore, despite the official workshops, the team had numerous contacts outside of the project, who were sometimes related to the project and at other times were not. Firstly, members frequently met to attend seminars, university meetings or art exhibitions, which were related to the project. For instance, we attended the Africa Day Memorial Lecture (2017) given by Paul Tiyambe Zeleza at the Centre for African Studies at the university, along with multiple meetings convened by the Student Representative Council (SRC) to update information on the de-registration issue on campus, by which some of the group members were affected. The team also participated in general assemblies convened by the university to provide information on the Shimla Park incident. Similarly, some members attended an art exhibition on campus related to LGBTQI rights. This was of interest as LGBTQI inequalities were raised at an early stage in the project as constituting an important form of inequality on campus. Further, the group even met for more informal meetings, such as watching a movie together or having casual contact just to catch up or help one another with personal matters. These spaces were relevant in that they provided a sense of belonging and family environment, as per their Ubuntu capability.

On the other hand, the combination of different knowledge systems, together with their continuous interactions, allowed the project not only to provide the members with epistemic access to scientific knowledge— as their insurgent epistemic capability valued—but also allowed the epistemic foundation of the project to be 'imperfectly' diversified. The project brought in other valued and relevant knowledge systems, as subsequent sections will highlight. The process of an ecology of knowledges (De Sousa Santos 2014) is not perfect when it is down-to-earth. It is a continuum where spaces for other knowledge systems are opened and debated, but also refuted through collective discussions and decision-making. Therefore, it is a process that requires flexibility for the diverse tempos among different individuals and space for collective decision-making in order to adjust the research in line with the group aims and paths of inquiry. Respecting these collective and organic learning processes and focusing on their valued capabilities and their group aims and aspirations, while simultaneously promoting a diverse epistemological base, sets us on the right path to articulate epistemological plurality. Consequently, the following sections will describe and explore each workshop, highlighting the different activities of the day and the decisions taken by the group, and focusing on their central capabilities and experiences as a result of being involved in the project.

## 6.2 'It Feels More Personal than Being Just a Participant...' (First Workshop)

The first workshop was the only one where I, as a facilitator, was fully in charge of the structure, planning, and implementation. The meeting consisted of establishing a first contact between the members. Despite the fact that the students were acquainted with me, and I with them, due to the individual and informal meetings conducted beforehand to identify their valued capabilities, the team had not yet had the chance to get to know each other properly. For this reason, the first activity of the day was for the members to prepare a brief presentation, a maximum of fifteen minutes each, to introduce themselves. They could talk, sing, show a piece of art, or give a conventional PowerPoint presentation. It was up to them to think about how to introduce themselves to the group. Two formats were most frequently used: oral presentations and PowerPoint presentations. Some of them talked about their friends, their families, their hobbies and/or their cultures. For instance, the in-depth explanation of her family name and family tree that one member gave were particularly significant. During the final interview, this member expressed how important this moment had been for her, and the significance of having the space to talk about herself and her family in her own way as this is not commonly done or promoted on campus.

Following the presentations, the group discussed what our lunch would be during the workshops. We all debated various options, and a decision was made by consensus. For every workshop, a different member would be in charge of this task, and therefore responsible for asking for the preferences of the group and taking the lunch order for the day.

The second activity of the day was to discuss justice and injustice. The activity started with a brainstorming session. One of the members volunteered to write on the flipchart for the group, featuring words such as 'circumstances', 'moral', 'government (positive/negative role)', 'power', 'ignorance', 'hierarchy', 'centralism/localism' and 'competition', which would form the core of our debates. The group discussed these points enthusiastically, relating the words to their experiences and the experiences of others they knew. After a while, one of the members proposed watching a video together about social justice (from TED Talks online) that was relevant to the debate the group was having. Thus, the group watched the video together and this helped to increase the number of ideas and concepts related to the debate about justice. Therefore, more words were added to our list, such as 'knowledge', 'conscience', 'proactive/action' and 'social classification (positive or negative)'.

After debating for a long time, I proposed a practical activity to better understand our different perspectives on justice. The group was divided into four small teams composed of two to three people each. All the teams were given the same issue and they needed to look for the most just solution and present it to the group as a whole at the end. The activity helped the group to continue thinking about justice and injustice, providing the larger group with different solutions based on diverse criteria of justice. Therefore, the whole group concluded the activity by understanding that justice can be assessed differently according to diverse criteria, such as values. However, it is important to investigate the circumstances surrounding that situation as a way to have a better-informed perspective. One of the students commented on this activity in the second interview:

> 'I got to understand social injustice. I never really understood it. It was just a word which I never really understood. But the first workshop... it just, it just helped me. What social injustice is... The little things that we don't think they... they are social injustices. That social injustice begins at home, academically here in varsity... It just helped me. It's just... It made me understand it even more. It, it gave me like a very broad understanding of what it really is.' (Bokamoso, second interview, May 2017)

This activity was designed according to the literature and the DCR principle of starting a research process with a common concern about injustices (De Sousa Santos 2010). Despite identifying which injustices were important for us as a group, it was necessary to grasp what justice meant for us in a certain way, and what we would use as an evaluative space to assess unjust situations (Sen 2009). This not only helped the group to expand their own understanding of justice, but also to find the common values that they had.

The following activity of the day was to agree on which injustices we were interested in, and which injustices the group wanted to investigate together. Writing on the flipchart, the members mentioned various issues, mostly related to their lives, such as racism, social privilege, social class, power asymmetry, gender inequality and sexual orientation discrimination. As the group was composed of twelve members, it could be divided into smaller working groups. Thus, the members agreed on three topics to be researched by three small groups: racism, gender inequality, and social inequality/power imbalance. The university would be our context to research these issues.

In this exploration of the specific concerns of the group, the valued insurgent capabilities were at the forefront of the process. One member expressed what this space to enhance their self-development capability meant for her:

> 'It feels amazing because at first you sort of think that... agggh... it is just some volunteering stuff... it's nothing, but becoming part of the project. It's... it feels more like, it feels more personal than just being a participant. [...] Personal in the sense of... that, for example, talking about certain topics, such as race, issues that we actually experience on a day-to-day basis, that we live... so... that's why I say it feels personal, it's like things we experience sometimes and issues that need to be tackled. And having the platform to do so, it's... it's just amazing.' (Minenhle, second interview, May 2017)

To finish the day, the last activity aimed to explore what the research meant for the members, and which options the groups had for exploring their topics. Therefore, as in the previous activity, the session began with a member writing on the flipchart and brainstorming possible research avenues. Ideas such as actively answering questions, collection of data by different means, searching for information, objectivity vs subjectivity, reading, surveying, theory and practice, science, mythology, evidence, and quantitative or qualitative research, were all discussed among the group.

The group continued talking about different methodologies, and the various ways to understand reality and knowledge. Although these were unfamiliar concepts for the group, they proved to be not only helpful for the development of the project, but also for their studies in general, enhancing their identified epistemic capability. This session provided access to the university epistemic system—which is denied and/or reduced, due to their colonial conversion factors—whilst also prompting discussions about which aspects of this epistemic system were adequate for them and the project.

One of the members expressed how this workshop was significant for her in that it enhanced her vocabulary, but also her awareness of the university epistemic system, and how knowledge is generated within its walls, which is not typical for undergraduate students in this context:

> 'Specifically... The first one it was... enhancing my vocabulary, I was like... I am used to natural science and biochemistry terms... so in terms of humanities... like... those definitions, it was something actually new for me. [...] It introduced us to the different terms: methodology, epistemology and ontology, so yeah... those two were really insightful.' (Iminathi, second interview, May 2017)

The team closed the workshop by agreeing on the date of the next meeting and individually exploring the ideas that we had been debating that day. At this point, the group had clear research themes that involved injustices that affected their lives, and had started thinking about how to implement the research in a more open way or guided by a more conventional strategy.

## 6.3 'There Is the World... Run Wild...' (Second Workshop)

The second workshop was intended to have two major functions: to progressively transfer the responsibilities of the project to the members, and to continue the process of ecologies of knowledge, by providing a diversification of internal knowledges.

In order to transfer the ownership of the project to the members of the group, two activities took place at this second workshop. First, as the project initially had a website page for the members to upload videos and information of interest, the group started the day with a website training session. Henceforth, they could not only create a new website for the project or update the current page, but also gain skills and use them for their own purposes, as part of their epistemic capability. In that training session, basic skills about how to create and design a website were taught. At the end of the activity, all of the participants had a basic website and had managed to work with the editing program for a while. However, no decisions about the project website were made at this point, as the group intended to make a collaborative website page at the end of the project to share its outcomes and create a platform for the larger community (see Workshop Nine).

Secondly, one of the strategies for transferring ownership was to start designing the following workshops as a whole group. What did the group want to do next? When? How? And who would be responsible for each activity? This helped to create a culture of communal decision-making, which was present until the end of the project, although not without challenges. One of the members said:

> 'I was telling Rethabile that [the facilitator] gives us so much rooming space... like... there is the world, run wild... yeah... so I was telling her, [the facilitator] gives us so much... how can I put it? Free... freedom in terms of getting there. She doesn't tell us no, you have to do this and think about this alone... So you actually get to expand your thinking... like... okay... So, I don't have to think in a little box.' (Iminathi, second interview, May 2017)

Nevertheless, she continues by saying how difficult this was for her when she was used to being given the exact work to be done and told how to do it and when, towing to her authoritarian educational experience:

> 'Mmm... I feel like, because we are so used to being given... like...this is the work...you're gonna write about it. That is what we are used to.' (Iminathi, second interview, May 2017)

This was definitely not the only comment on this subject; the transfer of responsibilities was not easy at all. Members mentioned several times that it was confusing to have the freedom to decide because they had spent more than twelve years in an authoritarian, post-colonial educational system that told them how, when and what to think. However, the project challenged these colonial conversion factors, and decision-making functionings were ultimately achieved, as the above quote highlights and other members' reflections indicate. Hence this progressive process, in which the co-researchers took more and more responsibility for the project, also impacted other important capabilities for them, such as self-development and human recognition.

In this workshop, the group agreed that they wanted to meet with individuals who might know about the topics they were interested in. Two groups were proposed: more students from the university, who could offer radical perspectives on the different issues under research; and scholars, who could give an academic perspective. A table was designed by the group with the individuals they wanted to invite, and the name of the group-member responsible for informing the person in question and ensuring that they would come to our next meeting. Initially, the third workshop was designed with three activities: first, jointly planning the next workshop; second, the scholars' meeting; and third, the students' meeting. However, the scholars' meeting was postponed until the fourth meeting, due to the fact that those individuals who had been invited to attend were unavailable on that day. The plan was to prepare relevant questions to be asked at each of the meetings relating to our three different themes, and to appoint a member of the group to be responsible for coordinating and facilitating the collective dialogue together, with another member to take notes of the discussion, despite the session being audiotaped.

Members of various social movements were invited to our second workshop to talk to us about the issues of concern to the group on campus. This idea arose because one of the members of the group was actively involved with several of these movements, and helped to select the student organisations, structure the dialogue, and facilitate the discussion for that day. Thus, the second part of the workshop was planned and scheduled with this member, who was in charge of contacting the pertinent organisations and arranging a meeting to explain the project to them and how they could help to enhance our knowledge about the issues the group was investigating. Three organisations were invited to this workshop for an open dialogue: 'Embrace a Sister'[1] (a feminist student organisation on campus), to talk to us about gender inequalities and racism, 'Unsilenced UFS'[2] and the Transformation Office of the Student Representative Council of the university, to debate inequalities and power struggles at the university.

For all the groups invited, the debate started with a brief explanation of the organisation, who they were and what they did, followed by questions from the members and an open debate about the ideas on the table. All of the debates were rich and extensive, covering a wide range of challenges, so our conversation was audiotaped and used as part of our data sets at later points of our research. What was obvious at this point was that there was racism on campus, as well as many gender inequalities affecting the student population in negative ways. Examples of this included the discussion about racist events that took place on campus during a student protests in 2015 and 2016, or the high incidence of sexual harassment and rape cases. In addition, controversial policies such as the 'No Student Hungry' (NSH)[3] campaign, or the language policy, both of which affect the most vulnerable students, were discussed (Dick et al. 2019; Sinwell 2019; Van der Merwe 2016).

Undoubtedly, this workshop was one of the most significant for the members. During the interviews, they referred to the second and third workshops as the most significant ones in the whole project. Iminathi mentioned the language policy and the fact that different conversations on that day changed the way she thought about these issues, enhancing her epistemic capability:

---

1    Embrace a Sister is a feminist student organisation founded at the University of the Free State in May 2012. Its aim is to focus on all issues pertaining to black woman and other minority groups. They challenge the set status quo that they are subjected to daily through oppression. Their activities are diverse, from the promotion of gender dialogues on campus, to protesting against rape culture and providing support to victims, among others.

2    Unsilenced UFS was born as a student organisation claiming justice after the Shimla Park incident at the UFS in February 2016 (see link for more information https://www.ufs.ac.za/docs/default-source/all-documents/ufs-shimla-park-report_27-february-2017.pdf). The organisation focuses on the unequal and constrained situation of black students on campus, performing artistic protests to highlight their demands (see the link for more information http://www.thejournalist.org.za/art/unsilencing-ufs).

3    For more information about this programme see https://www.ufs.ac.za/giving/unlisted-pages/lead-projects/the-no-student-hungry-programme.

'Remember when the SRC were here... and they started to touch... based on what is happening on campus, in terms of the language policy[4] [...] I remember they spoke about a lot of things, we spoke to Embrace a Sister... and... it literally... it changes you, because you have different perspectives like... even if I talk to somebody maybe before we met with the SRC and what not, and then we talked about the same issues after. I think, my opinion would be so, so, so different because now you hear different perspectives... so you understand... So, okay, this is how this person thinks. [...] It was very enlightening to hear other peoples' thoughts about certain topics as well... yeah. [...] It was actually an eye-opener for me, really an eye-opener... if I can put it that way.' (Iminathi, second interview, May 2017)

Another member, Siyabonga, uses similar words to refer to those conversations: 'Just hearing what they have to say... from a leadership point of view... it was... it was... enlightening...' (Siyabonga, second interview, May 2017). Or Khayone, for instance, who highlighted his learning on gender issues, 'I learned a lot of kinds of things, like that day when... it was those other people from Embrace a Sister... like we were having a debate about... the issues that women are facing and that those issues are not being addressed then.' (Khayone, second interview, May 2017).

Rethabile talked about how much she learned, enhancing her epistemic capability during these conversations because she was not aware of some of the issues that were discussed:

'The Embrace... and the SRC Transformation Office showed me a lot of things that I never thought about. Like... there... she... she... in a sense, like she opened my mind because there are a lot of things that you as a person, as a student, you are being ignorant to.' (Rethabile, second interview, May 2017)

---

4    The UFS was initially a bilingual institution with two main languages of instruction: English and Afrikaans. Programmes were offered in both languages. However, some questioned the equality of conditions for students when attending different classes presented in different languages, claiming that white students attending Afrikaans classes benefitted (see the link for more information about the language policy https://www.ufs.ac.za/docs/default-source/policy-institutional-documents/ language-policy.pdf?sfvrsn=0). This is not an isolated case, as this claim has been voiced in other traditionally Afrikaans universities in the country. Especially relevant is the case of Stellenbosch University and the viral video "Luister" (see https://www.youtube.com/watch?v=sF3rTBQTQk4).

Amahle equally highlights this workshop as the most relevant for her, due to the really rich and open dialogue. For her, the group discussed things that she was not fully aware of. She mentioned in the interview how this conversation had an impact on her, her way of being, her human dignity and self-development capability:

> 'That... it kind of changes my perspective at it... mmm... the last talk that we had... I think... yeah... it was like different people there... it was actually after that... that I left my hair in an Afro[5]... and [her friend]... was like "Oh no... it's actually really nice!" And I was like what?... Like how?... and then for once, it was just fine with my other black friends... "That looks nice"... I remember like those things... that's like... you are valid as well, even if like... It makes you feel that way and... that was the first time in my entire life that I ever just walked around with my Afro... it was so weird... but I also like it... I understand that it doesn't have to feel that way... that I must feel a little bit uncomfortable... but I was happy... that was a big, big thing.' (Amahle, second interview, May 2017)

This workshop was relevant for many of the members, not only because of the diverse perspectives presented and the knowledge emerging from the dialogues, expressed above as their epistemic capability. The workshop was equally a safe and open space to talk about sensitive issues enhancing their self-development capability, as expressed by Amahle. This was especially visible in this workshop and in the following one, in which racism and other delicate issues were discussed with other collectives. The members stated that spaces where they could feel safe and comfortable to participate are scarce on campus, especially owing to racial structures that impede them from doing so. Sometimes they even referred to classrooms as challenging spaces in which to participate openly, not even mentioning discussing sensitive subject matter with their peers. However, this epistemic injustice does not act in isolation. As this chapter will highlight, for many of the members, especially the female members, these colonial conversion factors intersect with their racial, gender and socio-economic identities, jeopardising their epistemic freedoms. Combined, they greatly inhibited their active participation,

---

5    Afro refers to when a black person wears her or his hair in its own natural state. This is a political feminist symbol which highlights the oppression of black women through hairstyles, due to the prevalence of white standards of beauty. It is a colonial conversion factor that affects their freedoms. See link for more information https://www.newstatesman.com/media/2014/01/politics-black-hair.

especially in the early stages of the project. Nevertheless, the transition observed from the beginning of the project to the end was remarkable for some of these members (see Chapter Seven). It is important to mention that even though these students participated more or less in their classrooms, the knowledge provided by the workshop greatly differed from that gleaned in the classroom. In the workshops their informational basis (Sen 1999) was being expanded, since they were now accessing new epistemic systems, different from the university ones, whilst being able to unpack the university epistemic system too (Grosfoguel, Hernandez & Rosen Velazquez 2016).

## 6.4 'The Solutions Need to Come From Us' (Third Workshop)

As the collaboratively pre-designed first part of the workshop (the scholars' meeting) had been delayed until the fourth workshop, the group used the first part of the morning to talk about the research project and next steps to take. The group talked for hours about what kind of research they wanted to undertake, how, and in which phases. Questions were asked about what academic research looked like, enhancing knowledge from previous conversations and ideas explained at the first workshop. The topics of research, paradigms, and diverse methodologies were among the wide compendium of ideas debated that morning.

Finally, the group agreed to work in three small groups according to their own interests, based on the initial divisions of gender inequalities, racism, and social/power inequalities on campus. For a few weeks, each group worked on a document that summarised what they had so far, and how to continue with their research plan. Hence, the three teams were to meet at the next workshop (the fourth) in order to have the opportunity to get feedback and advice on their research document from the other groups.

The second part of the day was dedicated to a dialogue with different students about the topics of interest to the group. This time they were not student organisations, but individual students. Five students from different faculties and levels joined the meeting. All of them had been invited to the workshop by the members of the group because of their different perspectives and opinions about the issues under research. One member of the DCR group, as usual, directed the conversation and acted as facilitator for the day, explaining to the guests what the group was interested in, opening the space for a joint debate, and leading the group conversation. In addition, all the members took notes and the conversation was audiotaped, as in our previous discussions.

The dialogue focused mainly on racism and inequalities, although there was a residual discussion on gender. Racism at university occupied most of the discussion. The various guests presented their own perspectives and experiences regarding racist issues and discussed them with the members of the group. Ideas such as white privilege, colour culture, black tribalism, university-specific racist issues (such as the Shimla Park incident),[6] gender-cultural traditions, oral history, oral knowledge, and inequality (in general), were debated, generating new insights into the research topics, with rich data from different perspectives.

This collective meeting and the previous one were those most frequently cited by the members as being significant moments in the whole project. For instance, Siyabonga said the collective meeting was important thanks to the different points of view we heard that day. He explained how this conversation was an eye-opener for him, enhancing his epistemic capability. Another member, Khayone, said this meeting was the most relevant one for him, due to the conversations we had about different cultures, gender, and politics in general. He said, 'I learned a lot from them' (Khayone, second interview, May 2017).

Furthermore, Karabo said this workshop had been important because she started applying the things she had learned in previous meetings, referring to the first part of the day and the discussion about research and next steps. Additionally, Kungawo talked about how powerful it had been to hear, for the first time, a white person recognise their own white privilege. This highlights the epistemologies of ignorance that this collective is used to enduring in the higher-education context (Steyn 2012). Kungawo said, 'It's very new to me to hear like a white person confesses white privilege and white... and all of these other things... It's... it was absolutely weird it was like... it just blew me away'

---

6    For more information see https://www.ufs.ac.za/docs/default-source/all-documents/ufs-shimla-park-report_27-february-2017.pdf.

(Kungawo, second interview, May 2017). Here Kungawo is reflecting on his own personally felt epistemic injustices as a black male in South Africa. He is reflecting on how colonial conversion factors affect his epistemic freedoms, and when the oppressor group often does not recognise their own system of oppression. In the literature this is referred to as epistemic exploitation (Berenstain 2016) or epistemic marginalisation (Goetze 2018). The oppressed groups subjected to these colonial conversion factors constantly have to explain their epistemic marginalisation, despite white communities having the available knowledge to understand it. For Kungawo this was the first time he did not have to explain his own marginalisation as a black student to a white member of the university community.

He added that it was also important due to the fact that they were able to bring diverse individuals together to talk in one place:

'It was important for me because first of all... I've never seen that in my life, all those kinds of people in one area, like I always told you that... you know... since I got here, to this university... I encountered racism and I know that I've been always told about it... but when I got here and I saw that was actually real... and... we spend too much time through this activism thing, we spend so much time trying to... to spend time to speak up about it, I told you that I'm from Unsilenced UFS and stuff... umm... and generally people, student leaders on campus and student activists try so much, so many times to put together people of these different kinds of thought to come together and talk about a solution... so the fact that we were... able to do it, it was amazing... and that's why we are even planning to continue the conversation to a larger audience, to other students. [...] Umm... for me that felt like a milestone... we were able to do that... and you know... then after the conversation, the people saying that... it was so useful... you know that we were doing something great... you know... I'm still meeting people around campus who ask me... are you still debating that stuff? People wanted to become, to join us and to do research stuff... it was amazing... because they think that... you know such a platform needs to... be created and... the solutions need to come from us because... you can say that the university... has... has... or it's institutionally racist... umm... but it is at the end of the day us because we are the ones, we have to deal with it on a daily basis, we are the subjects... you know of racism... on the daily basis, but... we... the students, both blacks and whites, we are part of the solution. [...] If... we as students... we just become independent and do our own stuff, and I almost swore then, but if we do our own things... you know be... outside management, outside of the institution management, we can go somewhere. [...] For me it was like a milestone, it was really important, especially because racism is important to all of us... and a lot of us had been subjected to it, so to hear white people speak like that... and actually confess that racism it's, it's, there is racism here... yeah, that was... yeah... that was, yeah.' (Kungawo, third interview, October 2017)

For Kungawo, this workshop and the research process as a whole challenged many conversion factors on campus, bringing together different groups to discuss sensitive issues. This impacted not only his epistemic capability but his own self-development and human recognition, giving him the platform to talk in more equal terms with those groups which had historically oppressed his communities.

Furthermore, Lethabo referred to this moment as being important, not only because it was an eye-opener for many of them and enhanced their epistemic freedoms, but also because it helped to solidify the group identity and enhanced their human recognition capability. He said:

'In one moment it gave us like a group identity, I guess, and the fact that the people we brought in were very... umm... well-spoken in terms of, the things that we wanted to talk about, you know, M-A, and the coloured lady, umm... yeah... I think specifically, the people we brought in... they really brought a whole new eye-opening dynamic to it all.' (Lethabo, third interview, October 2017)

Nevertheless, as Kungawo finally remarked, although it was important to listen to the students that came to talk to us, to listen to other members of the group was also part of the process of bringing different knowledges and influencing our epistemic freedoms. In his own words,

'Like I said again like... hearing like what people have experienced, yeah it's really, it's really interesting to me I don't know how to put it. Now it leaves me like... enlightened me to things like things I have never heard of before. And I know that the other guy, [referring to Khayone]. It's amazing when he talks like how he speaks of like South African history like that like for me... I need to shut up and listen to him speak because he knows a lot about African history. And then you get Lethabo who speaks about his Afrikaner experience and then you get someone like Rethabile.' (Kungawo, second interview, May 2017)

Clearly, the second and third workshop affected the group in various ways, enhancing several of their insurgent capabilities, and challenging their epistemic marginalisation, but also making them epistemic contributors. Firstly, due to the fact that they were discussing issues that were relevant to them personally, but which they did not have available platforms to discuss, the workshop was especially helpful for discussing racism happening at the university. Thus, the workshop enhanced and achieved different functionings of their epistemic capability. Secondly, because of the information provided there, and the different perspectives revealed during the dialogue, this being a safe space where they could openly participate, the workshops influenced their self-development as well as their human recognition capability. This was, in fact, a space of plural learning, where different perspectives were displayed and scrutinised by the members in an open and safe platform. They became more than just recipients of their university curricula.

## 6.5 'If We Make it...Too... Formal. I Feel it Will Lose Its Safeness' (Fourth Workshop)

The fourth workshop was designed by the group in two main parts. The first part was dedicated to discussion with scholars of the topics we were researching, and the second part explored the work done so far by the small groups over the past few weeks, and was used to create a document with their general research plan.

Surprisingly, after a really enthusiastic and active conversation with both of the scholars[7] who visited us that day and talked to us about the issues under research, none of the members referred to them during the interview as being relevant or significant during the project. Furthermore, the second part of the workshop seemed to be difficult and overly technical for them, as it was based on exploring the different phases of their research plan.

---

7    Two scholars working on campus visited us that day as guests. Both of them specialised in inequalities and racism. The first of these was Dr Marthinus Conradie from the Department of English, who has several publications related to critical race theory and social inequalities using discourse analysis. The second was Dr Luis Escobedo, who is a postdoctoral fellow at the Institute for Reconciliation and Social Justice and whose research focuses on whiteness and systemic racism. Unfortunately, the group was not able to find a third scholar specialised in gender studies at this stage of the project.

An interesting reflection was made by one of the students about this central phase, where much scientific knowledge was used, through conversations with scholars and some explanations about the use of scientific research:

> 'It's a debating context... you... know... but at the end of the day, I don't want us to lose that element of being like an informal settlement because if we go too formal it's gonna end up being back to that, it is not a space anymore... because now people are trying to really ... ummm... impress their ideas... and instead of us talking about it and developing new thought, changing or not changing, or just being exposed to new thoughts... if we make it... too... formal. I feel like it will lose its safeness.' (Siyabonga, second interview, May 2017)

The member was here referring to how an informal safe space, where everyone has the chance to express themselves in their own way, was somehow being transformed into a hostile space. This hostile space, which emerged with scientific concepts and ideas about research and complicated conversations about theory, made the members feel uncomfortable and, at times, lost. For them, it was like a return to their normal university settings. Lesedi said, during the second interview:

> 'Let me tell you something. [Laughs] Well while I was like... umm... there were a few words there. There were like D-whatever... I cannot even pronounce them right I was like... 'Oh my God these terms are so big, I am so lost,' so I am like, 'Oh God, okay! Calm down Lesedi, you got this.' (Lesedi, second interview, May 2017)

Their distance from these ideas and terms was emphasised by their unfamiliarity and hostility, which were not bad in and of themselves, but somehow served as a reflection of the group-members' epistemic marginalisation from the university epistemic system. The DCR process was a space for learning, and this learning combined their knowledges with other knowledge systems that were expressed in different ways, such as scientific theories. This combination created an ecology of knowledges in the process of learning and exploring. Therefore, it was important to investigate new ideas and concepts in order to allow the team to expand its informational basis as a dialogic space, e.g. a space in which to decide which direction the following steps of our project should take (Appadurai 2006; Rowell, Riel & Polush 2017; Sen 1999). Members decided that this kind of scientific knowledge production was important to them. After all, they were all students at the university and this institution used such frameworks to produce knowledge and, in many ways, to marginalise them. Hence they decided to explore these kinds of knowledge production to the extent that they could manage, to enhance their epistemic capability. Some evidence of this learning and the benefits of being exposed to this university knowledge will be shown in the following sections. Nevertheless, this was not ultimately how the members wanted to lead the project. This is why, in our fifth and sixth workshops, we looked for alternative approaches that could better reflect the research aspirations of the group.

During the fourth workshop, one of the members mentioned being confused about how to reference and access reliable scientific information. Other members were also interested in learning more about it, as they had not yet have been taught any research courses, or if they had, they had not gained much from them. As such, part of the workshop was spent talking about scientific sources of information and academic reference systems. Again, this was important, because despite the decision to take a less conventional approach in our research project, students were willing to learn more about the scientific epistemic system. This epistemic system is central in their lives, even if they are only the recipients of epistemic materials. Navigating and exploring further was a shared aspiration and valued capability, thus we dedicated time during this day to exploring these aspects.

Members mentioned during the interviews how beneficial this exploration of the academic knowledge system was for them, not only for the project, but beyond it. For instance, Siyabonga mentioned how this had helped him to look for reliable scientific information, which is framed not as the only source of information, but as a reliable space in which to look for information within this particular knowledge system. Similarly, other students stated how this helped them in their academic work. Minenhle said:

'The academic search engine as well, it makes things so much easier for me actually... because normally... I... I... normally took my information for my assignments... from... mmm... not so... umm... how do they say? I took it... from maybe blogs... I didn't know that I should not take information from blogs... and that doesn't mean that whatever they mean... is the right information... or... taking them from websites... or Wikipedia actually... so... and also... it is easier for me... in terms of the referencing, bibliography-wise... it really helped me... it made things so much easier for me... yeah.' (Minenhle, third interview, October 2017)

Lesedi corroborated this view:

> 'It helped us a lot, it helped with this academic search engine, you can use it for your academic work and it's something that nobody would be... you know... you are not taught in class, your lecture or your facilitator... who knows? They don't come to you and tell you "Hi, with this academic search engine if you need help with that and that and that." I did... I did more than four assignments with this academic search engine and I did very well with them so... it helped me that way... in my academic work and when I see that... I did perform well and it's something that it didn't take so much time to learn, and I didn't have to pay for it, because you have to pay for everything these days.' (Lesedi, third interview, October 2017)

The group talked very positively about these sources of information and the specific skills they had gained on that day. It is clear that accessing the academic epistemic system forms part of their aspirations and offers them a way to enhance their insurgent capabilities. Access is the only way to overcome the many colonial factors that jeopardise their freedoms, and those of their loved ones, in accessing higher education. Indeed, their epistemic marginalisation is central to the challenges they experience on campus and, more often than not, they face a unilateral epistemic relation with the university as a post-colonial and hostile institution. They are there to learn the coloniser codes but not to contribute their own knowledges and African conceptions of good (Mbembe 2015). They are situated on the wrong side of the epistemic line, as Ndlovu-Gatsheni explores (2018), and thus their insurgent epistemic capability needs to claim freedoms of epistemic access to the academic epistemic system. However, this is insufficient, and a redrawing of the epistemic lines is required in order for them to contribute their own epistemic material to this exclusive epistemic system (Fricker 2015). It is clear, thus, that colonial conversion factors are essential for an international reader to understand the oppression that these students experience on a daily basis. Hence, when I refer here to 'epistemic freedoms', this means fair access to Western epistemic materials, but also access to and respect of other epistemic systems, as both givers and receivers, as we will see in the following sections.

# 6.6 'I Didn't Really Feel, Like, Valid to Contribute...' (Fifth Workshop)

The interviews I conducted during the project and at the end of it provided an individual and collective perspective in the midst of the process. They were not only substantial in identifying difficulties and challenges for the group, but also in making these issues available to the group in order for them to be debated. These tensions, such as the issue of punctuality or power imbalances in the group, were mostly debated between the fourth and the fifth workshops.

During the second interview, I asked the members individually what they would change about the project. One of the participants mentioned punctuality and how that affected participation in the group. He said:

> 'Because sometimes people come late, and when they come late... they just sit... they don't even have an idea of what is really going on. [...] We have to be time conscious, when... when we say 9:30, make sure that we are here at 9:30, 9:45 at the latest, and then we start with everything.' (Khayone, second interview, May 2017)

Naturally, as this member observed, some of these delays were registered in my personal journal and the participant observation reports. One of the journal entries debated whether it was pertinent to initiate a debate with the whole group when it was only one member who was identifying this as a limitation. Nevertheless, the participant observation showed that this was in reality also a problem of active participation; thus, we dedicated some time to talk about it on this day.

The debate was started by Rethabile, who told us that we did not have a good excuse to be late and that it was not a question of meeting an hour later, but of being conscious of our responsibility to be on time. She also proposed that members always arrive an hour early in order to be able to start on time. For instance, she proposed that we should allocate responsibilities among the members, such as arranging the chairs and tables in the room, preparing breakfast, or setting up the laptop and projector. On the other hand, Lesedi proposed creating a punishment system; latecomers would not get the voucher for that workshop. This idea was not really supported by the rest of the group, so it was agreed that everyone would be on time for the next workshop and that the last person to arrive, together with her or his respective group, would be responsible for setting up the room the next day.

Secondly, equal participation was mentioned by the same member who highlighted the problem of punctuality, and who claimed that not everyone was contributing or participating equally. He highlighted that something which had to change during the workshops was 'contributions... it's contribution... everyone has to contribute' (Khayone, second interview, May 2017).

This response was quite surprising, as one of the questions everyone was asked at the second interview was if they were aware of power imbalances, or if they were provided with an adequate space to participate actively. Members attested that the research project helped them to be more secure in their opinions and to express their opinions in public more easily, thus enhancing their human recognition capability. However, the researcher journal and participant observation notes also recorded some observations that some members were more talkative than others, or dominated certain spaces during the meetings. In this case, the interviews helped us to investigate this matter from an individual perspective, highlighting that colonial conversion factors featured in these divisions of active participation. For instance, some examples are provided below:

> 'Because in a sense... that... you're still scared, that if I say this it might be wrong. Or, because in your mind it's always... I don't know, we have this mentality that "your answer is always wrong." So and then you know when you meet new people you're scared to share a lot of things.' (Rethabile, second interview, May 2017)

> 'For me, I am always that person who sits at the back. I just sit and listen to people talk. And then I agree. I am like... okay, okay.' (Bokamoso, second interview, May 2017)

> 'I wasn't so vocal. I know... I know that I am... ummm... I'm opinionated but most of the time, I keep it to myself... I felt... felt... something about certain issues... I just keep it to myself or I just tell a close friend.' (Minenhle, third interview, October 2017)

> 'I think... you remember... I was quiet at the beginning and I didn't really feel, like, valid to contribute and stuff.' (Amahle, third interview, October 2017)

In addition, Iminathi said that she did not like to talk and that she told her group that she preferred to do other kinds of work to contribute to the group, such as reading the material. She said 'I don't like approaching people, I tend to be like, I am angry when I am not, so I am like okay... I prefer to be reading' (Iminathi, second interview, May 2017).

Interestingly, this viewpoint was mentioned by six of the seven black female members of the group, which clarifies that there are sub-dimensions within colonial conversation factors, such as gender, race and class, among others, as sustained by post-colonial scholars (Lugones, 2003). A good example of this interaction is shown in the following quote by one of the (black female) members, who said:

> 'Yeah. Yeah, I do actually because I don't know, a friend of mine always says I suffer from insecurity, I don't really trust myself in terms of talking about your... sharing my thoughts... about maybe social injustices or maybe LBGTQI community, which is true because most of the time, when you come to varsity, when you come from a state school and you come to varsity, you feel like... no... uhh... Neliswa is smarter than me, and that [another person] is smarter than me, so I don't want to say anything because what if I say something stupid, something that might be stupid.' (Minenhle, second interview, May 2017)

This is a clear example of how epistemic injustices work due to colonial conversion factors in which different Western categorisations are at play, with intersecting forms of oppression, such as being a black woman in South Africa, where patriarchal, racial and class norms are part of the student experience on campus. These experiences vary widely from what a Global North student would experience, even if they might be subjected to oppressive norms and epistemic injustices in other ways. In a context such as South Africa, we are talking about colonial conversion factors because these students attend classes in a language that many do not know in their own country, their lecturers maintain the social norms of a dominant culture to which they do not belong (such as Western principles of professionalism, whereas looking directly into the eyes when talking might be seen as a sign of disrespect for many African communities). They are foreigners in their own educational system. As Berenstain (2016, 580) explores, this is an epistemic 'gaslighting'. She asserts that 'gaslighting functions to undermine a person's confidence in their grasp on reality leading to an overall sense of self-doubt and a lack of trust in one's perception. Gaslighting, thus, involves raising doubts about a person's ability to accurately perceive and understand events, and can thus harm them in their capacity as a knower'. This prevents them from participating and sharing their epistemic materials, thus affecting two of the major capabilities, epistemic and human recognition. Nevertheless, as Chapter Seven will highlight, some of these colonial conversion factors were challenged by the project, especially by female group-members, who noticed an expansion of capabilities and actual functionings in participation and voice. Moreover, these issues were debated by the group and addressed at different levels in an effort to compensate for the different positions that different members had, and the way in which that affected the functionings of participation.

The fifth workshop was held right after the winter holidays, in July. This was a special opportunity to collect knowledge and perceptions from the participants' own families, friends, and communities and to share them with the rest of the group. Thus, the group dedicated the second part of the day to sharing their knowledge of gender inequalities, racism, and power inequalities with the group through an open debate. Members collaborated in a broad discussion of the validity—or not—of this knowledge, and of how different values guide the assessment of these ideas. Equally, the ideas discussed previously in other sessions were raised and scrutinised by the group through audiotapes and notes taken of our conversations.

The group concluded the workshop by distributing the responsibilities and tasks for each group to bring to the following workshop. Each group was responsible for conducting a brief academic literature review, using skills from our previous workshop, about their topics.

## 6.7 'I've Learned More about Research than in those Past Two Years' (Sixth Workshop)

The members of each small group prepared a document which contained a brief literature review. The three documents from each group were printed and given to each of the members to read before the presentation. They had fifteen minutes to read the document before the group presented it to the plenary, and after every presentation there was a critical pause to debate the various points of the research, to propose changes or improvements, and also to resolve doubts.

This practical activity was beneficial for the participants' understandings of what scientific research is, how it is shared, and also of how the social issues they were exploring are framed by scholars. Some of the students mentioned these activities during the interviews:

> 'I feel that because they did not teach us in how to do research probably we end up not being able to take up the right information. It ends up... with this research process... it's teaching me to work through information and... yeah... it's quite beneficial for me. Because in my course they don't teach us unless you do your Honours, but when you do your honours... but it is not really guaranteed that you are going to do your honours because you need like a specific average, to qualify to do your honours, so it's quite difficult. Now you must wait for honours to do research and what not... but yeah... I think it is so beneficial to me.' (Iminathi, third interview, May 2017)

Amahle stated that, although she knew about research, she had learned more from the project than from her actual research module at her faculty:

> 'We did like a research module... first and second year... like... we do a project but I think in the past months, I feel like I've learned more about research than in those past two years... that... we used marks... and I did the test on it... and all those things.' (Amahle, second interview, May 2017)

As mentioned above, undergraduate students tend to be passive receivers of the academic epistemic system, and this is even more evident when talking about collectives that have been historically excluded from universities for generations and that still experience other types of epistemic marginalisation (Badat 2008). Information is given to them during their lectures but nothing is said about how this epistemic system builds its knowledge, or how knowledge comes to be knowledge in their classroom. Although this DCR project considered knowledge in a broad manner, it was important for these students to show, as their identified epistemic capability highlights, that access alone was not sufficient. They were claiming to be part of and contributors to this academic epistemic system, alongside other epistemic systems in which they actively participate.

On the other hand, to bring about an ecology of knowledges (De Sousa Santos 2014) is also to understand the different rhythms and learning processes that diverse individuals undertake, as well as their epistemic choices. In this regard, the project provided epistemic access to academic knowledge 'imperfectly'. Moreover, it equally provided space to explore and investigate other knowledge systems in the same context, in order to scrutinise them and decide on their epistemic paths. The members confronted the issues of how to propose a 'conventional' research project, how to look for academic and non-academic information, and how to implement a research project (in a broad sense) according to their personal interests, and thus this was sufficient to articulate an ecology of knowledges. Further, as Kemmis, McTaggart and Nixon assess, '[t]he criterion of success is not whether participants have followed the steps faithfully, but whether they have a strong and authentic sense of development and evolution in their practices, their understanding of their practices, and the situations in which they practice' (2013, 19). In a DCR process, it will be said that this 'strong and authentic sense of development' is assessed by the expansion of freedoms (capabilities) that these individuals have reason to value. Moreover, the process provides an adequate platform for their expansion and achievement (functionings). Hence, participatory research should not be assessed according to whether it follows particular stages, but rather with an expansion of valued freedoms and the articulation of an ecology of knowledges.

Hence, the group discussed whether to continue collecting data and analysing it in a conventional scientific way or whether to use an alternative way. The alternative path discussed was based on their own lived experiences and knowledge gained through the process, but also the knowledge collected during our discussions. Thus, together, the group analysed the viability of such an option, with two main considerations forming the core of this discussion. Firstly, the second semester is usually a really dense and short period of the year, which, in many ways, considerably reduces the free time available for students. In this case, it reduced the availability of the team members. On the other hand, two members of the gender group dropped out at this stage of the project, due to academic-related issues. Their leaving necessitated a redistribution of the members of that group into the other two groups— racism and power inequalities—which affected the original distribution of the team. Therefore, although a final decision was not taken on this day, we agreed to continue thinking about alternative possibilities and to discuss them at our upcoming workshop. And a final agenda point for the day was the discussion of a project t-shirt, which a few members had proposed in the previous workshop. One member brought a photo with a possible design for the t-shirt. This consisted of the logo of the project on the front and a slogan, the name of the relevant person and the words 'Researcher in action' on the back. The whole group was enthusiastic about the design. Some members then took on the responsibility of obtaining price quotes for the t-shirts, in order to have them as soon as possible. The group ended the day with an agreed plan to think about possible ideas to contribute to the next workshop.

## 6.8 'Now. Think Again. Are We Equal?' (Seventh Workshop)

The first part of the day was dedicated to brainstorming the ideas we had thought of for our research project, as we had finally decided not to adopt a conventional research approach. The group began with a discussion about how to continue with our research project, taking into consideration the time needed and our interest and preferences. Ideas such as using participatory video and participatory writing were the main proposals. Hence, we agreed that we would use participatory video, producing two final videos for the two principal themes: (1) racism and (2) power inequality on campus. Furthermore, we agreed that our written stories as part of the collaborative book would capture a more personal experiential knowledge level, with reflections on our experiences of injustices via the three themes (racism, gender inequality and power inequality). The final agreement was to create a new project website, where these resources would be shared and distributed. Hence, responsibilities were allocated and a schedule was designed to accomplish the deadlines and task before the end of the academic year. For example, these tasks included the creation and design of the website, and all members also had to work on a collaborative online document for their contributions to the book—according to the three main sections agreed upon. Finally, the group would partly use the second half of the workshop to start the participatory video process.

The group continued the workshop by exploring how to use the online program and how to work collaboratively on an online document until our next workshop. This program was proposed as a means of easily working together on our book. Further, a major benefit was that the program was available for free via an internet connection. Hence, a document was created and all of the members were added as editors. We displayed the program on the big screen and I provided a brief explanation about its use and main features.

To conclude, the group dedicated the last part of the workshop to the participatory video process, debating their themes and main ideas in their videos, and designing storyboards. They designed (in groups) one storyline on racism on campus named 'Thinking forward, moving backwards', and another on inequalities and power imbalances named 'Are we equal?'. The first video would interview different students and staff members around campus, discussing their perspectives about racism on campus. The aim of the video would be to highlight that even if some actions have been carried by the university (e.g. changing names of buildings), there are many micro-racisms underlying the relationships between actors in this institution. The idea, as proposed by the group, was to bring these micro challenges to the forefront but also to end with a message of hope, using Nelson Mandela's quote, 'It's always impossible until is done'.

The second video focused on power inequalities in a more intersectional manner. The team planned to interview students and staff members on campus. Besides an emphasis on students' financial constraints, the outsourcing of cleaners and other service providers, they wanted to emphasise the Shimla Park incident as a central event of the video. They wanted to conclude the video with a rhetoric question to the audience: 'Now. Think again. Are we equal?'

The workshop ended with arrangements for the agenda of our next meeting and the responsibilities for each member until then, and the decision that the eighth workshop would mainly be used to continue with our participatory video process.

## 6.9 'There Is No Place for Us, as Black Students...' (Eighth Workshop)

The storyboards were ready after some final feedback and reflections and the two groups only needed some basic training on how to produce video-clips, taking into consideration lighting, framing, and sound following their storyboards. This basic training was provided, together with an explanation on the basic use of the video camera and voice recorder. The groups had some time available before recording began, so they practiced in the room. Once roles had been allocated among the members, with consensus on who would take care of the video camera and who the recorder would be, the members were ready. They then went out to produce their videos.

The two teams returned in the late afternoon to edit the video-clips and audio pieces collected. Thus, as everyone had the video software, a brief training session, using some of the audio and visual material taken by the members, was provided. Basics skills, such as clipping footage, the introduction of layouts and text, or adding audio to a video, were provided. Thus, the groups used the rest of the afternoon to edit the videos according to their storyboards, and received continuous feedback and assistance throughout the production, even if this was not completed on that day.

During this workshop the videos started to take form and their arguments were constructed, through the inclusion of different positionalities from diverse collectives and their experiences on campus. Both videos ended up delivering a really powerful message about racism on campus. Throughout different interviews the team showed how racism is openly accepted on campus, how patriarchal norms define standards, and how homophobic prejudices about the LGBTQI+ community persist. In this regard, a statement given by one black student interviewed for this video was very significant. He said: 'It saw us, that there is no place for us, as black students at the University of the Free State, and that we still need to fight towards justice'. The videos presented many challenges that the university students were familiar with through their own daily experiences, although few platforms are provided to discuss them. The group felt that the videos and the collaborative book were tools to enhance their voices and make them properly heard by powerful actors. They as students are part of the solution too.

The editing of the videos took a long time, which is why the group worked until late during this workshop and decided to meet informally on another day to conclude their editing after the group feedback. They decided to set aside the last workshop to focus on the written pieces for the collaborative book and the website. Thus, the team met the following week, during a public holiday, to continue the editing of both videos, working on them for the entire day, and agreed to finalise the editing process by the next workshop.

## 6.10 '[I] Could Never Have Been Prepared for the Mental Adventure that Was About to Begin' (Ninth Workshop)

This day was mostly used to continue working on the book and to review the website together. The team worked on the book from morning to evening, using our online software on our laptops and reviewing the website together in deciding what to include or exclude. Siyabonga, one of the members in charge of the website, said during the interview that it had been a great experience to take on that responsibility,

> 'I learned how to make a website, which is quite great... I mean... the time might come when I need a website myself, and then it's really gonna help me.' (Siyabonga, third interview, October 2017)

However, this viewpoint was not restricted to him, and other members of the group also valued the opportunity to learn how to set up and design a website for free through the program. Lesedi said:

> 'We learned how to open up a website... it's great because when you think of a website you think... oh... I have to pay for that... like every month... or something and I just want to stay away from those things until you have your own job or what not, like... it's okay... it's not like that... you can just... learn and here is how... it was amazing.' (Lesedi, third interview, October 2017)

As Lesedi said, this program is freely available to use and not only allowed the members to create a project website, but also gave them the skills to be able to create their own websites, or to create websites for professional purposes in the future, at no additional cost. This is of relevance in a context such as South Africa, as these kinds of skills are scarce, and so this provided them with extra resources for facing the uncertain future. Although this may be seen as a mere skill transfer of access to and knowledge about the Internet, softwares, and computer literacy, technology helps humans to communicate, participate and exercise fundamental freedoms, like those that these students have reason to value. These skills are instrumental for the articulation of freedoms such as epistemic, human recognition and self-development, and facilitate an active and more equal participation in these virtual and interactive spaces.

The written stories were not finalised in this workshop, but it was agreed that they would continue working on them over the coming months. Even if this was officially our last workshop, we wanted to host a public event on campus in 2018 in order to engage with other students about the issues explored. Hence, before the end of the day we agreed that the written pieces would be structured in four main parts: in the first students would write about the DCR project, reflecting on their experiences as co-researchers in this participatory research. The second part would focus on racism and the third, would focus on gender inequalities. And the fourth and final part would focus on social inequalities and power imbalances. Furthermore, we decided to write the stories in a variety of different languages, from English to Sesotho, isi-Zulu, Afrikaans, and isi-Xhosa. The idea was that, although the major part of the text was in English (as our workshops had been), other local languages were given space in the compilation of the book, reflecting the linguistic diversity of the team. Moreover, once finished, the agreement was to upload the book and videos to the website, so that people could obtain free copies of the collaborative book and watch our videos.

Despite this being the last workshop of the project, the team knew that this was not the end. The project had perhaps concluded, but the group intended to continue working together informally, at least for the following year (2018). These ideas included holding a book launch at the university the following year, or continuing as a group of activists, and providing platforms at the university for different groups to discuss these issues together, or using social networks to promote awareness. The team continues to have informal meetings today even if not with all the members, as some have already left the university community.

I would like to conclude this last section with an excerpt of the collaborative book written by one of the members, which contains her personal reflection on her involvement in the DCR project:

'I am a twenty-one-year-old student at the UFS. I grew up in Durban in a family of five and felt like most of my worldview was shaped by my experiences earlier on in primary school, having had a very diverse group of friends and never being able to put my finger on the face of inequality and not being able to question it because no one else seemed to explain it in a way I could understand. I started debating in Grade Six but always had a very keen interest in politics and understanding the world and why it is the way it is. I really was that annoying kid who asked my parents bizarre questions like "why must I have a job? What if I want a job that doesn't pay? Does that mean I'm not making a valuable contribution to society enough to be able to afford to live?"

So, long story short, I ended up in Bloemfontein with the same questions unanswered. I think I have always surrounded myself more with people who ask the same questions rather than those who look like me or come from the same place. The participatory project happened, literally out of the blue. A friend of mine had seen posters about it and was very interested and could not shut up about it. So, I joined in the second week and could never have been prepared for the mental adventure that was about to begin. I feel incredibly lucky to have somehow found myself surrounded by such diverse, peculiar but very special people once a month at workshops discussing all of the questions that have plagued my mind for years. We had interesting discussions about everything but as you would expect from a group of individuals whose brains could not stop thinking even if they were rewired to do so, the topics ended up predominantly revolving around race, power and gender inequalities and the huge influence of these on our lives.

This project has given me tools to look at life from different perspectives and has enriched my knowledge of other people's experiences in a way that no other could. With the main objective of the project having been to explore social justice (the lack thereof) and to give us as undergraduates an opportunity to develop our ability to contribute to knowledge production unconventionally, I've learnt a great deal about research and the academic world and have also been able to see its flaws. The greatest question that this project has forced me to explore is value and how our place in life is hugely predetermined by the value boxes that different societal perceptions place us in.' (*Narratives on Social Injustices: Undergraduate Voices*, 2018)

Certainly, a project such as this DCR is a multidimensional project. It does not aim to advance knowledge for the sake of knowledge; but rather as a way to expand our limited frontiers of knowing, both personally and professionally. Working with undergraduate students in South Africa opened a door to other ways of seeing and experiencing the world, and the beauty of it is that our worlds connected with one another and bridged our differences, even if this was done imperfectly.

## 6.11 Conclusion

In conclusion, this chapter has provided a review of the activities undertaken by the group during each of the workshops that composed this DCR project. The combination of diverse epistemological bases made the promotion of an ecology of knowledges possible (De Sousa Santos 2014), bringing different sources into a common space for collective investigation and scrutiny. In this investigative space, research was considered as a capacity through which individuals can expand their own knowledge horizons about a matter that is important to them (Appadurai 2006). This is how this research process has mixed knowledges coming from different sources and adapting the approach according to the participants' aims, capacities and frames of reference (Chilisa 2012).

Furthermore, the ten sections have revealed how decisions were taken throughout the process, as well as the importance of the members' valued capabilities, situating them as the directors and owners of the project. This process has not been easy, and a variety of challenges have been highlighted. In addition, the chapter has shown how the members have benefited from the project in terms of their identified capabilities, and how significant some of the activities have been for the group due to the colonial conversion factors jeopardising their fundamental freedoms. However, this analysis is incomplete, and thus the next chapter aims to focus on two co-researchers' valuable capabilities and their expansion through the project, in order to better understand individual experiences of taking part in this project after a collective perspective.

## References

Appadurai, A. (2006). The right to research. *Globalisation, Societies and Education,* 4(2), 167–177. https://doi.org/10.1080/14767720600750696.

Badat, S. (2008). Redressing the colonial/apartheid legacy: Social equity, redress and higher education admissions in democratic South Africa. In *Conference on Affirmative Action in Higher Education in India, the United States and South*

*Africa*. New Delhi: Oxford University Press (pp. 19–21). https://www.ru.ac.za/media/rhodesuniversity/content/vc/documents/Redressing_the_Colonial_or_Apartheid_Legacy.pdf.

Berenstain, N. (2016). Epistemic exploitation. *Ergo, 3*(22), 569–590. https://doi.org/10.3998/ergo.12405314.0003.022.

Chilisa, B. (2012). *Indigenous Research Methodologies*. Los Angeles: Sage Publications.

De Sousa Santos, B. (2010). *Descolonizar el saber, reinventar el poder*. Montevideo: Ediciones Trilce.

De Sousa Santos, B. (2014). *Epistemologies of the South: Justice against Epistemicide*. New York: Routledge. https://unescochair-cbrsr.org/pdf/resource/Epistemologies_of_the_South.pdf.

Dick, L., Kruger, F., Müller, M., & Mockie, A. (2019). Transformative pedagogy as academic performance: #ShimlaPark as a plane of immanence. *Cultural Studies, Critical Methodologies, 19*(2), 84–90. https://doi.org/10.1177%2F1532708618807246.

Fricker, M. (2015). Epistemic contribution as a central human capability. In George Hull (ed.). *The Equal Society: Essays on Equality in Theory and Practice* (pp. 73–90). Lanham: Lexington Books. https://rowman.com/ISBN/9781498515719/.

Goetze, T. S. (2018). Hermeneutical dissent and the species of hermeneutical injustice. *Hypatia, 33*(1), 73–90. https://doi.org/10.1111/hypa.12384.

Grosfoguel, R., Hernandez, R. & Rosen Velazquez, E. (2016). *Decolonizing the Westernized University: Interventions in Philosophy of Education from Within and Without*. Lanham, Maryland: Lexington Books.

Kemmis, S., McTaggart, R., & Nixon, R. (2013). *The Action Research Planner: Doing Critical Participatory Action Research*. New South Wales: Springer.

Lugones, M. (2003). The inseparability of race, class, and gender in Latino studies. *Latino Studies, 1*(2), 329–329. https://doi.org/10.1057/palgrave.lst.8600039.

Mbembe, A. (2015). *Decolonizing Knowledge and the Question of the Archive. Aula Magistral Proferida*. Public lecture, Wits University (South Africa). https://wiser.wits.ac.za/system/files/Achille%20Mbembe%20-%20Decolonizing%20Knowledge%20and%20the%20Question%20of%20the%20Archive.pdf.

Ndlovu-Gatsheni, S. J. (2018). *Epistemic Freedom in Africa: Deprovincialization and Decolonization*. New York: Routledge.

Rowell, L. L., Riel, M. M., & Polush, E. Y. (2017). Defining action research: On dialogic spaces for constructing shared meanings. In Rowell, Bruce, Shosh & Riel (eds). *The Palgrave International Handbook of Action Research* (pp. 85–101). Los Angeles: Palgrave Macmillan.

Sen, A. (1999). *Development as Freedom*. New York: Random House.

Sen, A. (2009). *The Idea of Justice*. Cambridge, MA: Belknap.

Sinwell, L. (2019). The #FeesMustFall movement: 'Disruptive Power' and the politics of student-worker alliances at the University of the Free State (2015–2016). *South African Review of Sociology*, *50*(3-4), 42-56. https://doi.org/10.10 80/21528586.2019.1678070.

Steyn, M. (2012). The ignorance contract: Recollections of apartheid childhoods and the construction of epistemologies of ignorance. *Identities*, *19*(1), 8–25. https://doi.org/10.1080/1070289X.2012.672840.

Van der Merwe, J. C. (ed.) (2016). *Transformation and Legitimation in Post-Apartheid Universities*. Bloemfontein: AFRICAN SUN MeDIA.

# 7. Broadening Our Participatory Evaluations: A Southern Capabilitarian Perspective

All my life I have been taught to give respect, but to give the most respect to a white man.

My father is a farmer, finished matric at a young age, worked in a couple of jobs and ended on a farm. I do not know what life is like for my father, but, I can see the scars behind his smile.

Although my father finished matric with good grades, he came from a poor family; they could not afford tertiary education. I was already born by that time and as a father, he had to provide.

My father has worked for two or three farmers in his life. He has worked on the farms for more than twelve years of his life but all the time he made it look like it was great, he put a big smile on his face and guaranteed to me that everything was okay.

Years went by, everything was yet the same. But then my father began to change, his big smile didn't look the same. I only found recently what it was like for my father to work on the farms. You get insulted and called harsh names, you are kicked and slapped on the head and treated like less of a man. All you have to do is do as you are told, no questions asked. Although it hurts so much you have to go through all the pain just to put food on the table for your children. Most farm workers are underpaid, overworked and yet they have to stay and keep on working for their families.

Who will speak up for them?

How many people worked on the farms and were unfairly dismissed?

How many of them are still called kaffir?

Racism still exists, go to the farms and let the workers speak for themselves.

Who will be the voice of the voiceless?

We will not keep quiet.

*Narratives on Social Injustices: Undergraduate Voices*, 2018

 https://doi.org/10.11647/OBP.0273.07

# 7.1 Introduction

This chapter explores the experiences of two of the twelve co-researchers on the DCR project. These two members were selected to illustrate how the Capabilities Approach can provide a more adequate evaluative frame for participatory practices and fulfil the fifth principle of the DCR frame as part of the facilitator's role. Exploring a participatory project through a capabilities lens requires more than an evaluation of general capabilities, as presented in Chapter Five. Focusing on individual valued capabilities contributes to the expansion of co-researchers' valuable freedoms, as defined by the members themselves. It also contributes to the acknowledgement of invisible power structures that operate within the group, by highlighting differences among members. In this manner, the Southern potential of the Capabilities Approach, and its capacity to acknowledge different contexts and lived experiences, is enhanced.

Hence, the two cases displayed here demonstrate the potential of a capabilities evaluation. First, a broad explanation of each member's life experiences is provided in order to better understand their valuable capabilities. Second, each member's valuable capabilities are explored in detail in order to understand why they are important and how the project has achieved these capabilities, if indeed they have. The capabilities presented for each case are distinct, according to the formulation process by the participants. Furthermore, each case concludes with a summary reflection on how the project has contributed—or not—to the enhancement of each member's capabilities, aside from the general view explored in Chapter Five.

The chapter concludes by outlining the three main contributions of the Capabilities Approach to participatory evaluations. First, it expands the informational basis of the evaluative space. It expands the evaluation from an outcome perspective (functionings) to a freedoms-outcome perspective (capabilities-functionings), giving primacy to the valued capabilities of the co-researchers to evaluate the outcome. Second, it provides an individual, centred perspective, acknowledging power structures and differences among the members, if the facilitator wishes to do so. It captures the differences between members and shows how different colonial conversion factors affect their personal capabilities before and after the process. And third, it avoids a paternalist evaluation and Northern assessments, or evaluations drafted and implemented mainly and only by external actors. The Capabilities Approach does not provide an external or foreign evaluative frame. Conversely, it constructs an individual frame based on capabilities that are contextually valuable for the members and explores whether or not a practice has achieved valued functionings.

## 7.2 Shifting Our Informational Basis

Minenhle and Siyabonga, the two cases presented here, share some common features. For example, they both study at the same university as undergraduate students, they are black, and they live in a post-1991 South African context. These features cause them to share some similarities. However, Minenhle and Siyabonga are not the same. For instance, their gender and socio-economic status are different. These differences between them truly matter when it comes to evaluating our participatory projects and fulfilling our fifth principle of the DCR project. Thus, this chapter explores each of these individual cases, in order to understand what a capabilities evaluation of our DCR practices looks like, and what it brings to participatory evaluations from a Southern perspective. This shifts our evaluation away from generalities, to focus on the specificities of the team members.

### 7.2.1 Minenhle's Story

At the time of the project, Minenhle was a young woman of twenty-one years of age in her third year of studying political science. She comes from a township close to Bloemfontein, due to the racial segregation experienced by her family in the past. The township is relatively far from the city so every time she has to go to town, including to attend her university classes, this involves taking different taxis for over two hours, and traversing not-so-secure areas of the town. Besides this, the township is a lively place and constitutes a part of Minenhle's identity.

Regarding her family, Minenhle has a stepbrother, with whom she is no longer in contact. She identifies herself as Xhosa, even though her mother is Sotho and her father Xhosa. Minenhle never had the opportunity to spend time with her father because he was incarcerated and died while she was very young. Her childhood was not easy. She remembers her mother struggling to provide, even in terms of daily meals for the family, especially after the death of her father. Eventually, her mother moved in with another man and this situation did not benefit Minenhle. Minenhle's mother and her partner verbally abused her for years. Without a doubt, Minenhle would have wished for a more supportive mother due to all the challenges she has experienced in her life, but this was not the case.

Minenhle attended a public, fees-free primary and secondary school where the unofficial language of instruction was Xhosa. Both schools were deficient in resources and did not provide an adequate education for her to be able to access higher education easily, as happens with most of the children in her township. However, she fondly remembers a teacher at the high school who was supportive and helped her during that period.

In her community, she did not have much contact with white people. During high school, she did an assignment on racism, which, to some extent, made her feel frustrated and angry towards white people, because of all the horrible stories she heard from the individuals she talked to.

At university, she chose politics and started her first course of education in English, as the first person in her family to access higher education. She wanted to study politics because it is a male-dominated field and she wanted to demonstrate to her community that a girl can make it through even if you have to study in English, as she is certain to do. This desire in particular arises from all the negative messages that she received from her immediate community and family members, but also from all the barriers that she encountered in entering the local university. Minenhle was continually told that she would end up in jail like her father, and continually reminded of her insufficient economic status to pursue the education she wanted. However, none of these comments broke Minenhle down. On the contrary, she used them as a reminder of who she did not want to become, and who she did want to be, despite these difficulties.

Her first encounter with university was after her acceptance, when she arrived there with a friend to register as a student. This friend was looking for bursaries and knew someone who could help them.

Fortunately, this person was very helpful for Minenhle too. He paid her tuition fee—because she did not have the money for it—looked for accommodation on campus, and provided her with a bursary, which covered the entire three years of her undergraduate studies. This bursary, although not huge, was fine for her. She said, 'for someone who is from my background, it is enough'. Thus, in many cases she used part of this money to help other friends and her family. However, as the year of the project (2017) was her final undergraduate year, she was worried about how to finance her postgraduate studies, because she wanted to continue studying despite being unable to pay her tuition fees or her expensive student life. Minenhle understands the importance of education as a way to challenge her background, change her future and that of her loved ones, and as a way to overcome her financial marginalisation by accessing a decent job and helping others to do so too.

Minenhle's enjoyment of being on campus did not last very long, due to the racism she encountered there multiple times during her second year. She remembers some incidents that took place outside of her residence, such as one case involving security guards, and the incident at Shimla Park.[1]

Minenhle is determined to work hard to become the person she wants to be. She wants to be the first woman to become President of South Africa. She is really determined to fight against injustices and show other people that they can do it too. She thinks that it does not matter what has happened to you in the past, or how bad it was; you should not allow these circumstances to define you or determine who you are.

In conclusion, Minenhle's story determines her own valuable and insurgent capabilities, capabilities that are highly significant for overcoming her marginalisation. The context and the historical moment into which Minenhle was born are substantial for understanding what kind of life she wants to lead and the things she wants to do, as well as what is preventing her from achieving her goals. Minenhle is similar to many students around this campus, especially the majority of first-generation black students, but also different in many cases, having experiences that have shaped her in unique ways. Therefore,

---

1    See Chapter Five for more information about the Shimla Park incident.

her capabilities choices are better understood with an awareness of these abovementioned experiences. At the time of the project, Minenhle highly valued four capabilities. These were (A) Human recognition, (B) Ubuntu, (C) Self-Development and (D) Epistemic capabilities. However, these capabilities are not static, as the insurgent term highlights, nor are they entirely separate categories. These capabilities intersect with one another through functionings.

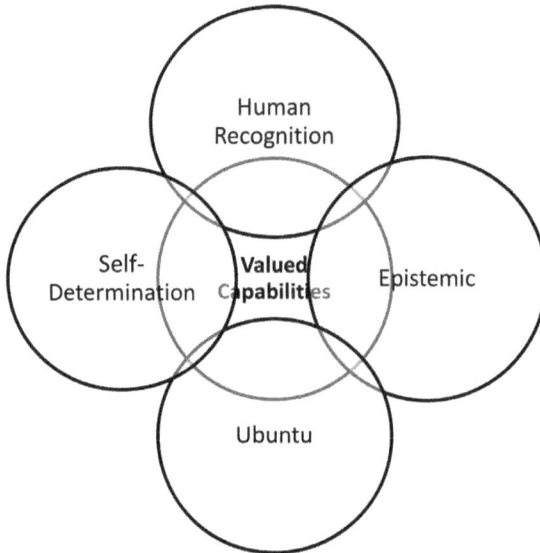

Figure 7: Minenhle's Valued Capabilities (image by the author, 2021).

The following sections will explore each of Minenhle's capabilities, first by showing why this capability is important for her and then continuing with an exploration of how the project has expanded the relevant freedom, if indeed it has.

## Human Recognition Capability

For Minenhle, human recognition is strongly linked to her life experiences and her past. The constant influence of the community, family members, and broader society on her self-perception acted as a degenerative conversion factor. Minenhle's freedom to be recognised as a full human being was significantly reduced by the derogative perceptions of her community. However, this still persists today, due to her context, and the different colonial conversion factors that make Minenhle more vulnerable than others. For instance, her racial group, gender, and financial status intersect, preventing Minenhle from exercising her own valuable capabilities, such as human recognition.

Minenhle has had multiple experiences which degraded her own self-perception; a situation which had been further reinforced by others in her immediate context. As mentioned in previous chapters, these constitute some of her colonial conversion factors as well as some of her epistemic exploitation and marginalisation (Goetze 2018). As Berenstain (2016) explores, what we are talking about here is not individual conversion factors, but rather colonial structures that gaslight individuals and distort their own perception. These undermine a person's confidence in their own understanding of reality, leading to a sense of self-doubt. In this case, Minenhle's security and self-perception are mediated by the derogative perceptions surrounding her, due to the circumstances of her life, thus minimising her own capability to value herself for who she is rather than what is around her or what people think about her.

The project had an effect on this capability. As she explained, the group was not a judgmental space; we respected each other and provided a space to value our opinions and ourselves. She said:

> 'The group... it does allow you to be yourself and obviously, they don't judge you...I never... they don't judge. That is one of the things that I love about it because I was worried...because I have this face that is like...I don't wanna talk to you...which...but...they are actually quite friendly... because at the beginning I thought...mmm...they will look at me...and...I don't know...but they are...actually...a bunch of friendly people and not so judgmental as...people that I normally meet with outside.' (second interview)

During the last interview, she said:

> 'The project did give me...some...value...in terms of...discussing certain issues and then...also being heard...also the...the other people...who I told my opinion, like how I feel about certain things...and to recognise that my opinions also do matter, like...other people's opinions...mmm... matter...' (third interview)

To a certain extent the project provided a space in which she felt relevant, and recognised as an individual who deserved to be heard. Moreover, this capability is closely related to outcomes—functionings—such as voice and participation. Minenhle wants to be an activist and participate in changing her society due to this insurgent capability. Therefore, she must acquire a position of leadership that allows her to do something about the inequalities she has experienced and continues to experience. However, the combination of different colonial conversion factors has reduced Minenhle's chances of raising her voice. Minenhle did not have many spaces or platforms in which to raise her voice or feel like a valuable person. Moreover, she did not, and does not, have appropriate spaces for active participation within the university context, nor many spaces to feel recognised and valued. She said during the interviews that, actually, the project helped her to find and use a voice for the first time:

'In the sessions I am able to say something, I have the confidence to say something and the environment allows me to say something and in classes there are a lot of people and most of them are not...so...they are very different from the normal setting that we have in the normal sessions [workshops], so I guess I would say I still don't have that confidence to say something in class but also the environment of the class does not allow you to say something because you feel like...I mean...in class...I am learning about something that I've never heard before, so...I don't really know anything and if I would say something what if they laugh at me, so...it's different in that sense and also...that in class you can say something at whatever, the topic that might be that day but he [the lecturer] being in front telling you what is right and what is wrong, so you can't really say "Sir I feel like this theory is wrong," or whatever, so it's different in that sense.' (second interview)

She said that the project had not only helped her to talk within the project meetings but also outside of them, and therefore it enhanced this valuable capability:

'It has helped with my confidence, just being able to speak in front of people and tell them my perspective confidently [...] It builds that thing of...if I can tell this to these people about this and that, then I am able to do so outside of the session which, it really helps.' (third interview)

She continues:

'So it also helped...in that because, now I'm able to stand up...for myself or for other people, [...] I'm able to participate on campus...with such things...like res [student residence], when they talk about...whatever that is happening, like feminism, I'm able to take a leadership position and stand up for what I know [...] Yeah...that's after...after...joining the project, when the project started...because before then I wasn't so vocal, I know...I know that I am...umm...I'm opinionated but most of the time, I keep that to myself...I felt...felt...something about a certain issue...I just keep it to myself or I just say it to a close friend...so that's how...I feel...that's not right...it really helped in giving me the confidence to...to stand up...not just knowing that...sorry...it gave me the confidence to... stand up in front of other people and tell them how...I feel about certain things...so yeah...it really helped.' (third interview)

The project not only helped Minenhle to find her voice and expand her participation freedoms in different spaces (as achieved functionings), but also expanded her capability of recognition, despite the degenerative colonial conversion factors surrounding her. In addition, the group helped her to be proactive in exploring issues that affected her from a leadership and activism point of view. For Minenhle, racism was really important due to her past experiences and the injustices surrounding her. To a certain extent, the project's research focus on racism provided her with a platform to explore these issues. While her context does not allow her and other students to openly discuss it due to colonial conversion factors, the project allowed her and the other members to openly discuss these issues:

'Race, I find race very relevant because of the current situation in... generally in the country, not only at the university. I find it relevant, which is something that I feel, it's something that needs to be discussed more, and not suppress it like it's not there, because it is there.' (second interview)

In conclusion, it seems that Minenhle was not able to fully exercise her recognition capability, and this impeded her from raising her voice among many other functionings. Therefore, this diminished her active participation in matters that were important to her, and also restricted her possibilities of achieving a position of leadership, which Minenhle valued. Conversely, the project acted as an interruption between some of her colonial conversion factors and her capabilities. She achieved certain functionings, and it also helped her to enhance her capability. Nevertheless, it must be said that this capability expansion is neither complete, nor perfect. It is actually fluid, according to both past experiences and future experiences that are yet to come for Minenhle. Human recognition was compromised by Minenhle's experiences and her own personal perceptions, and exacerbated by her marginalisation. The project helped her to understand herself differently and to achieve certain functionings, as well as considerably expanding her freedom. However, Minenhle still has to deal with the context and the society that surrounds her, which, to some extent, can limit her recognition capability in the present and the future.

## Ubuntu Capability

As Minenhle did not have her mother's support, nor care from the community or many family members, she highly valued support and care, due to her lack of this capability. One can see, however, that this capability was not entirely absent, as evidenced in the examples she provided of people who had given care, such as her secondary education teacher or the person that helped her to get a bursary for her higher-education studies. However, to a certain extent, this lack of care and support has continued throughout her current student life and the experiences that she has encountered when living in a new environment, so much so that her marginalisation is clear. Much of Minenhle's survival on campus depends on the people surrounding her and their willingness to support her in diverse matters. Nevertheless, the urgency of this for Minenhle does not necessarily mean that the context will automatically provide her with this substantial freedom. Conversely, as Minenhle's self-perception was diminished due to colonial conversion factors in place, this has influenced the way in which she engages with other students and individuals, directly affecting this Ubuntu capability, not necessarily as a giver but mostly as a receiver.

The research group provided a supportive space where many of the members were like family for her. Even though the purpose of us coming together was to implement our research, the members were also there to assist with personal issues. Minenhle said:

> 'When we come to varsity and we meet new people, or some of them, obviously... you meet different people, some of them were good for you, some of them not so much... they are just there for the sake of being there, and then... they don't really bring value into your life, but the

project... enabled me to meet some of the most amazing people who... have taught me so much about... even... about things... outside of the project like we do... talk about other things like life generally, so it did help in terms of affiliation... having that support, knowing that, if you need something sometime you are able to call one of the people within the group.' (third interview)

Minenhle also talked about how difficult it was for her to have female friends, and how the project helped her to meet other girls and challenged her own stereotypes,

'I normally say to people like... I don't get along with girls, I don't really have good friends who are girls... no... umm... but meeting the different girls in the group... like... it really taught me something, that not every girl is the same, not every girl is too dramatic... or... yeah [...] so... meeting... having those friendships with them, was really great and amazing... we always get along, which is something that I'm not used to... so yeah.' (third interview)

Moreover, the project helped Minenhle to understand herself differently, as seen in the previous capability. This contributed towards changing the way she usually relates to others, facilitating her affiliation, at least with the group members. She said:

'Actually, I cannot wait... for sure I cannot wait to... to... see them again... which is quite... which is quite interesting. Because one would say that... I am not comfortable with people that I live with, but I am not so comfortable with them, I am more comfortable with the group, which also they... they give you that thing to value yourself more... so yeah... yeah.' (second interview)

All of this permitted Minenhle to establish support networks that are basic and necessary for her to overcome the many colonial conversion factors that affect her life negatively. She said:

'In the group I know there's at least one or two people that I can actually come and say ehh, I don't have food, do you have food? Can I have... do you know what I mean... so that they're very supportive.' (second interview)

These networks helped her in different ways, as a way to ensure primary needs, as food security, but also to get valuable information about bursaries and knowledge that can benefit her in the future. She said:

> 'Yeah... it also helped, like finding bursaries... and... umm... just having the help... knowing people... like you who know where I can get certain knowledge about bursaries... or help with my academic work, or yeah... in terms of that it did... help.' (second interview)

And:

> 'Knowing that [the facilitator] can know where to find bursaries, finding what what what or what what... it was helpful... instead of being alone... not having someone to tell you that if you have financial problems you have to go to this institution or whatever place. It maybe... so it was relevant as well.' (third interview)

Therefore, Minenhle was able to expand this capability due to the project and achieved it through different functionings. Her enrolment in the group provided her with supportive networks. Nevertheless, this also expanded her capability for creating meaningful friendships and accessing networks of support in different ways, thus challenging the way she used to relate to others, at least in the university space and with this particular group.

## *Self-Development Capability*

The self-development capability discussed here supports the development of one's valuable life through critical thinking, which is closely related to Minenhle's case and her life experiences, particularly the negative social stereotypes that have been present in her life, and her desire to change her past and secure her capabilities in the future.

Minenhle's self-development was not a capability that was absent before the project. Her story says a lot about how she managed to overcome the negative effects of colonial conversion factors in her life. Her resilience and perseverance highlighted how this capability was available and how it was achieved, as evidenced in her desire to be different and her success in making drastic changes in her life, and becoming the first person to access higher education in her family.

Despite this capability already being available for her, the project managed to expand it a little further. She said, 'it really has changed me, it changed me, myself... yeah... because I got to learn, emotionally, intellectually, learn something about myself that I didn't know, so yeah...' (third interview). This is also evident in the second interview, when she stated, 'yeah... it helps your growth' (second interview).

To a certain extent, the project not only helped her to gain knowledge which had an impact on her, but also to learn from the time spent together and the shared experiences, so as to form an idea of who she is and what she wants for the future. She said:

> 'the group really motivated me to work hard, to better myself, be open-minded and not judge people because of their mistakes, or because of who they are and really... yeah... just be open-minded about... about things.' (third interview)

Minenhle was determined to lead her life in the way she wanted. However, the project expanded the information available to her in order to assess that life. Equally, it provided her with the spaces to achieve (functionings) some of her personal aims, for instance, the possibility to learn more about the issues that concerned her, or to provide her with an adequate platform to fight against these injustices in various ways.

## Epistemic Capability

For Minenhle, this capability is key, not only as an end, but also as a means of achieving other things that she wants to in her life. Ultimately, Minenhle wants to know more about the things she is passionate about, she wants to expand her critical thinking and be able to challenge her assumptions. On the other hand, Minenhle considers this capability as essential for her financial freedom, especially when talking about formal learning, and the educational system that has excluded her family for generations. Minenhle's life conditions did not make it easy for her to access higher education. There have been many colonial conversion factors on the way and others continue to exist. Nevertheless, she highly values her education as a way to gain the necessary skills and knowledge to access a job that can provide for her and her family economically, and, therefore, to challenge her present and past situation.

However, the university context was not always as open and plural as Minenhle wished. Colonial conversion factors such as the racism Minenhle experienced and the hierarchical structure of the institution, along with her gender, limited her capability to learn from other students and share her own knowledge, not to mention her opportunity to learn beyond Eurocentric frames favoured by the institution.

On this matter, the project provided Minenhle with a space for mutual learning as giver and receiver of epistemic materials (Fricker 2015). She said:

> 'It's been good... mmm... I've learnt a lot, especially from the other participants, yeah... It's been really great and really helpful.' (second interview)

This space for learning and gaining knowledge from each other was significant for her. Equally, hearing different perspectives from diverse individuals, among the group members and beyond, helped her to expand her own thinking, as well as to share her own knowledge with others:

> 'The people that we met and the team as well. Meeting the different individuals that I met, my knowledge... I was able to share my knowledge with them, and they also shared what they know, their knowledge, with me. So that allowed me to have a broader... umm... perspective on certain things... getting... having knowledge about... for example Kungawo... telling us about the LGBTQI community... which I didn't know what it meant... I didn't know... I didn't know fully what they go through [...] having other people that explained such things... to you, the knowledge they pass to you was really vital because you are able to think critically in the future.' (third interview)

On the other hand, as noted above, this capability is a means for Minenhle. Higher education can help her to achieve the dignified life that was denied to her family due to unfair existing colonial structures, which limited their access to sufficient financial means. In this way, the project had academic benefits for her, but it also provided her with skills that might be helpful for her employability in the future. In terms of academic benefits, she said:

> 'You talked to us about different methodologies, it was very important to me to know that, because I've been failing my assignments, so it was really important to me. Because it really helped me a lot. It helped me a lot with my assignments, because I always failed my assignments and for the first time I got above 60%.' (second interview)

Access to the epistemic system of the university was essential for her due to her hermeneutic marginalisation (Goetze 2018). Knowing how knowledge is produced in these institutions and somehow starting to become an active contributor affected this capability positively, as seen in the passing of her assignments. Moreover, the project also helped Minenhle to develop different skills, such as academic writing, research, or the use of different software that was useful for her studies, all of which increase her prospects of a career in the future:

> 'It did... especially in terms of... writing my assignments, it... it was an improvement with my references thing, how I go about my assignments... although I still have a lot of work to do, but it really helped me with writing my assignments, and doing research... so it helped me in that instance.' (third interview)

She continued:

> 'Definitely, definitely, timing... umm... Writing skills, critical thinking skills... umm... just... communication skills. And also the different programs... that you taught us how to use... that is gonna be really helpful [...]. The editing one, the video and also the one that you, that you normally do, like... voice thingy and then, you transcribe.' (third interview)

Minenhle not only expanded knowledge useful for her studies, but also knowledge helpful for her future, receiving and sharing knowledge as a multidirectional relationship with others; some aspects being more instrumental and others being ends in themselves. This is important because, as highlighted by her experiences, many colonial factors impede her from accessing epistemic systems such as the academic one, as well as from considering herself a worthy testifier and contributor to the pool of knowledge (Fricker 2015), which is essential for her identified capability. Moreover, the project allowed her to challenge her assumptions about those things that were important to her and others, in a space of mutual learning, bringing her self-development capability and epistemic capability into conversation with one another.

## Minenhle's Incomplete Story

Minenhle's story is an incomplete story, but that incompleteness does not impede us from understanding her circumstances, improvements and limitations. That is why, after this section which has explored the minor details of her capabilities choices, we can say that there are significant improvements in her Ubuntu and human recognition capabilities. Both of these capabilities were strongly affected by the conditions in which Minenhle lived, which impeded her enjoyment of them. For instance, we can see how colonial conversion factors produced negative effects in these freedoms before she began the project, as for instance in her educational background, due to her socio-economic background intersecting with other features such as her gender. During and after the project, we can see significant variations according to her own perceptions, as explored in the previous section. This is not to say that these freedoms are now available, but that she has managed to enhance them thanks to the fact that she and others in the research project have achieved certain functionings.

Equally, regarding her self-development and epistemic capabilities, we see how these are intrinsically linked in Minenhle's case. Minenhle came to the project already enjoying these freedoms in some way. Her self-development freedom was very evident, despite the degenerative conversion factors surrounding her, although it certainly grew somewhat during the project thanks to the contribution of her epistemic capability. We could also see that her epistemic capability was not absent, since she had managed to enter a higher-education institution despite her background. She clearly possessed and shared valuable knowledge before the project. Nevertheless, we can appreciate variation according to her perceptions, as reflecting about her enhancement of voice and participation. I will now introduce our second story, that of Siyabonga.

## 7.2.2 Siyabonga's Story

Siyabonga is a twenty-two-year-old male born in the Free State, who has lived in different parts of the country throughout his life. He is the middle of three siblings and maintains a good relationship with both his parents and his brothers. His father holds a higher-education degree and works as a consultant, providing for the family. His mother worked as a primary school teacher until he was born, then she dedicated herself to the children and home as a housewife. All three siblings, he and his two brothers, went to private primary and secondary schools, with English as the language of instruction. At home, all his basic needs were covered. However, Siyabonga's father was absent at important moments during his childhood, due to work commitments. Moreover, Siyabonga's mother suffered from depression, leaving Siyabonga with a deep concern for mental health.

He enrolled in various sports during his academic life, such as rugby, cricket, action cricket and squash. Thanks to these sports, he had the opportunity to travel overseas for tournaments. However, Siyabonga's childhood was not always easy, despite his well-off financial situation. As a black child enjoying a certain financial comfort, it occasionally put him in uncomfortable situations. Colonial conversion factors in South Africa work multidirectionally, and his economic comfort did not fully inhibit any negative impact on his freedoms, although it affected him differently than Minenhle. For instance, black friends accused him of being too white—in terms of lifestyle and comfort—and white students did not like the idea that he was going out with black friends. All of this situated him in an identity loophole, which still persists today.

Around the time of his matric year (the final year of high school in South Africa), he was very busy working alongside his studies and his mother had some health issues which affected him deeply, leading Siyabonga to fail matric. Thus, he had to repeat a year to increase his marks. In the end, in order to access the degree he wanted to study, he had to go through the extended programme at the university.[2]

In addition, Siyabonga did not play a very active role during his application process. His parents decided which university to send him to and took care of his application. His parents wanted him to stay away from distractions, so he could focus on his studies. Equally, his parents provided economic support for his education, giving him a monthly allowance, schooling materials, accommodation, transport and tuition fees.

Siyabonga enjoys his student life, especially during the year of the study (2017). He is relaxed as he is only studying a few modules. However, he is worried as he is repeating the modules he failed last year and this will be his last chance to continue with his studies. Actually, Siyabonga wants to finish his degree for his parents, to give them peace of mind that he can provide for himself. Nevertheless, he is thinking

---

2    The extended degree programme involves students who have insufficient access points upon entering the university. This programme adds an additional year to the mainstream degree.

about studying for an Honours degree while working in a bank, but he thinks there is no rush; he can always go back to his parents' house. Siyabonga is also considering saving for a few years while working as an accountant, and then investing that money to create an income. He also wants to create a company and become a CEO at some point in the future. In this way, he will be able to help his girlfriend's family and build big houses in which they can all live close to each other—his family and his girlfriend's family, along with them.

In this case, Siyabonga has a different compilation of valuable capabilities when compared to Minenhle, and less insurgent capabilities linked to his context and colonial conversion factors. He considered the following to be important capabilities: (A) Ubuntu, (B) Epistemic, (C) Human recognition, (D) Free time and leisure, and (E) Health.

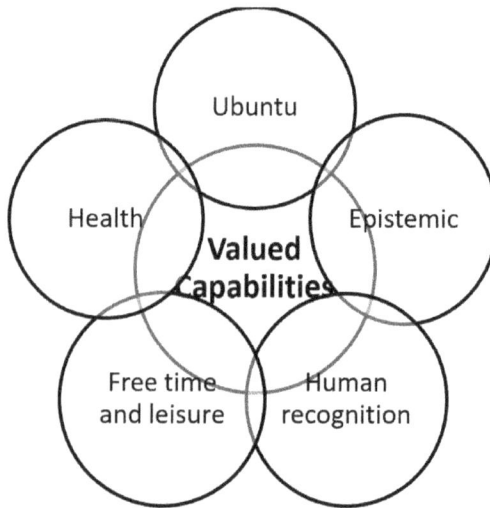

Figure 8: Siyabonga's Valued Capabilities (image by the author, 2021).

Like Minenhle, his capabilities are not clearly separated; they are interconnected. Hence, to explore these capabilities one by one, the following section investigates Siyabonga's capabilities and whether or not the project helped him to enhance or achieve them, exploring the colonial conversion factors that affected his valued capabilities, especially his conditions as a middle-class black student in South Africa.

## Human Recognition Capability

For Siyabonga, the capability of recognition was not absent in his life, or affected to the extent that it was in Minenhle's case. Siyabonga enjoyed a good, secure self-perception that influenced his way of approaching others. This positive self-perception also helped him to share and defend his opinions easily. In particular, his economic status and gender benefitted this capability in various ways. All of this was visible in the way that Siyabonga behaved within the group and the number of times Siyabonga intervened to give his opinion, in comparison to Minenhle.

Nevertheless, although Siyabonga's case differs greatly from that of Minenhle, the Capabilities Approach allows us to explore both cases deeply, uncovering colonial conversion factors that impede Siyabonga—to a much lesser extent than Minenhle—from fully enjoying his capability of recognition. In this case, Siyabonga valued his recognition capability not because of the low enjoyment of this capability in his life—as was the case for Minenhle—but due to certain structural, mainly colonial, challenges that prevented him from enhancing this capability to an even greater extent. These are nuances that will be difficult to identify without carefully exploring each case.

In Siyabonga's case, two major colonial conversion factors negatively affect his enjoyment of this capability. First, despite his comfortable socio-economic status, he still falls into the category of black, in a post-1991 context in South Africa, which is a clear colonial conversion factor (Mattes 2015). While he is able to enjoy this capability to a certain level, he still lacks certain aspects of this human recognition, due to the race structures surrounding him. Secondly, he is situated in a hierarchical and patriarchal society where respect for elders is a social imperative, especially for males, and this ultimately affects him negatively. As a young man, Siyabonga has to respect those who are older than him and show them respect to a point that diminishes his own recognition from other individuals.

To provide some examples of these structures that somewhat reduce Siyabonga's recognition capability, the text will first highlight some racial challenges in Siyabonga's life. Siyabonga spoke about incidents in high school:

'When I got to the school I was in, I was one of four or five black kids, but in Grade Ten I was like the only black kid, so I was like almost being indoctrinated into being a part of the whites, and seen as a white guy. So, because I was in a black school before I went to the white school, when my black friends came, I obviously still wanted to hang out with them. It wasn't because now I'm only around white people, I don't wanna hang out with them... like I'm better or whatnot. But that caused a lot of troubles in my life, because the white people were angry or my white friends were angry because I wanted to hang out with the black friends and the black friends were angry because they said I was too white, and I didn't understand their issues.' (third interview)

For Siyabonga, recognition was significant due to his identity challenges, and less related to self-perception and voice, as it was in Minenhle's case. To a certain extent, colonial conversion factors, such as racial division, do not allow individuals to be recognised above and beyond these racial categories. Therefore, due to Siyabonga's circumstances, he has to battle against both.

However, despite the double recognition Siyabonga deals with, at the end of the day his skin is still dark in South Africa, and therefore he does not have as much freedom as he would like to voice his opinions, especially when they are related to racial issues, because of colonial conversion factors:

'Back then... the people in power, the white people... if you ask too many questions, if you... if you... are talking too much, don't expect to be around next week, that's the truth about it... You will be killed or... whatnot... so... you know... also the older parents... who know how it was and how it still is. Kids keep quiet, you don't know... these people might not be happy with you talking about it... things might happen to you or whatever... so I think it is also a precautionary matter, like being careful what you say. You might say the wrong thing, to the wrong person, or about the wrong person, and things would happen.' (third interview)

Siyabonga did not generally lack this capability, as Minenhle did, but he was especially affected by his racial classification in the country, and the fact that he could not openly talk or make his opinions on social injustice heard, due to his country's past.

On the other hand, despite Siyabonga's gender, there are other hierarchical and patriarchal structures that can affect him, such as the issue of respect towards elders, or the educational level of the person he is talking to. These structures constrain the recognition of young voices and opinions, such as those of Siyabonga and Minenhle, to a much greater extent than those youth voices in the Global North. Explaining what would happen if he gave his opinion about racism to another adult person, he said:

> 'Ah... you are disrespecting me! Ah, you young people are disrespecting me! How can you ask? I'm your elder... whether you are right to ask or not. I am your elder, you should not be asking questions like that... yeah... it's one of those... taboos... you know.' (third interview)

Regarding educational level, he mentions having had a conversation with his father, who is highly educated, and how ridiculous it feels to him to talk from his position:

> 'Or for instance maybe speaking to my father about something like that... I wouldn't say dangerous but a little bit of... because of my dad is... highly educated or whatnot... He would say... hey you are naive, naive in your train of thought or whatnot... you know it's like when you speak... when you are speaking to like a rocket scientist but all you have is like grade eight math you... so how do I factorise? He is gonna be like... Ah... this is so beneath me.' (second interview)

Additionally, he mentioned a debate on the radio, which asked the audience whether students should or should not participate in political debates. He said, 'there was a topic on the radio the other day, it was speaking about should it be okay, or should students even be allowed to argue about politics? Because they are students!' (third interview). Actually, Siyabonga knew and had the voice to say that he had a right to discuss many of these political issues, despite contextual constraints. However, he identified the project as helping him to discuss sensitive issues that would be difficult for him to explore in other contexts, or outside of the project:

> 'How can I not debate that or speak about it? So... because I am a student I'm not allowed to speak about it... so... It [the project] helped me because I could speak about it, you know, yeah... it certainly enlightened me, it made me more aware, but it was also exciting because, I mean, it was... getting to work with people on topics that are quite hard, it's still... not really accepted in society [...] Those were the topics that we were looking at... so... yeah... it was exciting because I would say that was a taboo. Or... but it was exciting... when we get to talk about something that we are not allowed to talk about... and yeah.' (third interview)

Siyabonga's case is very different from Minenhle's case. While Minenhle had an initially low level of this human recognition that was significantly expanded by the project, Siyabonga, on the contrary, enjoyed more freedoms in terms of recognition due to his socio-economic status and gender. In Minenhle's case, self-confidence, voice, and participation were essential to enhance this capability. However, for Siyabonga, it was more a matter of identity and voice, referring to being able to discuss sensitive issues but also being recognised as a worthy member in a racially divided community (Cornell & Kessi 2017; Sutherland 2013). Therefore, the Capabilities Approach is able to mark an initial stage before the project and explore the transitions of different individuals. Moreover, a capabilities perspective is able to appreciate the redistribution of power and its implications for capability expansion and achievement within a group. While Siyabonga could not achieve a higher level of this capability, his presence as a member of the group contributed to the expansion of this capability in others. As highlighted in the previous sections, this is because capabilities are not stable categories; they are collective capabilities (Ibrahim 2006):

> 'I'm being recognised for what I believe in... I am being recognised and I'm recognising them or we are recognising each other. [...] No... you know... but in terms of a group... I think... yeah... we do... recognise each other and respect each other... that I think is great.' (second interview)

In this case, Minenhle and other members found themselves in a space where someone who was a male, went to a private school and did not have financial problems, was listening to them, recognising them and their opinions, thus, other individuals' freedoms were also being influenced.

## Ubuntu Capability

Without any doubt, when Siyabonga arrived at the project he enjoyed this capability, especially financial support, which was scarce among the members of the group. However, emotional support was notably deficient for him in the case of his family:

> 'I don't go to school with a bursary, my parents pay for me. So... you know... it just does... looking at the differences like, there are kids that are with a bursary, even my girlfriend is with a bursary. But I'm not...

but like my girlfriend her mum calls every day you know like they have that connection. I am financially stable, but I don't have that connection.' (second interview)

This emotional deficiency caused Siyabonga to give special importance to friendships, creating his own networks to fulfil the emotional support he needed in different ways. However, at times this was not easy, especially given Siyabonga's battle between two social groups that were antagonistic. Conversely, the project helped him to make new friendships, to engage with a group of people without it mattering where he came from:

> 'When I got to the group, we were strangers but we ended up being those people in each others' lives, who... umm... can care and support each other, especially... because we were disclosing personal, harmful... or... ahh... I don't know. If I can say... private things about ourselves... things that we felt and pains... so... we are those people for each other now... those friends that we are caring for and supporting each other.' (third interview)

Siyabonga enjoyed support within the project, in the sense that the issues he had in terms of identity were no longer issues in that space. The group was a family despite the colour of our skin, our socio-economic status, religion or nationality, even if we were conscious of our positionalities as blacks or whites. This allowed Siyabonga to create support networks easily, as well as supporting others and enhancing their freedoms.

To a certain extent, the project was also financially supportive, providing a small but significant contribution to the members. Siyabonga explained how he helped other friends and therefore this money was really useful for him. For Siyabonga, it was also important to care for and support others, beyond getting the support he needed, as this Ubuntu capability is conceptualised:

> 'There have been a couple of times that I've lent my friend my allowance, it was half of my allowance this month... so like I've been broke the past week so like you know this hundred bucks would be great cause I thought I'd like some cool drink, maybe I'll get some milk and some tea or whatever... and now I can go and get those things.' (second interview)

Therefore, Siyabonga was not lacking this capability in any way before the project. Conversely, this available capability allowed him to support others financially, while receiving emotional support in return. Thus, the project enhanced this capability, achieving some functionings through his new friendships within the group, the help that he was able to provide to others, and the help received from other members in the group.

## *Epistemic Capability*

Siyabonga's case differs greatly from that of Minenhle. Minenhle had extensive experiential knowledge about injustices, as she experienced them in different ways. Moreover, Minenhle understood knowledge as an end in itself, in the sense of being able to learn and to gain knowledge for knowledge's sake, not only as a means of ensuring a good life (which was nonetheless also important for her). Siyabonga has a more instrumental perspective of knowledge. He wants to gain knowledge in order to be able to provide a decent standard of living for his family and himself, especially for his girlfriend's family. For instance, he wants to pass his courses in order to be an accountant, and therefore have a stable job and good income. Moreover, this educational success was especially relevant for him because, despite having access to a first-class education, he was—and is—not doing so well in his academic work. Therefore, for him, knowledge for passing his courses and graduating was his main concern at the time of the project.

Nevertheless, it seems that the project provided him with a platform to reconsider knowledge beyond its instrumental advantages. Siyabonga said that the project provided an adequate space to expand his learning and knowledge in general:

> 'Looking at epistemologies and whatnot... methodologies. Actually doing research. So I feel like... I got to do a lot of learning and gain knowledge... that's not... although it's formal... education... formal... we were just coming and speaking to each other, doing a research project in our own time... so I feel like I learned a lot from the research project... from that aspect...' (second interview)

However, he also added that it was a space in which to challenge his own thinking and challenge other's opinions, and he enjoyed this aspect because it was actually something that he would not do in other company:

'I really enjoyed the workshops, yeah... I really enjoyed talking to other people... ahh... I... yes, you could say the joyful environment... where... you were challenging yourself and they were willing to challenge you... we really were able to... really... critically analyse stuff that maybe when you are with your friends, you wouldn't talk so deeply about... or whatnot... so I really enjoyed that.' (third interview)

Siyabonga had not previously been exposed to discussions about social issues in particular. To a certain extent, his lifestyle and undergraduate studies on finance limited his ability to engage critically with these types of challenges. The project expanded his knowledge of some of these matters. For Siyabonga, his learning about gender and LGBTQI inequalities was especially noteworthy, as he had not been aware of them before the project. For instance, he reflected on his positionality as a man:

'I don't know, looking at it in terms of gender... I'm a man, so I'm unintentionally, I'm already causing an inequality because of my... I can... you can say, the patriarchy or whatever... it's because I'm a man [...] it's something to learn from the project... or it was something that we help each other to understand.' (third interview)

Although Siyabonga presented very conservative ideas about gender roles and sexual orientation at the beginning of the year, the project helped him to challenge these assumptions and reflect on his own positionality. Equally, he had the chance to better understand the lives of other students:

'I feel like it's... it's just the way to remind myself that there are people out there struggling or whatnot... who would kill for the opportunity to be where I am so just keep working hard even if days are tough even if you feel like not studying just remember that one day something might depend on you... you know... because you went to school you have a salary, maybe you could send the kids to school, whatever, or do something so now that you're there try your best at what you are doing [...] Definitely, yeah... and learn more from them, not just look at them, like it was just a bad life experience.' (third interview)

However, despite the general knowledge about social issues surrounding him, Siyabonga valued learning useful skills for the future, skills that might enhance his capacity to find a secure job. He mentioned different skills developed by the project that could help him in the future in various ways, 'I guess the main thing I learned is being able to use the PC better, the laptop a lot better...' (third interview).

He added that team work was also an important skill gained from the project:

> 'I did definitely learn how to work in a team, because we have to work on a research project together. So I really got to learn the dynamics of working together in a team and working with people and working specifically with people that are doing different things so there are many different challenges... umm... and barriers... that get in the way of teamwork, and I really got to learn how to combat those barriers, umm... but ultimately it was about learning to work with people toward a common aim, and I feel like I definitely got to learn that from the DCR project.' (third interview)

Siyabonga not only gained knowledge that will benefit him in the future and will be applicable for other things that he considers important in his life. He also started to value knowledge for the sake of learning about—and understanding—the reality that surrounds him, and the many injustices that impact other members of his community, thanks to being part of the group and listening to others.

### Free Time and Leisure Capability

Siyabonga highly valued the capability of enjoying free time and time to dedicate to things outside his formal responsibilities. He valued his free time, and dedicated it to playing sports, as well as playing music with his friends. To a certain extent, Siyabonga enjoys and achieves this capability in various ways thanks to his family's socio-economic status and the circumstances surrounding him.

In this regard, the project allowed Siyabonga to enjoy his free time doing something that was significant for him. He did not consider the work done during the project as a job or a responsibility, but conversely as a leisure activity, and something that he was interested in:

> 'Although we were working on the project... it was a less stressful environment... where I was... still learning and increasing my knowledge... I was still participating and interacting with other students, not just people. And ultimately, you can see it as leisure time that we have spent, or easy time in terms of... I was doing something, that I was actually interested in... and at the end of the day—a hobby or something—you are doing something you are interested in... that

doesn't pretend necessarily to be work... that's very serious or stressful.' (third interview)

Therefore, the project in itself did not significantly expand this freedom for Siyabonga, as he already enjoyed the right circumstances for this capability in his life. Conversely, it could be said that the project helped him to achieve certain functionings related to this capability, such as being able to enrol in a leisure activity other than his formal education and existing hobbies.

## Health Capability

Siyabonga did not suffer from any serious illness, although his life was marked by his mother's mental health. This situation, together with the lack of emotional support previously mentioned, caused Siyabonga to highly value health in general, particularly the balance between mental and physical health. In this case, Siyabonga's capabilities, especially his free time and leisure and health capabilities, are related to his middle-class status in South Africa. These capabilities (free time and leisure and health) highlight how some communities have accessed and adopted capitalist, middle-class lifestyles, as well as the language to situate themselves in the society they live in, despite conserving certain other capabilities—such as insurgent capabilities—to struggle against their past and present experiences. Hence, Siyabonga experiences and makes sense of his life and valued freedoms in different terms than Minenhle does.

It is certain that his health capability was not expanded by the project, due to the nature of our work. However, this case can be seen as part of—or related to—the expansion of emotional support in the previous capability and how this has improved Siyabonga's general well-being. Thus, although both cases may refer to similar ideas, the context, conditions and understandings of their lives lead them to conceptualise these features within different categories. The middle-class status of Siyabonga influences his cosmovision as well as his capabilities and insurgent capabilities. For a black, middle-class undergraduate student, whose mother previously required counselling services, well-being might be associated with psychology and with health. Conversely, for Minenhle this is a self-development aspect and Ubuntu-related dimension that tells an individual to become better than they were and contribute to the betterment of others in the face of colonial oppression and its associated colonial conversion factors.

### *Siyabonga's Incomplete Story*

Siyabonga's story tells us that before becoming part of the project, his conditions were quite favourable. His capabilities were already there, to a lesser or greater extent. Siyabonga enjoyed his leisure and free time capability, along with the health capability, despite his mother's issues: they were possible because of the new, middle-class perspective to which Siyabonga was exposed. Furthermore, his human recognition, Ubuntu and epistemic capabilities were fairly protected by the conditions in which he had grown up, with some insurgent capabilities that reflected the oppression Siyabonga experienced despite his family having overcome the economic oppression of their elders. Despite some favourable conditions, we have seen that Siyabonga also experienced colonial conversion factors that diminished some of these capabilities for him, although not to the same extent as Minenhle. Siyabonga experienced discrimination from his friends and had to battle between two antagonistic identities in a difficult context such as South Africa, as is evident in his capabilities choices (Bhana 2014). Nevertheless, we can see how Siyabonga also benefitted from the project in some ways, although again to a different extent than Minenhle did. First of all, he was able to enhance his epistemic capability, enhancing his factual knowledge about certain matters, but also valuing knowledge in its own right. Furthermore, his human recognition was enhanced thanks to the relations between the members of the group, but also thanks to his Ubuntu capability of being able to help others, even if this was not always achieved in the exact way he wanted.

## 7.3 Discussing the DCR Contributions to a More Adequate Southern Participatory Evaluative Framework

The two cases presented above have highlighted that, actually, the same participatory process can affect diverse members of the same group differently. Thus, their experiences are divergent due to their personal backgrounds and the actual conditions under which they live. Participants begin the project with different valuable and insurgent capabilities, which they also enjoy to different degrees, as has been shown. Siyabonga and Minenhle both valued the Ubuntu capability, although the ways in which they enjoyed this capability before the project differed, and this is important to understand when assessing our participatory practices. The Capabilities Approach as a way to evaluate participatory practices adds a broader range of information that can capture Southern cosmovisions. This range of information not only expanded our own understanding of the DCR practice, but also oriented the practice as a way to improve the lives that the individuals involved have reason to value in different contexts, and with different aspirations.

Moreover, the Capabilities Approach does not simplify outcomes into a polarised distribution of advantaged versus disadvantaged. Conversely, it recognises the complexity of both cases. First, it shows us that, despite the better-off situation of Siyabonga, and the limited capabilities of Minenhle, both cases are worth exploring carefully, as different colonial conversion factors affect them in different ways. Thus, we need to understand these cases from a broader informational perspective that can capture how similar conditions affect different individuals. It can be generally said that the project has been more beneficial for Minenhle than Siyabonga. A capabilities analysis helps us to identify the complexities buried in our participatory practices and to show how individual personal experiences and challenges intersect with them, as well as how one individual's capabilities interact with the capabilities of others. This is basically to acknowledge that participants are not the same, by highlighting power dynamics within the group and how members of the participatory group are positioned in wider society, therefore acknowledging their own social and cultural specificities.

In conclusion, after a careful review of these two cases in this chapter, and the general analysis provided in Chapter Five, four main contributions can be highlighted, to defend the need for the facilitator to explore capabilities, but also to highlight the importance of capabilities in other participatory practices. From a capabilities perspective, these contributions are important for understanding the impact on co-researchers. The capabilities perspective contributes to the evaluation of participatory practices because it expands the informational basis of the evaluative space, through greater sensitivity to Southern perspectives. The evaluative space therefore moves beyond the tangible effects (achieved functionings) of participatory practices on a particular individual. For instance, without this perspective we would not have been able to understand Minenhle's individual definition of the human recognition capability, nor would we have known that this capability was important for her at that moment of her life as a reaction to certain colonial conversion factors affecting her capabilities. Equally, we would not have taken into consideration the initial positions of Minenhle or Siyabonga, which would have restricted our knowledge of their specific backgrounds prior to the project, and which would thereby narrow our understanding of the effects of the project on their valuable and insurgent capabilities.

The Capabilities Approach provides an individual and collective perspective. As the chapter has revealed, this can acknowledge both power asymmetries and freedoms of the co-researchers. The outcome of the same participatory practice might differ considerably among individual co-researchers. Hence, individuals and contextual group capabilities should remain at the centre of our exploration, with a particular focus on the lives they have reason to value, in order to recognise Southern perspectives. Thus, we, as facilitators, must ensure a deeply relational space in order to enhance and to achieve the capabilities that are important to them. The evaluative space does not aim to compare, but rather to explore and understand each case and its own complexities. It does so, as this chapter has examined, by not homogenising contexts and cultural aspirations. It does not simply say that the project has been more beneficial for Minenhle, but rather that it has been more beneficial for Minenhle in terms of the way she wants to lead her life.

Therefore, as with the previous point, it avoids paternalistic evaluations and Eurocentric assessments. Whereas evaluative spaces are mostly framed as determined by criteria external to the co-researchers and their contexts, the Capabilities Approach offers a set of criteria that are determined by the individual. These criteria, the valuable and insurgent capabilities that the individual has reason to value to lead the life they want to have, constitute the cultural and contextual evaluative space. Hence, this process contributes to the co-researchers' aims as opposed to external, institutional or universal aims, which are secondary or less relevant to their own lives, contexts and specific circumstances.

## 7.4 Conclusion

This chapter has explored two different stories, through two members of the DCR group. These two individuals presented different preferences, and therefore diverse valuable capabilities, at the beginning of the project. Each case has been analysed, exposing whether or not the project helped them to enhance their freedoms (valuable/insurgent capabilities), or to achieve functionings (tangible outcomes). Therefore, the chapter has revealed that adding a capabilities perspective to our evaluative space for DCR, following the fifth principle of the facilitator's role, is a gain in itself. It substantially changes the way we understand our evaluative spaces, orienting them towards the co-researchers' aims, and contextualising our participatory projects beyond institutional or universalistic goals. There are three major contributions of this capability perspective to the field of participatory evaluations and DCR. The first of these is the expansion of the informational basis, which moves beyond an outcome analysis and collection of information prior to the project to understand the members' individual cases and to be sensitive to their Southern perspectives. The second of these is the individual perspective that allows us to explore the complexities of each co-researcher and to better understand how a participatory practice affects each of the members of a group, whilst recognising asymmetries. The third is that the evaluative space is not determined by external or universalistic criteria, but instead the criteria are determined by the individual and/ or group, in the extent to which the project has helped this individual to lead the life they have reason to value in a deeply relational space.

Hence, to conclude, the chapter exploring these two cases presents how a DCR facilitator can undertake her or his evaluation of a DCR project alongside a more generic analysis as completed in Chapter Five. This enhances the ways in which current practices are assessed, and promotes a better Southern framework with which to democratise participatory practices through a Capabilities Approach.

# References

Berenstain, N. (2016). Epistemic exploitation. *Ergo, 3*(22), 569–590. https://doi. org/10.3998/ergo.12405314.0003.022.

Bhana, D. (2014). Race matters and the emergence of class: Views from selected South African university students. *South African Journal of Higher Education, 28*(2), 355–367. https://doi.org/10.20853/28-2-335.

Cornell, J., & Kessi, S. (2017). Black students' experiences of transformation at a previously 'white only' South African university: A photovoice study. *Ethnic and Racial Studies, 40*(11), 1882–1899. https://doi.org/10.1080/01419870.201 6.1206586.

Fricker, M. (2015). Epistemic contribution as a central human capability. In George Hull (ed.). *The Equal Society: Essays on Equality in Theory and Practice* (pp. 73–90). Lanham: Lexington Books. https://rowman.com/ ISBN/9781498515719/.

Goetze, T. S. (2018). Hermeneutical dissent and the species of hermeneutical injustice. *Hypatia, 33*(1), 73–90. https://doi.org/10.1111/hypa.12384.

Ibrahim, S. S. (2006). From individual to collective capabilities: The capability approach as a conceptual framework for self-help. *Journal of Human Development, 7*(3), 397–416. http://dx.doi.org/10.1080/14649880600815982.

Mattes, R. (2015). South Africa's emerging black middle class: A harbinger of political change? *Journal of International Development, 27*(5), 665–692. https:// doi.org/10.1002/jid.3100.

Sutherland, A. (2013). The role of theatre and embodied knowledge in addressing race in South African higher education. *Studies in Higher Education, 38*(5), 728–740. https://doi.org/10.1080/03075079.2011.593620.

Walker, M. (2005). Rainbow nation or new racism? Theorizing race and identity formation in South African higher education. *Race, Ethnicity and Education, 8*(2), 129–146. https://doi.org/10.1080/13613320500110501.

# 8. DCR for Socially Just Higher Education: Perspectives from the South

When I think of 'feminism' I see a woman, I see a strong woman. I see a very strong, 'white' woman, and then, I see a sub-category for myself. I see a dark room for me to shove my opinions in, a suggestion box that will never be opened. A voiceless young woman who'll never be intellectual enough, worthy enough, valuable enough and able enough to know more about politics than men do. Finally, I see a transgender woman who'll never be invited to a rally because she's not woman enough. What is gender equality exactly?

In my three years in varsity I got to learn that I, a young black woman, can suffer from sexism, homophobia, racism, classism, I can be raped, beaten and burned alive, and no one will ever look up to acknowledge my absence. I never knew what gender inequality was until I thought back to my past, during my high-school years. Studying history (humanities), which was one of my favourite subjects, I always got high marks. Male students in my class were always curious of what mark I got, until I realised that I was in competition with most boys in my class without really knowing it, it was funny. For me, it became an improvement type of competition but to them it meant more than that, it meant that they were not to be topped by a girl in any of the modules. One is probably reading through this text and wondering how is this narrative relevant to the topic at hand. This is the beginning of the male intellectual oppression towards women. It starts as a seed and slowly grows into the issue we now have of men believing women belong in the kitchen, raising kids, being submissive to their (men's) sexual needs. How ironic?

We live in a society that does not allow women to be cleverer than men, or to be sexual like men otherwise such a woman is considered to be promiscuous, be too successful, too opinionated otherwise. It is disrespectful not to allow a man to have the last word no matter how stupid the "word" is. Our society teaches girls to not be too ambitious.

     https://doi.org/10.11647/OBP.0273.08

I always wondered where this narrative of men being superior and women inferior came from. Then, I remembered a saying in Sotho that elders always used, "Monna ke mokopu oa mnama, mosadi ke cabbage oa ipopa", this allows men to have as many relations as they want but not the women. This, getting to the depth of it, perpetuates a lot of misinterpreted stereotypes that have landed us in the current gender issues we have. When a young girl is unable to sweep, cook or even clean our mothers always say "Who is going to marry you?" Our worth is always narrowed to submitting to a man, we are raised to be good wives while boys are raised to be successful.

The family would go to hell and back to raise funds for a boy in the family to go to university but not the girl. I suppose we are to be ambitious but not too ambitious as Chimamanda puts it, otherwise we are threatening a man's masculinity.

I as a girl am expected to pick up after my little brother's mess and see to it that his clothes are clean. Why not teach them at a young age to cook, clean and do their own laundry? What if he does not marry? What happens when their female caretaker dies? Will they starve because they can't cook? Live in mess because they cannot clean? No. They will learn how to do things themselves. Why not start at a young age? Besides "Thupa e kojoa esale metsi" (Literally: A stick is bent while it's soft (otherwise it breaks). Children are disciplined while they're still young.

Despite the society deeming the sole problem to be the perpetuation of gender inequality... Men. I, however, learned that women themselves are now perpetuating this narrow standard of mental capability. I remember when a friend of mine told me that a boyfriend's role in my life is to provide all my wants be it money-wise, clothes, food, airtime. I as a young woman am not allowed to assist my significant other financially because that's a man's role, how contradicting to the 'gender equality theory' that we so fight for but then again smash to the side like it is not a need but a want.

Being in a long-distance relationship requires money for two people to reconnect but this one particular visit my significant other did not have money to buy me a bus ticket; so I had to pay for my trip. Embarrassing to say, I was ashamed to tell my female friends that I had paid for my trip. I knew what they would have said, that he is either not man enough or that he was not worthy of having relations with me because he could not afford me. Are we now payable objects? Is that not us succumbing to the narrative that men are providers at all times? How is that equality? Is it equality when we deem fit?

We (women) are fighting a war that is never to be won as a result of the division between women. We do not have a united womanhood but instead we have a white woman, black woman, cis women and other non-white women. White women do not experience misogyny the same way non-white women do. The same way generally women do not experience misogyny the same way cis women do. It is acceptable for 'women' to protest against rape, any type of violence and gender discrimination. White feminism aims to close the wage gap between men and women, but what it fails to recognise is that most of the time non-white women earn even less than white women do. We women are divided by different racial struggles; we face, as a result, that "true gender equality" can never be accomplished.

Someone who understands my non-white struggle... The feminist movement (that fights for gender equality) does not belong to the non-white girl. I know everyone says that it is for all women but truth is it is not that way.

How can I fight with you for your rights when my black people have none?

I have to fight for black rights before I can even begin to fight for other people. How can I fight for your right to make the same pay as the white man when I don't even make as much as you?

I ask the feminist woman: "You want me to fight with you but where are you when I needed backup for my black movement?"

You want me to be free but you do not want me to be equal, or at least not free enough to mess with your white privilege." Black women think black struggle first. White women think race first. Gender inequality thinks gender first. That is the first division that disables women to fight side by side against gender inequality.

It is time that we recognise that there are more than two genders. Gender inequality is a fight for all women, all genders and all races.'

*Narratives on Social Injustices: Undergraduate Voices*, 2018

# 8.1 Introduction

After reviewing the valued capabilities and acquiring an understanding of the impact of the project in two cases, Chapter Eight reflexively aims to provide a Southern perspective of social justice and of how this DCR project might contribute to the goal of democratising participatory research beyond its evaluation. This chapter discusses the challenges, opportunities and lessons of the DCR project. Firstly, the five DCR principles are investigated, and their contribution to social justice after the South African DCR project is considered. A review of each principle is presented, highlighting how they were developed and implemented in this DCR project after their theoretical formulation. Following the review of these principles, the conceptualisation of DCR beyond the participatory practice is also considered. These final remarks will seek to clarify the two main roles within a DCR project—that of the facilitator and that of the co-researchers—and to show how these two elements imply different processes. The facilitator's task is to identify valued capabilities at the beginning of the project, to design a prospective way to lead the project towards the member's valuable capabilities, and to evaluate them at the end of the project. The task of the co-researchers is to develop their own research project in a democratic way with the facilitator. Furthermore, this section highlights that although this DCR project has applied both roles in a single project, they might be implemented independently, as the facilitator role can benefit, enrich and democratise other participatory practices.

The second part of this chapter explores the challenges and opportunities that emerged from the pilot DCR project. It explores the implementation of the case study, highlighting the complex academic space and the challenges for DCR's navigation of it, such as difficulties in co-creation. The following section will summarise some of the key points from Chapter Three and link them to the arguments discussed in this chapter.

## 8.2 DCR: A Southern Participatory Perspective for Socially Just Higher Education and the Democratisation of Participatory Research

Social justice is considered in this book from a capabilities perspective. However, this vision is interwoven with elements from participatory approaches and decoloniality. Firstly, a capabilities perspective, in the open-ended version of the CA sustained by Sen (1999; 2009), is not looking for a perfectly just society. Conversely, it seeks to identify injustices, to remove them or to expand capabilities, helping individuals and collectives to lead the lives they have reason to value (Sen 1999). Moreover, it has been shown that the constitutive elements of CA and decoloniality, in particular their understandings of social justice, are indeed aligned.

Several stages and various principles of Democratic Capabilities Research were presented in Chapter Four. The assumption is that by following these principles we can begin to democratise participatory practices from a Global South perspective. This is one way, among many others, to promote more socially just knowledge generation in higher-education institutions. This is mainly due to the centrality of co-researchers' capabilities and the expansion of the process in order to enhance them. Moreover, other elements, such as ecologies of knowledge or the promotion of more democratic spaces for knowledge production within the Western academic system, are essential to allow different ontological positions to be recognised.

This section will thus focus on and review the principles discussed in previous chapters. This section not only highlights their contributions to more socially just practices from a Global South perspective, but also explores how these principles were implemented in the South African DCR project.

## 8.2.1 Process as Capabilities Expansion

The first principle discussed here is the notion of the participatory process, DCR, as a space for capabilities expansion and achievement, which has two constitutive levels, prospective and evaluative. First of all, social justice has been framed as the expansion of capabilities that diverse individuals have reason to value (Sen 1999). Moreover, this is a normative positionality, from a non-ideal perspective. That is to say, we are not trying to expand these capabilities perfectly, but to explore the structural conversion factors, such as colonial conversion factors, that impede individuals from enjoying their valuable freedoms and assist them to enhance them. Equally, as argued in previous chapters, DCR research did not use universal or general lists. Rather, it identified valuable capabilities and insurgent capabilities that have enabled me, in my role as facilitator, to take strategic decisions about the DCR participatory project without compromising the collaborative research process. Therefore, this principle has two dimensions when applying a DCR process: the prospective and the evaluative dimension. Both are strategic, in the sense that they orient the DCR facilitator in their practice.

Focusing on the prospective aspect of this principle, Chapter Five argued that, from a DCR perspective, we have good reasons to design a contextual capabilities list for each participatory group. Several valued capabilities were identified, and a prospective table was presented, with recommendations and strategies for this South African DCR case. These strategies allowed the facilitator to align the DCR project with the elements that the members had reason to value, thus orienting the process to the preservation of diverse valued lives, and therefore to social justice, in an imperfect way.

On the other hand, the evaluative perspective was partly presented in Chapter Six and in Chapter Seven. These chapters presented the individual and group explorations among the members, which helped the facilitator to better understand the effects of the DCR project for each co-researcher. Chapter Seven explored the potentialities of evaluation through a capabilities lens, not only by understanding the valuable capabilities and insurgent capabilities, but also by exploring whether these individual capabilities had been enhanced or achieved by the project. This, to some extent, guides us to assessing our practices and identify them as more just than others, but also to situate them in a Global South context and perspective. In this way, by contextualising our capabilities we can understand Southern perspectives and worthwhile Southern ways of living that are not yet known to the Global North. This is proven by the identified Ubuntu capability and the means by which this group of undergraduates have valued, in different ways, the life that they want to pursue, and how insurgent capabilities played out in their preferences and experiences. This is not a unique Global South perspective, but it opens up new avenues for investigation of much more diverse Southern conceptualisations of capabilities from other geographical locations and other cultural cosmovisions.

As we have seen, the DCR project was able to achieve and enhance some of the valued and insurgent capabilities of this group, thanks to their involvement in the participatory project. Through a capabilities lens, this is one way to advance towards social justice, by enhancing or achieving valuable freedoms and functionings.

## 8.2.2 The Voiceless as Knowledge Creators

Moving on to the second principle, the term 'voiceless' is common in the participatory approaches literature (Cornwall & Jewkes 1995; White 2003). However, there are other ways to refer to certain voiceless groups, such as 'oppressed groups' (Fals-Borda & Rahman 1991). Nevertheless, if we view this voiceless person from a capability perspective, it would be someone who not only lacked a kind of human recognition capability, as these students have identified. Voicelessness relates to non-humiliation, a capability of control over one's environment in the political sense (Nussbaum 2011), diminishing one's effective participation, or their epistemic freedoms (Ndlovu-Gatsheni 2018).

These capabilities are central to the process of knowledge creation as a means of removing injustices, such as epistemic barriers that impede individuals from having epistemic access and/or becoming epistemic contributors (Fricker 2015). However, from a capabilities perspective, and also from the participatory or decolonial viewpoints, epistemic injustice has an impact on the achievement of global justice as a whole. De Sousa Santos claims that 'there is no global social justice, without global cognitive justice' (2014, 8), which is here referred to as hermeneutic and epistemic justice. Furthermore, linking these two ideas, Fricker argues (2015) that, beyond being receivers or having epistemic access, epistemic justice is integral to thinking about epistemic contribution as a central capability:

> The general idea that human well-being has an epistemic dimension depends on the idea that functioning not only as a receiver but also as a giver of epistemic materials is an aspect of human subjectivity that craves social expression through the capability to contribute beliefs and interpretations to the local epistemic economy. (Fricker 2015, 21)

Fricker (2015) links the idea of epistemic justice, which is heavily defended by participatory debates and decoloniality, to the Capabilities Approach, suggesting that it needs to be included as a central capability. What is important here is not that Fricker or other scholars say that, but rather that these students' valued freedoms align with this capability, and are therefore central for their insurgent capabilities. This leads us to the assumption that in order to advance social justice from a Southern perspective, as well in this case as epistemic justice, we must include individuals as epistemic contributors.

However, to see co-researchers as knowledge creators, especially those that are most excluded, we first have to recognise that they are dignified humans (Mpofu & Steyn 2021), and that they are not voiceless. Here 'voiceless' does not mean that these individuals are not epistemic contributors. They certainly are epistemic agents, in their own ways, epistemic frames and systems in the Global South, which differ from the scientific and Eurocentric epistemic frames. That is why these ideas are especially relevant in discussions of formal knowledge production by professional scholars. If we accept that they are epistemic contributors, the discussion here guides us towards a more flexible and inclusive approach to understanding research and knowledge production. Research is then seen as a capacity to 'make systematic forays' beyond our current knowledge (Appadurai 2006, 179). Therefore, considering this broad perspective, it makes sense to promote knowledge production and research beyond a scientific frame or context. It is about leading research with those who are excluded from these processes and constrained in their own access to powerful epistemic systems. We refer, therefore, to those who have been marginalised from becoming epistemic contributors in these privileged spaces (Fricker 2015). The point is that they are epistemic contributors and exercise their epistemic freedoms, but in marginalised spaces or subject to hierarchical epistemic structures, thus, the angle shifts towards inclusion and recognition from powerful epistemic positions.

In the DCR case, a group of undergraduates were selected as co-researchers of the project in a South African university. This decision was guided by the aforementioned main DCR principle. In terms of participation in knowledge production, these undergraduate students were mostly treated as passive receivers of their 'teaching and learning' university programmes, as their stories and experiences have shown. They appeared highly passive until reaching post-graduate level, whereupon they were considered as academic knowledge producers. Moreover, various examples illustrating this can be found in the interviews and data collected for this research project, highlighting the role that the students themselves think they have in the university. Kungawo said: 'Classes are just you hearing that person speak, the person who has the... the fancy degree or master degree or doctorate or whatever. They speak to you and then you listen for the entire hour' (Kungawo, second interview). Amahle stated: 'we all sit right at the back, moving from the back forward and then the lecturer speaks, then it's done, and maybe they try to force us to answer a question to show that we are actually involved' (Amahle, second interview). Minenhle mentioned how she perceives the lecturer: 'He's at the front and telling you what is right and what is wrong, so you can't really say "Sir, I feel like this theory is wrong" or whatever' (Minenhle, second interview).

All of this highlights the secondary role of these particular undergraduate students in this specific context, and their participation as listeners and empty recipients of an epistemic system that is external and strange to them. They seem not to have anything to contribute to the university context (Freire 1972). This applies not only to the classrooms, but also to their undergraduate programmes and their informal culture, which is very different from the cultures they come from and the cosmovisions with which they grow up. This is important to be aware of, not only for Global South institutions and academics but also, even more so, for colleagues and institutions in the Global North. Global South students' knowledge matters.

In conclusion, a research process should consider the voices of students who are excluded from formal knowledge creation processes, and who are not considered as worthy epistemic contributors. This is a means of challenging knowledge inequalities, as well as paying attention to a central capability, as Fricker (2015) has highlighted above, and the students of this group have also corroborated. It is a means of fighting against epistemic barriers and expanding the capability of these individuals as knowledge producers in pursuit of social justice.

## 8.2.3 Injustice as an Initial Issue

The third principle arises from the decolonial debate, along with elements discussed in Chapter Four, such as diatopic hermeneutics (De Sousa Santos 2010). I will cite De Sousa Santos to clarify how this relates to social justice and the case study presented here:

> The diatopic hermeneutic does not only call for a different form of knowledge, but also a different process of knowledge creation. It requires that the production of knowledge be collective, interactive, intersubjective and in networks. It should be pursued with full awareness that this will result in black holes, areas of irredeemable mutual intelligibility that, in order not to result in paralysis or factionalism, must be tempered through inclusive common interests in the fight against social injustice. (De Sousa Santos 2010, 81)

What De Sousa Santos (2010) is trying to highlight is that, as argued above, we need alternative ways to create knowledge, as Appadurai defends (2006)—collective processes in which we can come together with a common interest, guided by injustices against which we want to fight. These injustices are important because they are translated across cosmologies. They are the spaces in which different individuals and groups with different ontological and cosmological perspectives can achieve mutual understanding and advance knowledge in a multi-epistemic foundation.

The Capabilities Approach is aligned with this idea, in the sense that our agency is our focus on the pursuit of things that we want to do (Sen 1999). Therefore, this can be linked to ideas of fighting against social injustices that limit other individual capabilities or our own experiences of being constrained by conversion factors, as the case of these students has shown (Sen 1999).

Nevertheless, this principle presents a challenge to how academia works and funding is allocated, and impedes practices that are fully participative or collaborative, as has been explored in this book. Understanding research in this way means that it is the group of individuals decide the object under research and guide the process together. The group needs to decide which injustices are important to them and are worthy of research. This is well defined by one of the categories of participatory approaches, Community-Based Participatory Research. Vaughn et al. (2017) acknowledge that:

> [CBPR] is an approach built upon equitable collaboration among all research partners, including researchers and community members, in all aspects of the research process [...] It is not a specific research method but is an orientation to research that seeks to create an environment of shared authority among community and stakeholders that encompasses the entire research process, from the idea generation and data collection to dissemination and implementation of research findings [...] involving the target community in all phases of research so that the work is informed by their lived experience; building the capacity of the local community to address issues that affect them and the capacity of researchers to conduct culturally relevant research. (Vaughn et al. 2017, 1457)

Therefore, this is how this principle is conceptualised in the DCR process: through research of injustices that matter to the team members. In this way, DCR demands not only the methodological space—the strategies to create knowledge—but also the democratic formulation of the issue under research; it is an ontological, cosmological and metaphysical matter. This significantly assumes that the conceptualisation of the research issue is an ontological statement that might strongly influence the research process as a whole, and thus a substantial element in democratising research from a Global South perspective. This is because the decision on the issue under research normally comes from the dominant voices in the North, although the cosmovisions and cultures in the South might see these same challenges differently, or even consider them irrelevant. Hence, providing an incomplete ontological space is part of the democratisation of knowledge and the inclusion of Southern perspectives and knowledges. The point is to allow different perspectives—Southern perspectives—at this ontological level, and not only from a method or methodological level.

Furthermore, as the South African case has presented, having the freedom to decide which issue to research, by themselves, had a significant impact on the DCR participants, expanding the capabilities linked to their research, and making them view the project as something personal. It positioned agency and their insurgent capabilities at the core, and this was visible throughout the interviews, in statements like 'We choose topics that are relevant to us' (Iminathi, second interview); or 'It's very, like, personal' (Lethabo, second interview).

In conclusion, the principle of injustice as an initial issue seems rather central for advancing social justice and democratising knowledge, as the question of who decides which issue to research is important for an understanding of unfair power dynamics between the Global North and the Global South. It is even more important in order to preserve epistemic freedoms in the Global South and to allow populations in the Global South to theorise and understand the world according to their own cosmovisions (Connell 2014).

Nevertheless, this does not deny the importance and relevance of participatory approaches and the use of other methods and methodologies in academia. Conversely, it highlights that when using the Capabilities Approach and participatory practices to create a practice such as DCR, it is better directed to the advancement of social justice. It does not only expand capabilities but considers individuals as capable of identifying, investigating and resolving their own concerns. Furthermore, it recognises their power to fight the social injustices they experience, but also to understand and theorise them according to their own frames of reference (Chilisa 2012).

## 8.2.4 Uncertain Horizon (Democratic Space)

The concept of an uncertain horizon is apt for the previous section in the sense of providing democratic spaces where decisions are taken together. I have discussed in this book whether 'participatory' is an ambiguous word within the field of participatory approaches. This is intimately related to the different schools of thought on participatory practices. DCR was conceptualised in a clear way, in the sense that it is not a practice to include co-researchers in several stages of the researcher's project but to allow them to be the protagonist, along with us, as explored above. To defend this idea, I used the Capabilities Approach and the concept of democracy, as we need to move in the direction of more inclusive frameworks, in which co-researchers do not participate in the research. Conversely, members are sharing spaces of knowledge creation with scholars. Here, knowledge creation is not only for the sake of contributing to the expansion of a discipline's knowledge, but also for the sake of using different knowledges in combination to bring about a change in members' lives. It is the capacity to influence members' lives and future horizons.

Therefore, this principle is aligned with the previous principle highlighting that DCR is a democratic space where decisions are taken by the group, not mainly guided by a facilitator who elaborates an academic project before meeting the research team. Coming back to the ideas presented above about Community-Based Participatory Research, DCR represents an orientation for research. It is a way to start, create and finalise a research project with others in a broad sense. This collaborative aspect is discussed in detail in Chapter Six. It involves exploring how decisions were taken during the project and demonstrating that the members of the group were making these decisions over time, by walking through the process together. Only some actions were undertaken by the facilitator during the DCR process, as a way to either expand or achieve members' capabilities and to follow the prospective plan designed from the capabilities analysed at the beginning of the project.

In conclusion, participatory practices and more democratic practices like DCR seek to advance socially just higher education by fighting knowledge inequalities and epistemic injustices. DCR is here situated in a space, which is more closely related to the expansion of capabilities for the co-researchers than other participatory practices in the broader field. DCR allows the agency and capabilities of the participants to be at the centre of the process, guiding the project towards the things that matter for us, creating more democratic (although imperfect) spaces for knowledge production. This allows Southern populations to really engage in genuine collaborations as opposed to paternalistic or instrumental practices that do not enable them to make sense of their world from their own perspectives.

## 8.2.5 Internal or External Diversity (Ecology of Knowledges)

The principle of internal/external diversity is more intricate than the previous ones. First, the CA talks about the need to have diverse voices heard in the sense of having better-informed choices, as well as a moral definition of what inclusive public scrutiny would look like (Sen 1999). This position was aligned in Chapter Four with the term 'subjectivities of intersubjectivities' (Dussel 2007), showing how both positions talk to one another. This perspective represents what knowledge production is when we are able to understand knowledge beyond the scientific discipline contribution (Appadurai 2006), or equally, when we understand it as also contributing to the social pool of knowledge (Fricker 2015). In this sense, as noted in earlier chapters, by including as many knowledges as possible we are able to investigate better. The process fosters an 'ecology of knowledges', the epistemic diversity needed to challenge the dominant structures of knowledge creation (De Sousa Santos 2010). Nevertheless, although some theoretical concepts can be easily grasped, it is not the same when these concepts are put into practice. An easy way to better understand these concepts is to explore practical examples of how they have been understood by scholars in the past. In this case, the ecology of knowledges was implemented through the Popular University of the Social Movements (UPMS).

The UPMS looked for the 'potential to exchange knowledge, alternating with periods for discussion, study and reflection as well as leisure periods' (UPMS proposed methodology, 4). Throughout the workshops this will involve a shared space made up of militant intellectuals (one third), such as scholars or artists committed to social movements, and activists, or leaders of social movements or NGOs (two thirds). The idea of this itinerant[1] university is to confront the different perspectives of each collective on the same issue, as a way of building epistemic bridges between groups, and in order to 'overcome the separation between academic and popular knowledge and between theory and practice' (UPMS proposed methodology, 2). That is why the UPMS methodology document states that 'the ecology of knowledges is an attitude that transcends the prevailing logic of the production of knowledge and encompasses a pedagogical process for the production of knowledge aimed at mutual enrichment, combining knowledge emerging from struggle and knowledge emerging from committed academic work' (UPMS proposed methodology, 4). This way of implementing ecologies of knowledge will be considered (in the terminology of this study) as internal diversity, where different individuals sit together to explore their common concern.

The DCR project was slightly different. It used four groups of very different commitments, taking one as the principal. The first of these was the group of undergraduate students, who primarily decided the issue to be researched and formed the internal or permanently active group. Secondly, four more collectives were externally added, in the sense that they made visits to the DCR group for conversations, which situated them as external groups. These groups were: social movements (university organisations such as Embrace a Sister and Unsilenced UFS), institutional groups (Student Representative Council, Transformation Office) and intellectuals committed to the issues under research (two scholars from the university),[2] as well as the knowledge from local communities introduced later on in the project.

As explained above, the UPMS brings together different groups for knowledge creation in one space, which according to my criteria would be 'internal diversity'. This is, for instance, an idea, which could be taken further in subsequent DCR practices by carefully exploring the way relations are constructed among the different groups and the

---

1    I refer to the UPMS as itinerant because it is not framed as being located in a campus, particular institution or space. The UPMS can be proposed by any individual and can be organised in different places around the world, as has been the case since 2000 (see http://www.universidadepopular.org/site/pages/en/about-upms/history.php for more information).

2    See Chapter Five for more information about these individuals/groups and their participation in the DCR project.

expansion of their capabilities. However, due to the passive role of the undergraduate students on campus (in terms of their not being viewed as legitimate knowledge contributors), and the need for them to make some central decisions about how to proceed with the research (in terms of capabilities expansion and agency), I framed it as external diversity. In this way, the central group that represents the most marginal position, in this case the undergraduate students, is situated at the centre of the process, guiding it by themselves and bringing different groups to the conversation.

In conclusion, whether we use the internal or external epistemic diversity—as I did in this DCR case—as a way to introduce an ecology of knowledges in the research process, the question of justice relies heavily on the diversity of perspectives presented and the possibility to expand the informational basis. This is substantial for the Capabilities Approach, as well as participatory approaches and decoloniality. It highlights how we can create more democratic spaces for knowledge creation, including other knowledges, especially those from Southern locations and historically ignored or marginalised locations.

## 8.2.6 Final Remarks

The five principles discussed above highlight how DCR is a participatory practice that aims to advance socially just higher education from a Global South perspective, even though it is situated in an imperfect context. DCR generates a context that continuously interacts with members' capabilities and with the impossibility to create a 'perfectly just' research processes, whilst aiming to preserve and enhance Southern cosmovisions in the process of knowledge generation. To a certain extent, this 'imperfect practice' is not a limitation but a particular perspective of understanding what counts as knowledge, and what research is, orienting us to understanding the limitations and challenges surrounding our participatory practices. Therefore, when we talk about the process as a space for capabilities expansion, the voiceless as knowledge creators, injustice as an initial issue, the democratic space for knowledge production, or the need for internal/external diversity (ecology of knowledges), we refer to broad principles that can guide us towards a research practice that is more rooted in the South. And this assists us in advancing towards more just (rather than less just) higher-education systems. Hence, this is achieved imperfectly and not necessarily via major structural changes, but rather through changes to a level that makes sense in the precise context and the Southern location where relations and human relationalities are defined by local cosmovisions, such as Ubuntu.

Furthermore, now that the principles have theoretically been revised after the case study in South Africa, these five principles also imply the role of two different actors: the research facilitator, and the participants. That is why the following section will elaborate on this distinction and its implications for the conceptualisation of DCR as a whole.

## 8.3 Democratic Capabilities Research and Beyond

Initially, DCR was conceptualised as a collaborative research project that, although specifically conceived for this South African DCR case, could be implemented in different ways, thanks to the flexibility of its principles. However, this book has also presented certain stages to be undertaken by the facilitator. This has highlighted the fact that there are two central roles in the DCR process: the facilitator's role, and the DCR group members' role. Perhaps it is this division that is not yet clear in many participatory processes and much of the participatory literature, which lacks a clarification of how the facilitator might guide the process and to what extent she or he is able to modify or intervene in the process.

After the implementation and exploration of DCR in this book, this division is clear. The facilitator in this particular DCR process assisted a group of students to research a topic of interest to them in different ways, guided by the principles explored in the previous section. Furthermore, the role of the facilitator included valued capabilities exploration at the beginning of the project and designing a frame to guide the process according to the group's valuable capabilities, as shown in Chapter Five. In addition, the facilitator explored the evaluation of valued capabilities after the implementation of the project (Chapters Six and Seven). Therefore, two main roles are identified: the facilitator conducts capabilities-centred exploration or promotion of locally valued capabilities, and assists with the collaborative practice and what the group decides to do.

However, beyond acknowledging the separate roles required to implement a DCR project, we should consider DCR as an integrated tool, as we have done in this book. Moreover, DCR can also be used separately if the facilitator exploration is applied to any other participatory practice, as a prospective-evaluative framework. DCR can be used at two levels that can be combined or applied separately, depending on the interest and circumstances surrounding the research project, as a case study exploration.

In some ways, this division resolves the scientific tensions that have been discussed throughout this book, whether we are following scientific lines of research or using a more radical research approach. Both are valid and necessary, but might not be so in all cases and all situations. Certainly, the tension between both lines is resolved by the provision of a rigorous research process that is able to accommodate the scientific standards of disciplinary contribution, i.e. the facilitator's roles. In this case, DCR is a tool for identifying locally rooted capability as a scientific contribution to the field of capabilitarian scholarship. Furthermore, DCR also innovates in finding ways to analyse and evaluate our participatory practices within the AR literature, providing an alternative theoretical framework to equip us with other frames of reference that might be more adequate for Southern locations and experiences of oppression. Secondly, DCR provides a flexible research process, challenging traditional approaches and including groups traditionally marginalised from accredited networks of knowledge creation, thereby understanding knowledge as the expansion of co-researchers' knowledge frontiers, which is the participants' role. In this second aspect, the lines of research will be determined by the participants, so they will decide how conventional or transgressive our practices are and what will be the most adequate means to disseminate our findings and conclusions.

## 8.4 A DCR Reflection: Challenges and Opportunities from the South African DCR Project

This section explores some of the key issues and opportunities that arose from this group involved in a DCR research project at a South African university.

As expected for a first-time practice, many challenges arose in this DCR project. However, these challenges helped me to better understand the fields in which DCR is situated and to rethink some aspects of the practice. I will start by highlighting some general elements and opportunities that are probably familiar to the reader, as some of them have been mentioned previously in other parts of this book.

In relation to the co-creation of the process with the participants, this was not an easy stage, as explored in Chapter Six. Although theoretically ideal, in that it allows new elements and ideas coming from the group to be a central focus of this research process, it was a tremendous responsibility for the members of the group. Iminathi mentioned the difficulties of adapting to a new way of working and learning, coming from a 'given' system. The participants noted difficulties in appropriating and leading the project. They were not used to autonomous or self-driven learning-work, and this delayed and obstructed the transfer of leadership throughout the project. This was not only caused by their being part of a highly hierarchical and culturally external education system, but also by the substantial deprivation in certain of their insurgent capabilities, such as human recognition and epistemic capability. For instance, the participants did not feel confident enough to talk, especially at the beginning, mentioning that they felt that they had insufficient knowledge due to a constant deprivation of their freedoms which had affected their self-perception, as I have explored in other sections of this book. To a certain extent, this was resolved by long-term engagement with the participants. However, this highlights that understanding the freedoms of the communities we work with can help us, as facilitators, to identify these limitations in the early stages of our projects and to put forward measures that allow the group to overcome 'unfreedoms' that impact ownership and active participation within the project.

In terms of power structures within the group, active participation seemed at the time to be unequal, especially for the female group-members. As raised in Chapter Six, when meeting together, the imbalances in terms of the freedoms they enjoyed as part of their human recognition capability were visible in functionings such as voice. Male members who came from more advantaged backgrounds tended to dominate conversations and decision-making from the beginning of the project. During the interviews, the female members—especially those who tended to participate less—justified this imbalance by their lack of knowledge or personal insecurity (Chapter Five). Nevertheless, as mentioned above, this was an opportunity for the group to discuss the issue together and to reflect on the internal dynamics of the group, exposing the conversion factors to which they are subjected in their daily lives and experiences on campus. Debating unfreedoms was a gain that the capabilities analysis provided for the group. Despite the facilitator having taken responsibility for this aspect of the project, debate is a potential tool for discussing power inequalities within the group, rather than erasing unequal relations, which in any case will not be fully possible. However, the point is to bring awareness about these dynamics to the group and to debate with them about how to minimise them as far as possible, given the circumstances.

Perhaps one of the major limitations for this DCR project was its being situated in a specific timeframe, as the project was envisioned to last throughout the 2017 academic year so that I would conclude the 'official' project by the beginning of 2018.[3] This timeframe created a challenge with several unforeseen consequences. For instance, it made me rush at times, owing to being overwhelmed by deadlines and occasionally forcing decisions within the group, such as the decision to finalise the official project at the end of 2017. This was certainly a major limitation, as the group had a particular timeframe and they were confident in continuing the project for as long as they envisioned. However, the need to set aside time for interviews, transcriptions, and analysis in order to conclude my individual analysis in 2018 affected the project in several ways. Initially I thought that agreeing with the members to continue with the project but on a more informal basis would resolve the challenge, however, this did not work well. It created a feeling among the co-researchers that the project was finished, although the agreement was to continue informally during the following year. Indeed, respecting group time is essential for DCR practices and something to take into careful consideration when we are constrained by funding schedules or submission timeframes. Perhaps, if we are unable to avoid this, an option could be to anticipate this situation with the group, and to ask the group about what we should do if we have to suddenly conclude

---

3   In South Africa, the academic year begins in February and ends in December of each year.

the project. Therefore, although this limitation could be resolved by applying these practices and considering a flexible timeframe which could adapt to different circumstances and processes, as DCR requests, when this is not possible we will need to have some conversations and anticipatory planning strategies.

Another limitation observed during the DCR project was the participation rate. Participation dropped slightly towards the end of the project, causing two members of the group to leave the project, although only provisionally, as they kept in contact and came back for the late meetings in 2017 and early 2018. When exploring the causes of this issue in the interviews, although responses focused on motivation in general, they were more specifically concerned about their academic calendar, in the sense that the students viewed the second semester as being extremely demanding. They reported struggling to combine their academic responsibilities with the project duties. This might be a central point when starting a group, i.e. bearing in mind that whilst the facilitator might have the time available to guide the process, this might not be the case for the co-researchers. Again, it seems essential to have some strategic conversation before starting the project, in order to anticipate challenges such as this, or constrained timeframes that have to be met by the facilitator. A process such as DCR is time-consuming and we should be conscious about that from beginning to end.

In terms of capabilities expansion and achievements as a crucial part of the facilitator role, analytically, capabilities are difficult to identify. They are dynamic components of an individual's life and those categories that are not achieved are ascribed 'potential' status, as Chapter Five has explored. In this sense, we could say that, empirically speaking, we can create approximations of the enjoyment of a particular capability through functionings (achieved capabilities) or subjective accounts of capabilities expansion, as explored in Chapter Seven. In the project, these functionings reflected the available choices for the individual, as well as those of the participant to achieve it, providing valuable outcomes in order to assess our practices. However, we know it will be difficult to accurately measure a particular capability for a particular individual beyond subjective perceptions. It is exactly this subjective perception that we use as a frame of reference in addition to their achievement and perceptions of achievement, as this book has explored. Thus, when using capabilities and functionings to evaluate our participatory practices, and practices such as DCR, we can only talk about approximations of their valued capabilities through their subjective perceptions and facilitator observations. In these cases, it would be what we need and what we need to know to acknowledge and respect the fluid aspect of capabilities and fluctuations in valued capabilities. We are not aiming for a precise measure as that would contradict our basic understanding of capabilities as dynamic. What we do is to take a picture of the valued capabilities at the time we meet with the individuals, review them again collaboratively in order to prevent our own cultural assumptions, and assess their expansion after the project. We are not claiming that these capabilities are infinite, or central for every human being. Contrary, these capabilities are instrumental for understanding contexts, as in the Global South, where perceptions of the world and knowledges have been marginalised and therefore are unknown to many scholars in the North. Investigating capabilities in this way, we claim their partial observations and thus, more contextually and culturally related explorations and results.

Regarding the Ubuntu capability for this group and the implications of it as a group insurgent capability, students mentioned this concept of Ubuntu during the interview and the project. They explained how the meaning of this African philosophy directs their lives towards caring for others, or seeing themselves as interconnected individuals. This caused the Ubuntu capability to form part of their capability list and made me carry out a follow-up interview after the project had ended (2019) in order to better understand its relevance. However, it is necessary to acknowledge some limitations of this notion being conceptualised as a single capability. The capability of Ubuntu presented here seems limited and conditioned and in need of richer exploration and consideration. For instance, and as highlighted in Chapter Five, we need to understand the extent to which this capability impacts other capabilities, or the extent to which it could be considered as an especially generative, fertile capability or a cosmovision that is a meta-level, as an Ubuntu agency. The data shows that Ubuntu is a foundational capability for these students, and we see how aspects of Ubuntu are presented in other valued capabilities. Hence, this Ubuntu aspect needs to be explored, not only due to the literature gap, in which these types of capabilities are residual, but also so as to carefully consider and question the real implications of Southern cosmovisions from a capabilities perspective.

Thus, this presents a necessary avenue to examine more deeply in future questions such as: Are there different capabilities levels for Southern populations? How can a Southern cosmovision such as Ubuntu come into a real and horizontal conversation with the Capabilities Approach? Is Ubuntu a type of agency for these students?

To finally conclude this section, I would like to focus on the challenges presented by the ecology of knowledges in the DCR process, exploring the difficulties when this is applied to a real and non-ideal participatory experience. To promote an ecology of knowledges, where all knowledges are treated as equal, requires a perfectly equal society (which does not exist), as well as a deep and critical understanding of knowledge and academic knowledge production. However, our societies are complex and our terms of reference are different from place to place, to the extent that it is a challenge even to share an understanding or a basic agreement about what knowledge is and how epistemic inequalities take place. This seems to be even more difficult to maintain when working with a group of individuals that are not familiar with these debates, despite embodying much of this epistemic marginalisation. In the DCR project, students came to the research with their own ideas and beliefs, which were very different from each other. Some students from biochemistry or the natural sciences generally understood the positivist scientific method as the only way to achieve truth, although their knowledge about how to do so was limited and their epistemic access to this system was constrained. Other students relied on and believed in witchcraft, and the majority had a combined vision, mixing different knowledge systems but relying heavily on their spiritual, localised and experiential knowledge. This multiplicity of perspectives seems to highlight that the main element when talking about an ecology of knowledges outside of the academic and theoretical scope, is not necessarily about equal evaluation of knowledges, but about introducing and assessing different knowledge systems—including scientific truths—according to the circumstances of the group. It relies on questioning the limitations of each knowledge system presented during the research project. It is about presenting their potentialities and deciding which one is adequate or which combination of various knowledges is adequate for us as a group, respecting our frames of reference. Hence, in a DCR practice, we will need to have conversations about what we believe, what other groups believe, what we want to believe, and what the criteria to consider something believable, as a group, are. This is in order to promote an ecology of knowledges, not to represent all types of knowledge and present them as equal, but to reflect and decide together about the knowledge systems available and which ones we want to use in order to bring justice to our positionalities and contexts. Therefore, in the DCR case, experiential, cultural and spiritual knowledges were much more frequently used than scientific knowledge, due to the composition of the research group. In this way, an ecology of knowledges seems to have been achieved not by the extent to which 'all' knowledges are presented equally in a project, but by the way in which the various knowledges, whichever ones we are using (scientific, conceptual, experiential, intuitive, local, Indigenous, cultural, prepositional and so on), are questioned and scrutinised by a collective rationality (Sen 2009). Thus, this rationality is not understood in a modern rational frame, but instead is considered in an extended manner.[4] In this ecology of knowledges the research project would question any knowledge presented, but at the same time would use the types of knowledge that were more appropriate and relevant for the participants involved in the process.

## 8.5 Conclusion

This chapter has mainly discussed challenges and lessons in promoting Southern perspectives of social justice and capabilities expansion in this DCR project. In doing so, the first part of the chapter has focused on the five principles since their application in this South African project. It has reviewed each of them by exploring their implications for social justice from a Southern perspective. The second part has investigated the roles involved in the implementation of a DCR practice, clarifying and concluding the conceptualisation of DCR. This section has highlighted the two roles involved in the DCR practice by separating the facilitator's role (identification and evaluation of valued capabilities) and the participant's roles (leading the research process on those things that matter to them).

---

4   As for instance Hoffman and Metz refer to rationality, as understood by Sen: 'If rationality were a church [...] It would be a rather broad church' (Sen 2009, 195 cited in Hoffman and Metz 2017, 2).

The second part of the chapter investigated more general challenges and lessons that emerged from the case study. It has explored aspects such as the intricate academic space of DCR, the challenges of co-creation, the difficulties in equal participation among the members, the time constraints, the challenges to capabilities identification and expansion, the incompleteness of the Ubuntu capability, and reflections on the use of an ecology of knowledges in this case study.

Therefore, after concluding with this chapter, Chapter Nine will summarise the argument of this book, focusing on the contributions of this research, methodological challenges, dissemination, and potential directions of future research. It brings about possibilities to contribute strengthen (rather than weaken) the democratisation of knowledge production, especially for those situated on the wrong side of the epistemic line.

# References

Appadurai, A. (2006). The right to research. *Globalisation, Societies and Education*, 4(2), 167–177. https://doi.org/10.1080/14767720600750696.

Chilisa, B. (2012). *Indigenous Research Methodologies*. Los Angeles: Sage Publications.

Connell, R. (2014). Using southern theory: Decolonizing social thought in theory, research and application. *Planning Theory*, 13(2), 210–223. https://doi.org/10.1177%2F1473095213499216.

Cornwall, A., & Jewkes, R. (1995). What is participatory research? *Social Science & Medicine*, 41(12), 1667–1676. https://doi.org/10.1016/0277-9536(95)00127-S.

De Sousa Santos, B. (2010). *Descolonizar el saber, reinventar el poder*. Montevideo: Ediciones Trilce.

Dussel, E. D. (2007). *Materiales para una política de la liberación*. Buenos Aires: Plaza y valdés España.

Fals-Borda, F., & Rahman, M. A. (1991). *Action and Knowledge: Breaking the Monopoly with Participatory Action-Research* (No. 300.720172 A2). London: Intermediate Technology.

Freire, P. (1972). *Pedagogy of the Oppressed*. London: Harmondsworth.

Fricker, M. (2015). Epistemic contribution as a central human capability. In George Hull (ed.). *The Equal Society: Essays on Equality in Theory and Practice* (pp. 73–90). Lanham: Lexington Books. https://rowman.com/ISBN/9781498515719/.

Mpofu, W., & Steyn, M. (2021). The trouble with the human. In Steyn, M. & Mpofu, W. (eds). *Decolonising the Human: Reflections from Africa on Difference and Oppression*. Johannesburg: Wits University Press.

Ndlovu-Gatsheni, S. J. (2018). *Epistemic Freedom in Africa: Deprovincialization and Decolonization*. London: Routledge.

Noffke, S. E., & Somekh, B. (eds) (2009). *The SAGE Handbook of Educational Action Research*. London: Sage Publications.

Nussbaum, M. C. (2011). *Creating Capabilities: The Human Development Approach*. Cambridge: Harvard University Press.

Sen, A. (1999). *Development as Freedom*. New York: Random House.

Sen, A. (2009). *The Idea of Justice*. Cambridge, MA: Belknap.

Vaughn, L. M., Jacquez, F., Lindquist-Grantz, R., Parsons, A., & Melink, K. (2017). Immigrants as research partners: A review of immigrants in community-based participatory research (CBPR), *Journal of Immigrant and Minority Health*, 19(6), 1457–1468. https://doi.org/10.1007/s10903-016-0474-3.

White, S. A. (ed.) (2003). *Participatory Video: Images that Transform and Empower*. London: Sage Publications.

# 9. Redrawing Our Epistemic Horizon

## 9.1 Introduction

The main purpose of this final chapter is to clarify and summarise the major elements of this book, reflecting on the different contributions, and future directions of this research project. Therefore, this chapter reflects on the findings presented in this book and highlights how the project contributes new ways of knowing to the field of higher education and development research. Thus, the first section explores the key findings and conceptual, empirical and methodological contributions of this book, and concludes with the final contributions to pedagogical practices and education policies in higher education.

## 9.2 Conceptual and Empirical Contributions

The major contributions of this book are its conceptual and empirical contributions, based on the combination of three fields of study to conceptualise, develop and implement a capabilities-based participatory research. The central point was the conceptualisation of the practice, as well as a review of its application following a South African project. Furthermore, the use of the Capabilities Approach in this study has intentionally focused on a particular Southern perspective in order to better understand its potential to acknowledge its Southern application. The Capabilities Approach claims to focus on actual lives. However, this focus seems at times to be secondary, particularly when using aggregations of individuals and the quantification of human development indices. However, as Sen and Muellbauer claim:

https://doi.org/10.11647/OBP.0273.09

> The passion for aggregation makes good sense in many contexts, but it can be futile or pointless in others. Indeed the primary view of the living standard, as argued earlier, is in terms of a collection of functionings and capabilities, with the overall ranking being a secondary view. The secondary view does have its uses, but it has no monopoly of usefulness. When we hear of variety, we need not invariably reach for our aggregator. (1988, 33)

This book brings back the centrality of individuals and local groups in the process of choosing valuable capabilities and the question of how to assess practices such as DCR in terms of these valued capabilities at a local level.

Nevertheless, various claims can be made about this book's contributions to several aspects in the three fields—the Capabilities Approach, participatory approaches and decoloniality. First, in terms of its conceptual contributions—which are interwoven with its empirical contributions—three major points can be highlighted. The first of these concerns the exploration of the limitations of Western participatory approaches and the limitations of participation under this critical view. Second, this book has proposed an innovative type of participatory research—Democratic Capabilities Research (DCR)—and has thus managed to link these three research areas to present a participatory capabilities-based research, an undertaking which had thus far not been achieved in the literature. Third, as a result of this conversation between the three research areas, the book has presented the conceptualisation of DCR as an incomplete and open-ended tool, following the decolonial and Southern influences of the Capabilities Approach. Thus, it assumes that our theoretical frameworks need to be incomplete in order to adapt to the dynamism that characterises societies, and in order to allow other Southern cosmovisions and knowledge systems to enter our research practices and theorisations.

Additionally, in terms of conceptual contributions—which are equally interwoven with empirical contributions—three main points are important. The first of these concerns the understanding of contextual valued capabilities as dynamic and the visual placement of them as a continuum, stretching from active to latent capabilities. This representation supports the argument of dynamism and also challenges the use of a universal list. Second, the use of contextual valued capabilities is advocated as a means of generating recommendations and assessing DCR in order to expand current evaluative spaces within participatory approaches. In this view, the participatory process is not only guided by the things that the participants have reason to value but, ultimately, the process is also assessed in terms of the things that matter to them (Sen 1999). And finally, the identification of the insurgent character of some of these identified capabilities is highly relevant for the well-being of these students due to the oppressive structures that surround them.

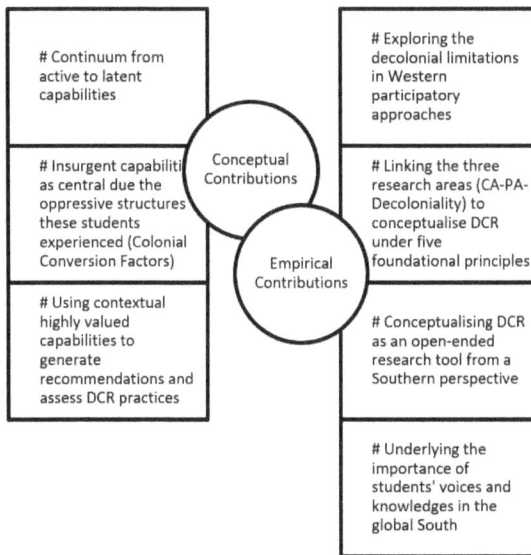

Figure 9: Conceptual-empirical contributions of this study (image by the author, 2021).

Further, a major and general contribution of this book is the underlying importance given to students' voices and knowledges throughout the process. An implicit aim of this study was to challenge and interrogate arbitrary liminalities in the process of knowledge production. Moreover, the aim was to amplify the voices of those students who are often considered recipients of knowledge rather than architects and actors in higher-education institutions. This research project questioned the limited epistemic space in scientific knowledge generation, highlighting the relevance of other knowledge systems. Thus, the book defended the introduction of these knowledges into our academic participatory practices, as a way to democratise participatory research from a Southern perspective.

## 9.3 From a 'They Are All Stupid' to a 'We Are All Stupid' Paradigm

The DCR collaborative research process calls for epistemic and methodological considerations that go beyond conventional scientific standards (Chilisa 2013). It questions the structures of knowledge production and the knowledge gap between different epistemic systems, urging the need to build bridges between them (Ndlovu-Gatsheni 2018). Furthermore, the case study highlights that qualitative research is still of value and necessary to advance this epistemic diversity, not by removing traditional processes, but by combining them and acknowledging knowledge asymmetries. The methodology—the case study—was validated as a way to continue creating relevant knowledge and politically involved research in ways that have been historically dominant. This combination of both processes (the collaborative DCR process and the case study exploration) required both inquiry paths of knowledge creation. Despite their imbalances, they were both necessary and substantial for challenging the epistemic barriers present in some of the most traditional schools of thought within the sciences. Citing an instructive argument highlighted by Nanay (2018), the idea is to switch from a 'they are all stupid paradigm' to a 'we are all stupid paradigm' in which we, as scholars and scientists, can acknowledge our own limitations regarding rationality and truth. As much as we want to believe that we know more, we still need the knowledge and perspectives of others to embrace the multiplicity of ways in which knowledge can be created.

In summary, the major methodological contribution of this study was the implementation of these theoretical principles (DCR), through a case study. This study made all of these ideas tangible, showing how something works in practice and what its limitations might be in such cases. It provided an alternative path to a known challenge and demonstrated a feasible application—although not necessarily a unique, better or perfect application.

## 9.4 Education Policies and Pedagogical Possibilities: DCR for What?

Another important point to consider as a contribution of this book concerns the possible applications of DCR in university classrooms, pedagogies and educational policies. Firstly, the current debates on decolonising universities in South Africa, as well as in other countries in the South, forces us to re-think our institutions. In this transformation, the representation of diverse kinds of knowledge in classrooms is a question of social justice, and practices such as DCR can introduce this diversity. There are many ways of introducing DCR into classrooms, and one of them is using DCR as a pedagogical tool with a project-based approach[1]. DCR can contribute its collective nature—such as working in small groups—to these project-based pedagogies, as well as emphasising the central need to introduce knowledges that are not necessarily scientific into higher-education learning programmes. The point is to combine knowledge systems, especially in contexts such as the Global South, where an oppressive history has meant that traditional epistemologies have been marginalised and ignored (De Sousa Santos 2014). On the other hand, this is also crucially important for higher education in the North, as possible collaborations with Southern institutions can be a way of bringing an ecology of knowledges into their classrooms as well, for instance, by promoting cross-cultural research projects that will expand Northern students' understandings of their own ontologies and other cosmovisions around the world.

Another relevant rationale for the use of DCR within the classroom is to introduce valued capabilities as central for the design of curricula, programmes or courses, and the pedagogical process as a whole. In this case, lecturers can use students' valued capabilities to guide the content and relationship with them, as shown by the role of the facilitator presented in this book. This is an interesting point for a Southern context, such as that found in South Africa, as it leads to questions like: How can our classroom promote a valued capability such as Ubuntu? In this

---

1   Project-based pedagogies are based on the acquisition of skills throughout the development of activities/projects by the students. Normally, students are assigned an open project, in which they choose a theme and decide how to go about it, with just a few guidelines given by the lecturer.

case, perhaps exams will not be important anymore, and collaborative learning and support between students and the larger society will be central to the pedagogical process. What about Global North institutions using Southern cosmovisions in their educational institutions? If not a complete change, small introductions could be made, for instance in what a classroom would look like under an Ubuntu cosmovision. What about a classroom under a 'Buen vivir' cosmovision?

Certainly, we still have a long way to go until we can talk about real plurality, but somehow DCR can help to create educational paths that until now have not been available options. DCR assists us to create alternative pathways that have not yet been placed on the table. This is important, especially for Global North institutions expanding their educational practices and cosmovisions beyond the dominant Eurocentric ones. In this view, participatory research is not only a knowledge generation tool, but also a pedagogical tool that can transcend research spaces for classrooms and other higher-education spaces. Knowledge is not detached from our lives, and nor should our educational experiences be; we are, indeed, living knowledges.

Regarding educational policies, DCR can offer an alternative to conventional policy generation, as some participatory monitoring and budgeting practices have done. In using the DCR perspective, what educational policies are aiming for is not a unique universal/global trend—replicating policies from the North and implementing them in the South—but the development of policies using local aspirations and interests, in order to connect the local with the global. Therefore, one way of using DCR for policy generation could be to explore local capabilities, as this study does, in order to contextualise policies to the local space and cultural specificities of where they are used, as done by Velasco and Boni (2020) in the context of Colombian Higher Education. Alternatively, DCR can also be used as a collective research process— including those collectives that are currently excluded—in order to investigate, design and implement policies, bringing diverse sectors of society together in one space. What DCR really questions about educational policies is the top-down, Eurocentric approach in which they are traditionally designed and applied. DCR provides a bottom-up process that can be combined and can generate more relevant Southern policies that align with students and local collectives' aspirations and ways of living, rather than the Eurocentric system. Research is no longer an end but a constant democratic means needed to enhance our plural and contextual knowledge to resolve complex and intricate global and ecological challenges.

## 9.5 DCR beyond this Book

The future directions for this DCR practice are the most exciting part of this project and book. To a certain extent, DCR represents the beginning of a conceptual connection between different research fields and this gives us, as scholars, endless opportunities to inquire and achieve a better understanding within this frame. The DCR principles might be applied to rethink and explore different practices or DCR as a research process. This may be done, for example, by implementing the internal knowledge diversity (internal ecology of knowledges) and comparing this practice with the external processes used in this research. Alternatively, DCR could be applied in other higher-education contexts—for instance, in the Global North—in addition to other contexts beyond higher education.

To conclude, networks will be substantial for the future of DCR, and for bringing this work to other scholars interested in participatory practices and capabilities as a way to contribute to further practice and theorisation. Currently, there are a variety of intersecting networks required to initiate this expansion of DCR, such as some of the thematic groups of the HDCA association, or other networks within participatory approaches, such as ARNA, CARN or PRIA. Thus, the future of DCR will depend on its use and expansion following this book, and our capacity, as scholars, to understand the power of other contexts and their knowledge systems to democratise our participatory research practices.

## 9.6 Conclusion

This final chapter has endeavoured to conclude a long and diligent thinking process by discussing the main contribution of this research project to different fields, as well as clarifying the main arguments maintained throughout the book. The conceptual/empirical contributions section has highlighted that, even though the conceptualisation of this capabilities-based research process (DCR) is a main element, the book contributes on a variety of levels and in other terms to the expansion of knowledge and innovation within the study's different fields. Furthermore, this chapter highlights other contributions, such as epistemic or pedagogical contributions, and identifies the possibilities of using DCR in higher-education classrooms or for the planning and implementation of educational policies.

This chapter has also examined future directions for research and highlighted the importance and relevance of taking this DCR frame forward on different levels, for instance by using this DCR proposal as the starting point of a particular participatory framework, as has happened with other participatory practices such as CPAR or PALAR. Although we do not know the extent to which this proposal can cross the frontiers between fields and become a widespread approach, the idea is to continue developing the tool at different levels. In order to do so, this study will require networks and deep public engagement on different levels. The future development of DCR will depend on the joint work of scholars and practitioner networks who are interested in developing and shifting the use of a participatory capabilities-based orientation to research towards a more grassroots, decolonial and Southern use of the Capabilities Approach.

# References

Chilisa, B. (2012). *Indigenous Research Methodologies*. Los Angeles: Sage Publications.

De Sousa Santos, B. (2014). *Epistemologies of the South: Justice against Epistemicide*. New York: Routledge. https://unescochair-cbrsr.org/pdf/resource/Epistemologies_of_the_South.pdf.

Nanay, B. (2018). *Stupidity is Part of Human Nature: Why we Must Scrap the Myth of Perfect Rationality*. Iai News. Changing How the World Thinks. https://iai.tv/articles/why-stupidity-is-part-of-human-nature-auid-1072.

Ndlovu-Gatsheni, S. J. (2018). *Epistemic Freedom in Africa: Deprovincialization and Decolonization*. New York: Routledge.

Sen, A. (1999). *Development as Freedom*. New York: Random House.

Sen, A., & Muellbauer, J. (1988). *The Standard of Living*. Cambridge: Cambridge University Press.

Velasco, D., & Boni, A. (2020). Expanding epistemic capability in participatory decision-making processes: The Universidad de Ibagué capabilities list. In *Participatory Research, Capabilities and Epistemic Justice* (pp. 27–57). London: Palgrave Macmillan.

# List of Figures

## Chapter Three

1. Participatory Families (image by the author, 2021).      45
2. Diagram of Lewin's Action Cycle (image by the author, 2021, based on Fieldman 2017, 127).      47
3. Four dimensions for Indigenous research (image by the author, 2021, based on Chilisa 2012, 13).      53

## Chapter Four

4. Principles of Democratic Capabilities Research (image by the author, 2021).      97

## Chapter Five

5. Dynamic and Contextual model of valuable capabilities (image by the author, 2021).      114

## Chapter Six

6. Workshop schedule (image by the author, 2021).      136

# Chapter Seven

7. Minenhle's Valued Capabilities (image by the author, 2021).     176
8. Siyabonga's Valued Capabilities (image by the author, 2021).     188

# Chapter Nine

9. Conceptual-empirical contributions of this study (image by the     231
   author, 2021).

# List of Tables

## Chapter Three

1. Typologies of participatory approaches.                                    43
2. Features of Educational Action Research (based on Kember    55
   2000, 30).
3. Purposes of Pedagogical Action Research (based on Norton    58
   2009, 59-60).

## Chapter Four

4. Comparing Decoloniality and the Capabilities Approach.      86

## Chapter Five

5. Co-researchers' valued capabilities.                        113
6. Comparison of Nussbaum's capabilities list vs the DCR group's   127
   valued capabilities.
7. DCR case study prospective framework.                       129

# Index

Action Research  vii, 35–37, 42–44, 46, 48–50, 53–58, 61–64, 89

adaptive preferences  113–115

Africa  8–10, 13, 121, 129, 137, 150, 157

agency  2, 5, 17, 20, 68, 77, 80, 83–84, 92, 96, 111, 116–117, 122, 210, 212–213, 215, 217, 223–224

apartheid  9, 105, 115, 122, 125

aspirations  9–11, 93, 115, 123, 125, 138, 153–154, 199–200, 234

capabilities  6, 12–13, 15–18, 20–22, 76–77, 80–81, 83–87, 91–95, 97, 109–126, 128, 138, 140, 143, 150, 153–154, 158, 160, 167, 172–173, 175–177, 179, 182, 185–186, 188, 192, 197–201, 205–209, 212–215, 217–218, 221–223, 225–226, 229–231, 233–236. *See also* epistemic capabilities; *See also* human recognition; *See also* Ubuntu; *See also* insurgent capabilities; *See also* latent capabilities; *See also* valued capabilities

Capabilities Approach  vii, 4, 6, 13, 16–18, 20–21, 68, 76–78, 80–81, 83–87, 90–92, 94, 110–111, 131, 172, 189, 192, 199–201, 209, 212–214, 217, 221, 224, 229–230, 235–236

collaborative research process  207, 232

collective decision-making  91, 138. *See also* decision-making

collective dialogue  143

colonial conversion factors  5, 21, 79–80, 88, 109, 114–115, 117–119, 121–123, 125, 141, 143, 146, 149, 154, 156–158, 167, 172, 177–180, 182–183, 186–190, 198–200, 207

colonialism  2–5, 7–11, 13–14, 17, 20–21, 30–32, 34–36, 42, 51–52, 66–67, 79–80, 83, 88, 92, 109, 114–115, 117–119, 121–123, 125–126, 129, 141, 143, 146, 149, 154, 156–158, 167, 172, 177–190, 198–200, 207

communities  2–5, 8–9, 14–15, 18, 30, 32, 44–45, 50, 52, 60–61, 67, 78, 80, 88–89, 93, 106–107, 120, 125–126, 142, 149–150, 157–158, 163, 165, 174, 176, 180, 184, 192, 196–197, 212, 216, 220

conversion factors  4–5, 21, 78–80, 88, 109, 114–115, 117–119, 121–123, 125, 141, 143, 146, 149–150, 154, 157, 167, 172, 177–180, 182–183, 186–190, 198–200, 207, 212, 221

cosmologies  32, 34, 85, 88, 96, 212

cosmovisions  30, 79, 87–88, 90–91, 117, 197, 199, 208, 211, 213, 217, 223, 230, 233–234

DCR (Democratic Capabilities Research)  vii, 4–5, 12–13, 18, 20–23, 76, 90–91, 94–98, 109–112, 114, 117, 121, 124, 127–128, 140, 148, 152, 159, 165, 167, 172–173, 196, 198–199, 201, 203, 205–208, 210, 212–214, 216–226, 230–236

decision-making  17, 60, 80, 91–92, 97, 119, 126, 136–138, 142–143, 153, 160, 162, 167, 207, 210, 213–214, 217, 220–221. *See also* collective dialogue

decoloniality  6–8, 10–14, 16, 19–20, 23, 31, 33–36, 42, 44–45, 52–53, 63, 67–69,

76–77, 79–92, 95, 123, 206, 209, 211, 217, 230, 236
decolonisation 7, 10, 13–14, 19, 37, 49, 52–53, 63, 233
democracy 4, 6, 10, 16–17, 20, 35, 43, 46, 48, 52, 64, 66, 76, 78, 83–88, 90–94, 96–97, 105, 107, 115, 206–207, 213–215, 217, 235
democratisation of knowledge 4, 6, 14, 31, 37, 45, 49, 68, 92, 213, 226, 233

ecology of knowledges 14, 16, 20, 22, 34, 84–85, 87–88, 92–93, 96, 136–137, 141, 149, 152, 159–160, 167, 207, 215–217, 224–226, 233, 235
engagement 7, 17, 50, 76, 90, 220, 236
epistemic 5, 12, 17, 20–21, 23, 31–34, 36–37, 76, 78, 82, 84, 86, 91–92, 95–96, 109, 112–115, 118–123, 127, 129, 137, 141–142, 144–146, 148–154, 157, 159, 176–177, 184–186, 188, 198, 209, 211–213, 215–217, 226, 232, 236
epistemic access 137, 154, 160, 209–210, 224
epistemic capabilities 118–122, 137, 141–142, 144–46, 148, 150–151, 153–154, 159, 185–186, 194, 198, 220. *See also* capabilities
epistemic contributors 118, 151, 209–211
epistemic exploitation 119, 177
epistemic freedoms 5, 95, 121, 146, 149–150, 154, 209–210, 213
epistemicide 31–32
epistemic injustice 17, 80, 146, 149, 157, 209, 215
epistemic line 23, 154, 226
epistemic system 5, 12, 17, 32–34, 48, 68, 76, 82, 115, 141, 147, 152–154, 159, 184–185, 210–211, 232. *See also* Western epistemic system
epistemologies of ignorance 148
Eurocentrism 7–8, 13, 17–18, 31–32, 53, 66, 77, 81, 90, 121, 184, 200, 210, 234

facilitators 13, 16, 21–22, 95–98, 109, 111, 128, 131, 136, 138, 142, 148, 154, 172, 182, 199–201, 206–208, 214, 218–223, 225, 233

freedom 21, 77, 109, 115, 118–122, 124, 126–128, 142, 176, 180, 186, 190, 197, 213
freedoms 1, 4–5, 9, 17, 20, 22, 77–79, 81, 84, 86–88, 91, 94–95, 107, 109, 114–115, 119–122, 125, 127, 146, 149–150, 154, 160, 165, 167, 172, 179, 186–187, 192–193, 197, 200–201, 207–210, 213, 220
functionings 5, 77, 94, 97, 143, 151, 158, 160, 172–173, 176–177, 179–180, 182–183, 186, 194, 197, 200–201, 208, 220, 222, 230

gender 2, 10, 19, 22, 51, 75, 78, 123, 140, 144–148, 151, 157–158, 160–161, 165–166, 173, 177, 183, 186, 189–190, 192, 195, 203–205
Global North 7, 11, 18, 21, 31, 34–35, 78, 80, 123, 157, 191, 208, 211, 213, 234–235
Global South 3–9, 11, 16, 19, 21, 29–31, 33, 35, 78, 80, 83, 87–88, 92, 109, 115–116, 118, 131, 191, 207–208, 210–211, 213, 217, 223, 233

hegemonic 9–10, 20, 30, 32, 34, 36, 50–51, 67–69, 87, 96, 115
hegemony 12–13, 31, 126
higher education 4–11, 14, 19, 22–23, 30–31, 33–35, 58–59, 92, 115, 117–119, 121, 148, 154, 174, 180, 182–184, 186, 207, 214, 217–218, 229, 231, 233–236
human development 19–21, 76–78, 80, 85, 88, 109, 219, 229
human dignity 1–2, 125, 146, 220
human flourishing 85
human recognition 112–114, 120, 123–124, 127, 143, 150–151, 156, 158, 165, 176–177, 180, 186, 188–189, 192, 198, 200, 209, 220. *See also* capabilities

imperialism 30, 36, 76
Indigenous 3, 7–8, 12, 32–33, 41–43, 45–46, 51–53, 62–63, 67, 78, 89, 96, 225
individualism 84, 86
inequalities 10, 13, 31, 83, 88, 94, 105, 108, 123, 129, 137, 140, 144, 147–148,

151, 158, 160, 162, 165, 178, 195, 211, 215, 221, 224

insurgent capabilities 5, 109, 115–119, 123, 125, 131, 140, 150, 154, 175, 178, 188, 197–201, 207–209, 213, 220, 223. *See also* capabilities

knowledge 1–6, 8–12, 14–17, 20, 22–23, 30–34, 37, 62, 68, 78, 82, 84, 87, 91–94, 96, 98, 118, 120–122, 129, 137, 139, 141, 146–149, 152–153, 158–161, 167, 181–186, 194–196, 198, 200, 209–213, 215–217, 219–221, 224, 226, 230–235. *See also* democratisation of knowledge

knowledge production 3–6, 11–12, 15, 17, 20, 23, 34, 78, 88, 92–93, 96, 152–153, 166, 207, 210, 215, 217, 224, 226, 231–232

latent capabilities 230. *See also* capabilities

learning processes 12, 54, 60, 138, 159

marginalisation 2, 10, 17, 33, 53, 78, 96, 115, 117–119, 122–123, 126, 149, 151–154, 159, 175, 177, 180, 184, 210, 217, 219, 223–224, 233

methodologies 3, 14–15, 42, 47, 50, 53, 58, 61, 63, 88–89, 95, 141, 147, 184, 194, 213, 216, 232

methods 8, 14–15, 42, 52, 55, 58, 66, 88–89, 213

onto-epistemological 31, 83, 87

ontological 3, 16, 31–32, 52, 84, 92, 121–122, 141, 207, 212–213, 233

paradigm 30, 36, 52, 61, 147, 232

participants 21, 47–48, 50, 55, 60, 63, 67, 93–94, 96–97, 109–112, 116–118, 129, 131, 142–143, 155, 158–160, 167, 172–173, 184, 199–201, 206, 210, 213–215, 218–222, 225, 231

participation 20, 36, 78, 86, 91–93, 124, 127, 129, 146, 155, 158, 178–179, 192, 209–211, 216, 220, 222, 226, 230

participatory 6, 13–15, 17, 20–23, 35–36, 68, 76, 81, 84, 88, 90–95, 109–112,

114, 116–117, 160, 172–173, 198–201, 205–209, 212–214, 217–219, 223–224, 230–232, 234, 236

participatory approaches 6, 14–15, 19, 35–37, 41, 43, 45–46, 49, 51, 61, 64–66, 68, 81, 84, 88–89, 91, 93–95, 206, 208, 212–214, 217, 230–231, 235

plurality 4, 6, 11, 18, 35, 138, 234

pluri-verse 34, 82–83, 86–87. *See also* uni-verse

pool of knowledge 185, 215

post-colonial 2–5, 9–11, 13, 30–31, 42, 51–52, 143, 154, 157

power 3, 5, 14, 22, 30, 41, 48, 56, 75, 83, 93, 98, 105, 107, 124, 129, 139–140, 144, 147, 155–156, 158, 160–162, 165–166, 172, 190, 192, 199–200, 213, 220–221, 235

power inequalities 22, 147, 158, 160, 162, 221

prospective 21, 78, 80, 109–110, 112, 114, 116, 128, 206–208, 214, 219

public scrutiny 10, 84, 88, 93, 215

racism 29, 41, 123, 140, 144, 146–149, 151, 158, 160–162, 165, 171, 174–175, 191, 203

rationality 12, 32, 67, 83–84, 111, 225, 232

reason to value 20, 22, 77, 81, 83, 87–88, 91, 94–95, 111, 116, 126, 160, 165, 199–201, 206–208, 231

research 6, 11–12, 14–15, 17, 22–23, 33, 35, 37, 76, 78, 81, 90–98, 138, 140–141, 143–144, 147–153, 158–159, 161, 180, 185–186, 194, 196, 205, 207, 210–214, 216–220, 224–226, 229–236

scientific knowledge 1, 3, 12, 16, 137, 152, 225, 231

self-determination 112

social justice 4, 6, 12, 14, 16–18, 20, 23, 31, 33, 35, 37, 61–63, 67, 80, 88, 124, 139, 166, 205–209, 211, 213, 225, 233

South Africa 1, 6–11, 14, 18–19, 21–23, 29, 109, 114–115, 119–120, 122, 125, 135, 149–150, 157, 164, 173, 175, 187–189, 197–198, 205, 207–208, 210, 213, 218–219, 225, 229, 233

South America 8, 13, 49

Southern perspectives 11, 17–18, 20–21, 23, 34–35, 68, 76, 79, 89, 91, 109, 111, 128, 173, 200–201, 205, 208–209, 213, 215, 225, 229–230, 232

student experiences 157

system of domination 14, 30–32, 34–35, 68

system of oppression 3–5, 16–17, 33, 80, 88, 106, 109, 116, 125–127, 144, 146, 149, 154, 157, 198, 219

transformation 6, 9, 29, 55, 105, 233

Ubuntu 21, 52, 109, 112–114, 119, 121–127, 130–131, 137, 176, 180, 186, 188, 192–193, 197–199, 208, 218, 223–224, 226, 233–234. *See also* capabilities

undergraduate students 6, 13, 18, 114, 118–119, 135–136, 141, 159, 166, 173, 175, 195, 197, 208, 210–211, 216–217

unfreedoms 4, 77–78, 87, 116, 220–221

universal 3, 21, 23, 31–34, 76, 81, 83, 87, 109, 111, 117, 123, 127, 201, 207, 230, 234

uni-verse 34. *See also* pluri-verse

universities 1–3, 5–6, 8–11, 19, 29, 33–34, 41, 55, 59, 77–78, 105, 107–108, 125, 137, 140–141, 143–145, 147–149, 151–152, 154, 159, 165, 173–174, 178–179, 183–184, 187, 204, 210–211, 216, 219, 233

University of the Free State vii, 29, 105, 107, 136, 144–145, 149, 163, 166, 216

valued capabilities 21–22, 97, 109, 112, 114–116, 125, 127–128, 131, 136, 138, 153, 167, 172, 188, 205–206, 208, 218, 223, 225, 230, 233. *See also* capabilities

voiceless 16–17, 20, 45, 93, 96, 171, 203, 208–209, 211, 217

well-being 4, 77–78, 80, 83, 85, 125, 197, 209, 231

Western 20–21, 30–34, 36, 76, 84, 86–87, 90, 92, 109, 111, 117, 120, 129, 154, 157, 207

Western epistemic system 5, 33–34. *See also* epistemic system

Western power 30

white privilege 6, 148, 205

workshop 14, 22, 136–139, 141–144, 146–148, 150–151, 153, 155–156, 158, 160–163, 165–167, 178, 195, 215

# About the Team

Alessandra Tosi was the managing editor for this book.

Melissa Purkiss copy-edited, proofread and typeset the book in InDesign.

Anna Gatti designed the cover. The cover was produced in InDesign using the Fontin font.

Luca Baffa produced the paperback and hardback editions. The text font is Tex Gyre Pagella; the heading font is Californian FB. Luca produced the EPUB, AZW3, PDF, HTML, and XML editions—the conversion is performed with open source software freely available on our GitHub page (https://github.com/OpenBookPublishers).

# This book need not end here...

## Share

All our books — including the one you have just read — are free to access online so that students, researchers and members of the public who can't afford a printed edition will have access to the same ideas. This title will be accessed online by hundreds of readers each month across the globe: why not share the link so that someone you know is one of them?

This book and additional content is available at:

https://doi.org/10.11647/OBP.0273

## Customise

Personalise your copy of this book or design new books using OBP and third-party material. Take chapters or whole books from our published list and make a special edition, a new anthology or an illuminating coursepack. Each customised edition will be produced as a paperback and a downloadable PDF.

Find out more at:

https://www.openbookpublishers.com/section/59/1

# You may also be interested in:

**Wellbeing, Freedom and Social Justice**
**The Capability Approach Re-Examined**
*Ingrid Robeyns*

https://doi.org/10.11647/OBP.0130

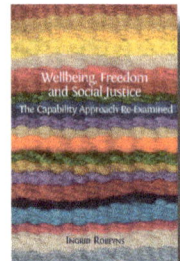

**Delivering on the Promise of Democracy**
**Visual Case Studies in Educational Equity and**
**Transformation**
*Sukhwant Jhaj*

https://doi.org/10.11647/OBP.0157

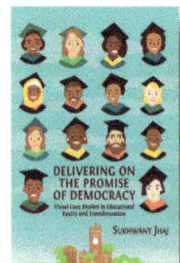

**Open Education**
**International Perspectives in Higher Education**
*Patrick Blessinger and TJ Bliss (eds)*

https://doi.org/10.11647/OBP.0103

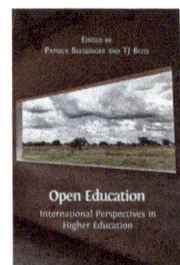

www.ingramcontent.com/pod-product-compliance
Lightning Source LLC
Chambersburg PA
CBHW040148270326
41929CB00025B/3421